THE PRACTICAL COUNSELOR

Elements of Effective Helping

THE PRACTICAL COUNSELOR

Elements of Effective Helping

Philip Lauver

University of Arizona (Emeritus)

David R. Harvey

Counseling and Consulting Services, Inc.

Brooks/Cole Publishing Company

I(T)P® An International Thomson Publishing Company

Pacific Grove • Albany • Bonn • Boston • Cincinnati • Detroit • London • Madrid • Melbourne
Mexico City • New York • Paris • San Francisco • Singapore • Tokyo • Toronto • Washington

Sponsoring Editor: *Lisa Gebo*
Marketing Team: *Jean Vevers Thompson and Deborah Petit*
Editorial Assistant: *Lisa Blanton*
Production Editor: *Laurel Jackson*
Production Assistant: *Mary Vezilich*

Manuscript Editor: *Patterson Lamb*
Interior and Cover Design: *Terri Wright*
Art Editor: *Kathy Joneson*
Indexer: *James Minkin*
Typesetting: *Joan Mueller Cochrane*
Printing and Binding: *Malloy Lithographing, Inc.*

For more information, contact:

BROOKS/COLE PUBLISHING COMPANY
511 Forest Lodge Road
Pacific Grove, CA 93950
USA

International Thomson Publishing Europe
Berkshire House 168-173
High Holborn
London WC1V 7AA
England

Thomas Nelson Australia
102 Dodds Street
South Melbourne, 3205
Victoria, Australia

Nelson Canada
1120 Birchmount Road
Scarborough, Ontario
Canada M1K 5G4

International Thomson Editores
Campos Eliseos 385, Piso 7
Col. Polanco
11560 México D. F. México

International Thomson Publishing GmbH
Königswinterer Strasse 418
53227 Bonn
Germany

International Thomson Publishing Asia
221 Henderson Road
#05-10 Henderson Building
Singapore 0315

International Thomson Publishing Japan
Hirakawacho Kyowa Building, 3F
2-2-1 Hirakawacho
Chiyoda-ku, Tokyo 102
Japan

Printed in the United States of America

10 9 8 7 6 5 4 3 2 1

Library of Congress Cataloging-in-Publication Data

Lauver, Philip, [date]
    The practical counselor : elements of effective helping / Philip Lauver, David R. Harvey.
        p.   cm.
    Includes bibliographical references and index.
    ISBN 0-534-34349-X
    1. Counseling—Study and teaching. 2. Counselors. 3. Counselors and client.   I. Harvey, David R., [date]   . II. Title.
BF637.C6L38 1996
158'.3—dc20
                                                                96-12007
                                                                CIP

To the memory of Joan Lauver
P. L.

To the memory of Raymond B. Harvey
D. H.

and
To our students, colleagues, and clients who
have taught and inspired us over the years

Contents

CHAPTER 2

Thinking Like a Counselor   13

CHAPTER 3

Underlying Assumptions and Beliefs   25

CHAPTER 4

Counselor Intentions 35

CHAPTER 5

The Counseling Process Model 43

PART 2
The Counseling Process Model 51

CHAPTER 6

Step 1: Initiate Counseling Relationship 55

CHAPTER 7

Step 2: Understand Counselee Concerns Empathically 77

CHAPTER 8

Step 3: Negotiate Counseling Objectives   99

CHAPTER 9

Step 4: Identify Plan for Achieving Objective   137

CHAPTER 10

Step 5: Support the Plan   165

CHAPTER 11

Step 6: Evaluate Counseling   183

PART 3
Professional Development   211

CHAPTER 12

Promoting Professional Growth   213

Preface

There is a world which is happening all the time.
Our experience is that portion of it which is happening to us.
—George Kelly

The Practical Counselor: Elements of Effective Helping is a text for people learning how to be professional helpers. We believe that the elements of effective helping presented here are applicable wherever a service provider works with someone who is seeking help with problems in living. Although the material in this book was developed primarily while training counselors, it has also been used with psychologists, marriage and family therapists, nurses, and other human services professionals.

As the title implies, this text provides educators and students with a practical, functional model of the counseling process. We are committed to a view of counseling that emphasizes a client-centered, outcome-referenced approach to helping. Further, we conceive the model presented here as a foundations resource with no particular theoretical allegiance. We also acknowledge our biases as authors and hope they are responsibly articulated.

The Practical Counselor is organized into three parts. Part 1 involves students in identifying and exploring the values and concepts that support caring and respectful professional helping relationships. Part 2 presents a six-step counseling process model, guided by three questions fundamental to professional service. The model provides a map that represents a counselor's tasks and delineates the skills needed to perform them. The Counseling Process Model is intended to guide the counseling student through a client-centered and outcome-referenced professional helping process, with each task an orienting benchmark of progress along the way. Part 3, "Professional Development," focuses on using counseling experience to improve the counselor's effectiveness. We also address the demands of real-world settings and implications of the "counselor culture."

Our intent is to bridge the gap between *reading about* counseling and *being* a counselor. With this purpose in mind, we present the Erikka Transcript, a demonstration counseling session, to exemplify each step in the Counseling Process Model. Each interview segment is preceded by samples of self-talk that counselors would use to prepare themselves for a session. This is followed by a debriefing that consists of questions and the counselor's responses.

In each chapter, we suggest activities designed to integrate the concepts presented in the chapter and to promote hands-on experience with the concepts and skills that constitute the elements of effective helping. We have also included "Consultation Time" segments in Chapters 6 through 11 to bring readers in touch with some of the real-life experience, choices, and questions prompted by professional practice.

We have chosen not to segregate professional ethics, cultural issues, and problem categories into separate sections but rather to present these aspects of practice as integral to the counseling process. We hope that learning and practicing the Counseling Process Model will foster learning and practice of ethical behavior, maintenance of a responsiveness to the "culture" of the client's experience, and application of methods that effectively assist clients in realizing desired outcomes.

This book grew out of 25 years of teaching the beginning course in counseling. In the counselor education programs we are familiar with, students start with a first counseling course. This is followed by courses that cover a selection of the many theories, techniques, and approaches to counseling, as well as the related empirical literature. Students face the daunting task of somehow arriving at a personalized synthesis of counselor beliefs and skills that gives them some basis for believing they can help potential clients. (Those of us who recall our first counseling practicum can remember how fragile our sense of professional counseling efficacy was when we met our first "real" client.)

The six-step model of counseling presented here evolved partly as an attempt to give students a map of the series of counselor tasks basic to helping clients. We hoped that, in their subsequent encounters with counseling theories, strategies and techniques, this map would give them a useful basis for deciding what to include in their own counseling style. Our aim is to persuade students to think less in terms of "Is that a good counseling technique?" and more in terms of "What are we trying to accomplish?" and "How can we accomplish it?" It's hard to make good choices regarding means when our destination is not clear to us.

Thus, the counseling process model is meant to be a practical guide. We present counselor tasks in everyday language, with descriptions and examples that make clear what we mean when we use terms like *understand* and *support*. Further, we indicate that the performance of counselor tasks is ultimately assessed in terms of observable client behaviors. Counseling is less about doing things than about facilitating client accomplishment. When we find ourselves in the client role, hoping to be served, we appreciate our encounters with people who seem sincerely interested in helping us have a satisfactory experience.

In this book, we speak of *elements* of effective helping. Again, our focus is on the basic counseling skills needed to accomplish each step in the counseling process. The counselor who wonders what to do next always has a task to accomplish and requires tools with which to do it. (Where are we going? How can we get there?)

In the midst of the explosion of professional literature that has appeared in the last decade, we continue to rely on some of this relatively young field's "old masters" in presenting the philosophical and theoretical underpinnings of the Counseling Process Model. Carl Rogers, George Kelly, and Leona Tyler were among those who most strongly influenced the basics of our counseling approach. The work of some less familiar figures, such as Wendell Johnson, has been helpful to us in conceiving and articulating our ideas about such issues as confrontation and culture. Our reliance on the "old masters" provides a thread of continuity and a vantage point in our rapidly developing field of diverse theoretical and applied counseling approaches. However, our focus is not intended to diminish the influence of other pioneers, such as Perls, Ellis, Meichenbaum, and Beck. Just as a computer's basic operating system is compatible with specific, refined software applications, so the specific counseling viewpoint presented in this book will help students and counselors articulate the variety of counseling theories and methods that abound.

George Kelly believed that we do not really "learn from experience"; rather, the learning *constitutes* experience. We are grateful for the opportunity to learn from our students and clients. Further, we hope this text conveys that experience to readers and encourages them to learn from the people whom they will be helping.

Much of what we know about counseling we've learned from those whom we've taught. We would appreciate hearing of insights you've gained or experiences you've had in applying the material in this book. If you would like to share any of your comments or recommendations with us, you can reach us at the following addresses:

Philip Lauver
1801 East Spring Street
Tucson, AZ 85719

David R. Harvey
1665 Lost Canyon Court
Tucson, AZ 85745

Acknowledgments

Over the years, hundreds of students, thousands of counselees, and many colleagues and associates have contributed to our shaping and expression of the view of counseling presented in this book. Thomas Froehle of Indiana University contributed much to our initial conceptualization of the counseling process as a series of counselor tasks, and, 20 years later, his thoughtful review of the present manuscript has been most helpful. We received helpful feedback on early versions of the manuscript from Anne Corbishley and Michael Ponce, both practitioners, and from Betty Newlon of the University of Arizona and Michael Salzman of Lewis and Clark University, Portland. Luz Harvey provided encouragement and validation at just the right times.

We are especially thankful to those who carefully reviewed earlier versions of the manuscript. Their comments, questions, and suggestions helped us improve the focus and clarity of presentation. These reviewers include Diane H. Coursol, Mankato State University; Thomas C. Froehle, Indiana University; William Lynn McKinney, University of Rhode Island; Ron Partin, Bowling Green State University; Terrence Patterson, University of San Francisco; Charles Mack Porter, Slippery Rock University; Ann Puryear, Southeast Missouri State University; and Patricia M. Raskin, Teachers College, Columbia University.

The members of the Brooks/Cole team for this book were professional, personable, and encouraging in their efforts to create the most readable, useful text possible. Lisa Gebo has been enthusiastic and supportive throughout the project. Laurie Jackson's editing and management of the production process have left readers with a far more accessible resource than our own talents could have offered. Others who contributed their time and talents to this text include Lisa Blanton, Carline Haga, Kathy Joneson, Deborah Petit, Kelly Shoemaker, Jean Thompson, and Mary Vezilich. We also wish to thank designer Terri Wright for the elegant design for this book.

We want to add a special note of thanks to our copy editor, Patterson Lamb, whose empathy with our intentions and whose skill with language contributed greatly to the coherence of the present text.

And, once again, we owe a debt of gratitude to Claudie Hensley. Her assistance with the manuscript preparation was invaluable, and her moral support was, as usual, unflagging.

—*Philip Lauver*
David R. Harvey

PART

1

Conceptual Foundations

CHAPTER 1

Becoming a Counselor

If a man will begin with certainties, he shall end in doubts, but if he will be content to begin with doubts, he shall end in certainties. —Sir Francis Bacon

A basic tenet of professional counselor practice is informed choice for clients. The basis for this belief is that individuals (clients) make more satisfactory decisions when they have information about the potential consequences of each possible course of action. And having made a choice, this advance information helps them anticipate what's coming and adapt to it advantageously.

In that spirit, we want to share with you some of our observations about what happens to people who decide they want to learn how to be counselors. From working with counseling students, we have discovered how the learning process works and what students seem to find along the way— about themselves and about their emerging identity as counselors.

Learning to be a counselor involves change, not only in what you know and what you do but also in who you are. We believe that if you are knowledgeable about the learning process, if you are given informed choices, you will be able to anticipate these changes in a way that will help you move more smoothly and rapidly toward your ultimate goal of becoming a counselor.

How Does Counseling Competence Develop?

In the process of becoming a counselor, you will acquire knowledge, skills, and an awareness of your own personal qualities. Counseling competence develops from the merging of these three elements: the person, counseling knowledge, and counseling skills (see following figure).

By *person*, we mean the aggregation of attitudes, values, beliefs, needs, abilities, and expectations that you bring to the task of becoming a counselor. *Person* is all that is included when you think "I."

Counseling knowledge refers to the body of information that defines counseling: ethical standards, research, authoritative opinion, theoretical counseling models, personality theories, the reasons people seek counseling, counselor intervention strategies, and so on. It is what we *think we know* about counseling. We say "think we know" as we remember Gary Zukav's (1979) observation about *knowledge*: "The history of scientific thought, if it teaches us anything at all, teaches us the folly of clutching ideas too closely" (p. 267). Thus, "knowing" something can blind us to other, possibly more fruitful, possibilities. Zukav's insight applies equally well to counseling knowledge. We therefore prefer that you use this book as a starting place rather than as the last word.

Counseling skills are those needed to perform intentionally, sensitively, and creatively in the counselor role so that the client's goals are met. Within skills, we include how counselors think as well as what they do and say.

Counseling competence emerges as personal qualities, *knowledge*, and *skill* become integrated, allowing the individual to perform effectively in the role of professional counselor. Counseling competence grows as differences and inconsis-

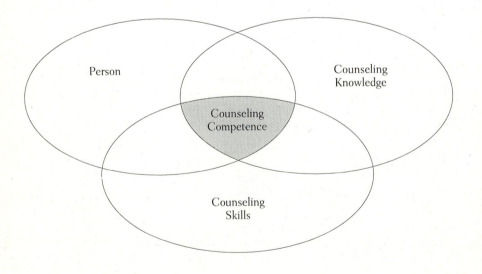

tencies between personal and professional attitudes and beliefs come into awareness through experience and are resolved. It strengthens as the counselor becomes more knowledgeable and better able to perform those functions that contribute to client success.

What Happens to the Person Who Is Becoming a Counselor?

Perhaps you want to become a counselor because you've found helping others to be rewarding and now you want to upgrade your capabilities as a helper. You will no doubt become a more skilled helper but other things may happen, too. As shown in the figure on page 4, the person becoming a counselor is involved in and therefore *changed by* the process. You can expect to experience challenge, change, and ultimately personal satisfaction as you learn counseling.

The first area we address is challenges to your personal values and beliefs that you may experience. As you begin actual counseling, personal issues will arise that must be addressed, and this is to be expected. Occasionally, people resolve their conflict between personal values and professional role demands by deciding not to become a counselor after all. The second area we address includes the personal implications of being in constant change during the learning process. We talk about two modes of coping: some fasten their seat belts and keep flying; some try to bail out. A third area we highlight involves the importance of building your confidence and satisfaction in performing as a counselor. Finally, we expect you will become known as a beginning counselor within your circle of friends, and we want you to be ready for this shift in perceptions within your social network.

Accepting Challenges to Personal Values and Beliefs

Counselors are challenged by conflict on the boundary areas. Recall the Person/Knowledge/Skill elements in the figure on page 4. One type of conflict occurs where the boundaries of these elements meet—for example, where you, *person*, encounter *professional knowledge* or *skill*. Conflict can occur when personal ideas, values, and skills are *different* from those expected of the professional counselor.

An issue that often arises on the *person* and *professional knowledge* boundary involves the client's freedom of choice. One reason people give for becoming counselors is to help others to live happier, more satisfactory lives, and most of us have personal convictions about how best to live. In a counseling relationship, *professional* ethics mandates that the counselor serve the best interests of the client, and in a democracy, people have the right to decide what's best for themselves. Therefore, as a *person* I may believe I know what's best for my client, but as a *counselor*, I must not usurp the right of clients to make their own choices. As counselors, we must continually monitor our impulses to "help" that spring from other helper roles—as friends, parents, or life partners. (This is "dual relationship" territory, discussed later.)

Issues can arise on the *person-skills* boundary as well. We all have long-established habits of thought and speech. Although these have served us well in the past, some of these habits may conflict with effective counseling practice. For example, beginning counselors often must struggle to break the closed-question habit in favor of open leads (Chapter 6). Another common difficulty of learners is to shift focus from inquiring *why* something occurs to *how* it occurs as they try to understand or explain life events (Chapter 6). As you get a better grasp of what you are trying to accomplish, you will more easily see the old habits that conflict with the modes of speech and patterns of thought characteristic of the effective counselor.

Becoming a counselor is a continuous process of encountering and dealing with conflicts; a number of these will arise because you are a *person* who at the same time is striving to think and act like a professional counselor in a counseling relationship.

Coping with Change in the Process of Learning

Sometimes the change involved in learning brings discomfort that can inhibit growth. You may remember when, in the process of learning something, you experienced the following four stages:

1. *Unconscious incompetence:* I don't know that I don't know how. (You can't imagine how difficult roller skating is if you've never tried it—had no strong feelings here.)
2. *Conscious incompetence:* By trying, I learned that I cannot perform as well as I expected. (I tried roller skating and found I could barely stand up—felt dumb, frustrated, incompetent.)
3. *Conscious competence:* I can perform with minimal competence, but only if I concentrate every effort! (With practice, I'm skating better, but it still takes lots of concentration—felt awkward but determined; I may look OK but I'm really shaky inside.)
4. *Unconscious competence:* I can perform competently; appear spontaneous, smooth, effortless, and natural. (I'm not really as aware of how to *do* it as of how to *achieve* my goal—can put less focus on what it takes and more focus on getting it done.)

Many learners report discomfort in the middle two stages. The comments we get from students when we ask for feedback about an interviewing assignment include statements like these: "It didn't feel natural"; "It felt mechanical"; "I wasn't comfortable." Then, other people in class say things like "No pain, no gain."

Learning to walk probably felt awkward and uncomfortable. But you tumbled, scrambled to your feet, and persisted because walking was important to you. You learned to walk because you wanted to get somewhere. You are learning counseling to reach a goal, too. Keep your eye on your intentions.

We tell our students: *Don't* practice listening skills except in situations where you can truthfully tell yourself you *want* to listen and understand. Expect that it will take *many* repetitions to acquire competence in counseling skills.

We build on recognized achievement. Focus on your intentions and what *did* go well. Almost any learning trial contains something that can also be observed in an expert performance; look for these achievements from the first so you can recognize, repeat, and build on them. (Becoming skillful at recognizing the positives in a situation is something you can use with every client.)

Recognizing Unhelpful Responses to Stress

Learning is change and change is stressful. For counseling students, the change involves learning and performing in front of at least one other person. Public performance can be tough. You get to practice piano in private and perform when you're ready, but in counseling, the practice *is* the performance. How do you deal with the possible discomfort and stress that accompany being in an environment that calls for new behaviors? How can you handle the discomforts of *conscious incompetence?*

COPING WITH DISCOMFORT BY WHAT WE TELL OURSELVES

Some people distract and discourage themselves with irrational statements like the following. Such statements can steal incentive and effort, and stifle openness to learning. We offer challenges to each irrational statement. Use these or similar ones when you need something to get you through a trying situation.

> *Discouraging statement:* "I'm not okay if my performance is not flawless."
> *Challenge:* To err is human. Truly flawless performance is very rare, even among experts. At no time can I do more than my best at this moment. The Cub Scouts are in touch with reality with their motto: "Do Your Best." That's all that is ever possible.
> Discouraging statement: "I'm not okay if anyone dislikes, criticizes, or disagrees with me."
> *Challenge:* Someone will *always* take an opposite view. Even so, expressions of others are *never* more than human opinion. Everything appears different from another perspective. Different does not mean bad.
> *Discouraging statement:* "Everyone else is better than I am."
> *Challenge:* A gross overgeneralization like this ignores our multiple capabilities and unique talents. Most of all, it's irrelevant! Everyone can make *some* contribution. (Even the poorest spoon holds more soup than a fork!)
> *Discouraging statement:* "Keep a low profile and you won't get hurt."

Challenge: Learning is performance. Remember that the turtle can't move unless he sticks his neck out. Nothing ventured, nothing gained. *Counseling is performance!*

The first three statements preceding also distract learners from noticing and acknowledging their own accomplishments and the needs of their clients. Counselors who are engrossed in their own world don't have much attention left for the people they should be helping. It's important to those who will seek your help in the future that you build confidence in your skills, based on your self-observed achievements with clients.

The fourth statement indicates giving up. How people ever expect to perform as counselors without practicing the skills baffles us. Visual imagery is a widely used and effective rehearsal technique. Imagining what we may say or do can help us cope with an anticipated event. But your client can't be helped by your visual imagery alone; counseling is performance and counselors-in-training must practice their skills while being observed by their peers and instructors.

USING THE WAYS WE THINK ABOUT FEELINGS TO COPE WITH STRESS

When we ask students to demonstrate a counseling skill in class, a ripple of manifest feelings goes around the room. When asked, students say they were nervous, tense, worried, even scared before and during a demonstration.

We prefer to think and talk about the feelings that accompany communications exercises, simulated counseling interviews, and other learning trials as simply excitement. We notice excitement in ourselves when we prepare to demonstrate counseling before a group. We notice excitement in our students when we call on them to demonstrate a set of skills.

Terms such as *nervous, tense,* and *worried* carry unpleasant connotations. As we hear and use such terms, the unpleasant feelings they suggest tend to snowball. So, unless you want to feel bad, don't use them. As we understand it, what we experience in a new situation is excitement. If we *expect* a sensation to be unpleasant and give it a name that includes the expected unpleasantness—such as *tension, nervousness,* or *worry*—we feel bad. So, why do it?

Before a classroom counseling demonstration, we are aware that our heart rate goes up, breathing becomes shallower and faster, and our palms get sweaty. We believe it is helpful—and more accurate—to recognize these symptoms as evidence that the organism is getting ready, becoming energized, for a special performance. We prefer to acknowledge our "old friend" excitement something like this: "This energy will help me do my best during the performance. I'm glad I still get excited in situations like this; if I didn't, I might not do as well."

As an aside, some counselors use the term *reframing* for this technique of giving something a different name. We think this label is not very accurate. It sounds as though you are simply putting a different frame around the same picture. To us, the example involving worry/excitement demonstrates the substitution of a more accurate description for one that had been distorted (e.g., Goldfried & Goldfried, 1980). For observing, describing, and reporting behavioral events, we prefer terms that describe without built-in judgments.

As you monitor your experiences in the process of becoming a counselor, we suggest that you become a more objective reporter and less a judgmental editor. Think and talk about what happened at a descriptive level; become familiar with the data. You'll know you're at the descriptive level when the language does not evoke the same visceral reactions you get from blame or praise. Things happen, or they don't. Goodness and badness, the language of political rhetoric, can be added to the description later if that serves a purpose.

Building Confidence in the Counselor Role

The best counselors we know do what they do because it somehow realizes their personal ideals. They get satisfaction from using their skills to help other human beings find ways out of their quandaries. The best counselors earn the liking, trust, and respect of their clients—powerful reinforcement for counselors. We certainly enjoy the good feelings that come from meeting our own standards of practice and from being of help to someone else.

You will build your counseling skills through exercises, simulations, and practice counseling sessions. We hope you will use some of these skills in other life situations where listening accurately and communicating effectively are important. Good things will happen that we hope you notice and appreciate. People will tend to talk longer with you; they will talk about personal issues; and as they experience your intent listening, they may share things you'd rather not hear, painful things. These are indications that liking, trust, and respect are there and growing. You must be doing something right! You need to develop a reality-based conviction that your skills are developing and are effective with people. Your confidence in yourself is a real resource for your clients.

We need to offer a caveat at this point. When practicing listening skills and finding themselves hearing about someone's predicament or pain, the listeners sometimes feel pressure to help, to relieve, to solve. Our advice is that you not unilaterally shift from listener or friend to helper/counselor/fixer. If you find yourself distracted from listening by impulses to help, you might discuss this with the other person. If the pressure you're experiencing includes not having the foggiest idea of what would be helpful, you might also mention that. Perhaps you renegotiate your role; perhaps you continue as listener. In any case, the decision will be by mutual choice. Isn't this mutual consideration what you would prefer if the roles were reversed?

Counselors sometimes seem to let their need to be well regarded by clients distract them from client goals. This is one of many reasons that regular supervision can be useful for every counselor.

Accepting Changes in Your Identity

Learning is *change*, and change produces varied and sometimes surprising effects. Change is the natural order of the universe. And isn't it curious how hard we sometimes work to block it? As evident in the figure on page 4, who you are affects the counselor you can become; but this process is a two-way street. Your idea of who *you* are will undergo some change.

Even if you don't seem any different to yourself, you will very likely be perceived differently by others, especially by those in your support network. Your closest sources of support encouraged you to become a counselor, but the *you* they encouraged is being changed by the learning process.

How will they respond to the new you? Students in the past have reported a range of responses. Sometimes people become wary. Sometimes people say, "Don't practice any of that counselor stuff on me!" People may approach you seeking advice. Probably the best you can do is be prepared to pay more attention to maintaining relationships with your significant sources of support.

In summary, learning to be a counselor, like learning to perform any role, means change. Learning requires entertaining new ideas and performing new acts. The *process* of learning can be uncomfortable for those who hold themselves to standards of inhuman perfection, and it can be rewarding as you equip yourself to realize valued personal ideals.

People who are "running scared" through the learning process are likely to be more interested in "getting it right" ("How am *I* doing?") than in learning to do it effectively ("What are we *accomplishing*?").

Monitor what you tell yourself about the tasks involved in the learning process. Hold yourself to expectations that are rational for someone *beginning* to learn a highly complex role. Include the expectation that learning this role will take many repetitions. Admonish yourself to do only the best you are capable of *today*. Focus on recognizing what you've added to your repertoire, and use what you learn today to improve your performance tomorrow.

We'd like to offer this thought, brought to our attention by one of our students: "Self-doubts indicate we are stretching, striving, and that we have placed ourselves in territory that is unfamiliar but ripe with opportunity" (Shelley Levitt, *Cosmopolitan*, July 1989, p. 193).

Counselor or Therapist?

Some of you want to become therapists or psychotherapists. Many practitioners refer to themselves in this way and describe their work as doing therapy. We have no quarrel with this terminology. At other times we have used the terms *counseling* and *psychotherapy* interchangeably. Our choice of terms in this book reflects our own habits of thought and speech. We pretty consistently refer to clinicians and their practice as counselors and counseling.

Words mean different things to different people. To us, *therapy*-related terms have connotations of treating illness and pathology. We prefer what seems the connotatively cleaner term, *counseling*, without the implications that those who seek it are sick or impaired. We acknowledge that as counseling and related helping professions become more specialized, there is a commensurate increase in specialized training and education programs. These programs define various criteria of accomplishment and expertise through certification as marriage and family therapist, hypnotherapist, strategic family therapist, and other specialists.

 ## SUGGESTIONS FOR INTEGRATING ACTIVITIES

1. Some of you may currently be keeping personal journals. Journal writing can be a private way of noting, commenting on, discussing and venting about the day's highlights, low spots, challenges, issues, and frustrations. Keeping a journal helps me discover what I'm thinking about, what's important in my day, feelings I haven't acknowledged before, what I need to do. Journal time can help make personal sense of some aspect of your day.

   The right way to keep a journal, initially, seems simply to get in the habit of doing it. You'll find in the process of doing it what's best for you. What to write? Some people do it as if writing a letter about their day to themselves or someone close. We suggest that part of your journal be about your journey toward becoming a counselor—as though you were making notes about what you had noticed today. For instance, you've no doubt found some things in this chapter that you question, that you disagree with, that aren't clear, or that you really liked. Your journal could be in the form of a dialogue with yourself, or with us, around your personal reactions to the materials and experiences that lie ahead.

2. Why is becoming a counselor attractive to you? When, where, and how did it first occur to you? Did someone suggest it to you?

3. Have you been a counseling client? If so, what did your counselor seem to want or need from you?

4. Find one or two people who work as counselors and ask them what's most satisfying about what they do—and what's hardest to live with. Then get a bit more specific: In your professional life last week, what was the most satisfying moment? Hardest moment?

5. How do you cope with situations that call for "performing" in front of others? Have you been in situations where you were actively supervised? Critiqued? Coached? How do you respond in such situations? What parts of your responses help you keep going forward?

6. Complete each of the following three sentences in ways that reflect your present beliefs. Write down at least three endings for each sentence stem.

   • The counseling relationship should be . . .

- The relationship between friends should be . . .
- Counseling relationships differ from friendships in that . . .

Now, find several other classmates and compare your statements. See whether you as a group can write consensus statements for counseling and for friendships. You may want to discuss in class similarities and differences in these two kinds of relationships. Those who have experienced both might comment on the realities of their relationships with counselors.

Finally, look at your classmates from the perspective of a client seeking a counselor. Would your experience as a client be affected by which "counselor" you selected? Begin to think about what you would like *your* counselor to bring to the table. You might want to record some of your thoughts in your journal, if you're keeping one.

REFERENCES

Goldfried, M. R., & Goldfried, A. P. (1980). *Helping people change* (2nd ed.). New York: Pergamon Press.

Zukav, G. (1979). *The dancing wu li masters*. New York: Morrow.

SUGGESTED READING

American Counseling Association. (1995). *Code of ethics and standards of practice*. Arlington, VA: Author.

Corey, G., Corey, M. S., & Callanan, P. (1993). *Issues and ethics in the helping professions* (4th ed.). Pacific Grove, CA: Brooks/Cole. Chapter 2, "The Counselor as a Person and as a Professional," includes questions and discussion of issues arising from demands of the counseling profession and needs of its practitioners.

Mahoney, M. (1991). *Human change processes, the scientific foundations of psychotherapy*. New York: Basic Books. Chapter 13, "The Person and Experience of the Psychotherapist," highlights variables affecting the person of the therapist, such as motives and stresses of the helping role. Mahoney offers suggestions for self-care, including 23 "reflective questions" for periodic self-assessment (e.g., *How happy are you most of the time?*) and 23 guidelines for quality practice (e.g., *Whenever possible, let the client do most of the work*).

CHAPTER 2

Thinking Like a Counselor

There is nothing so obvious that its appearance is not altered when it is seen in a different light.
—George A. Kelly

The clinician is always part of both the problem and the solution. —S. B. Sarason

In Chapter 1, we described the process of becoming a counselor as one in which professional knowledge and skills are melded within the person. We also noted some of the emotional implications of participating in that process. In this chapter we focus on certain aspects of language and related behavior that we believe are quite important in learning to think and act like a counselor.

As adults, we each have extensive experience as language users and with other behaviors. Much of our language behavior and other behaviors have become invisible to us in the sense that we aren't very aware of them; habits of thought and speech are pretty well established. Counselors need to be especially cognizant of language, behavior, and their relationship if they are to understand and help others. Thinking like a counselor requires most people to think about language and behavior in new ways.

Listening in a Special Way

When counselors are consulted, it's because something in the client's current situation is no longer tolerable. Counselors advertise their ability to help people move from an unpleasant present to a more satisfactory future. Counselors are in the business of helping people change. Thinking like a counselor about what the client is seeking means being very interested in learning as much as possible about these complementary aspects of the client's world: what the client finds currently intolerable, and what the client desires. These issues are the professional counselor's reason for being.

We believe counselors need to understand the client's responses to *What brought you to counseling?* in a special way, suggested by these two comments from Wendell Johnson (1946):

> The language of distress might be part and parcel of the distress. (p. 16)
>
> Before a problem can be attacked effectively it must be stated with reasonable clarity. And as soon as it has been so stated, some kind of solution to it becomes more or less apparent. (p. 16)

These two observations reflect the importance of our words in shaping our experience. Johnson's ideas have helped us think about the role of language in maintaining problem situations and in affecting the counselor's ability to empathically understand client experience.

Listening in a special way is sometimes a difficult idea to grasp. Johnson (1946) observes, "Scarcely anything is more difficult to learn than something that is obvious" (p. 47). This observation applies to counselors and listening. Many of us grew up hearing some version of "Be quiet and listen." The message was that listening meant being silent, simply not talking. A second piece completed our instruction, "Look at me when I'm talking to you." Listening meant being still and looking attentive. We learned that life went best when we were quiet, looked attentive, and thought about what we would say when *our* turn came. We became adept at listening *defensively*, in the service of our own agendas. And these are very useful skills that served us well at many times and places, but not as counselors.

Listening in a special way means learning, for specific clients, what brought them here, what they hope for, and what resources are available to effect change and meet their goal. Because the desired change is to occur in the client's world, the counselor needs to develop the clearest possible understanding of that world to help the client better direct his or her own life. The clients are the expert sources of information about their world, the only ones who have actually experienced their world. Counselors need to learn from their clients where the clients are, where they want to be, and what resources are available that can contribute to the change.

Developing a sense of another person's experience is fraught with difficulties. We find that understanding our own world is sometimes challenging. Understanding someone else's world, at an empathic level, as though one were "in their shoes," is even more challenging. You cannot see with their eyes, hear with their ears, feel with their skin. We rely on language: "Tell me about it." Language is the counselor's usual means of access to the client's personal experience and to what the client has made of it.

The Language of Distress

Accurate communication is not assured, however, just because both counselor and client are fluent in the same tongue. Let's go back to Johnson's first observation, "The language of distress might be part and parcel of the distress." What is "the language of distress"? It's like these familiar statements:

Ronald Reagan: "I can't recall."
George Bush: "I misspoke myself."
Bill Clinton: "Why is everybody picking on me?"
You and me: "I'm in deep trouble," or "I'm depressed."

These complaints are like most of the language of distress we hear in at least three ways. First, they are reported in terms so general that they could be true for anyone. Second, the language conveys no idea of what you might have actually seen or heard if you had been there at the distressing moment. And finally, the statements carry no clue about how one might relieve, avoid, or end the distress. To the extent that these statements reflect the self-understanding of the persons who made them, chances are these people will find themselves using those words again and again. Distress expressed in such general terms as these is quite likely to persist. Thus, how we think and talk about our troubles contributes to their persistence in our lives.

The Importance of Stating Problems Clearly

Johnson's second observation provides some help for counselors, "Before a problem can be attacked effectively it must be stated with reasonable clarity." We think this is profoundly important for counselors. The Erikka transcript, which accompanies Chapters 5–10, contains many examples of a counselor working hard for a clearer problem statement.

What do we mean by "reasonable clarity"? "The problems of knowing and of understanding center around the relation of language to reality, of symbol to fact" (Johnson, 1946, p. 91). A "reasonably clear" problem statement will consist of words about some event, some piece of human experience, something that happened to a person at a place at a moment in time. The problem statement consists of words selected to represent experience with the greatest possible fidelity. A reasonably clear problem statement can be like a series of word pictures of some experience. For example, Erikka, in the counseling transcript following Chapter 6, says, "I'm getting terrible, terrible headaches which I've not gotten in the past." Does this statement represent a reasonably clear description of what's going on in Erikka's life?

All we have at this point is Erikka's words, but the picture of Erikka's reality that these words evoke is in broad outline rather than clear detail. To learn more about what Erikka has experienced, we'd like to know what she means by words like *terrible, terrible headaches.* If we could have been in her shoes last week, we'd know better what these words represent. If we had experienced what only Erikka experienced, would we describe it like she has? Reasonable clarity, we think, has to do with the fidelity with which words describe experience.

But words are symbols, not experience. The question with any verbal description is how accurately it reflects experience. The clarity of Erikka's problem statement can be improved, and the transcript shows some ways the counselor works to do this. In brief, the counselor keeps checking the words against Erikka's experience, validating her problem statement by asking Erikka to report elements of the problematic experiences of the past week.

The Map Is Not the Territory

A linguistic device that we have found useful in reminding us of the difference between words and experience, and the importance of validating verbal descriptions, is the map/territory metaphor. In the following paragraphs, Wendell Johnson (1946) describes Korzybski's map/territory metaphor more fully.

> What we call a map is an example of a kind of language, symbols arranged in some kind of order. Now for a map to be useful to a traveler it must be coordinated with the territory. Its structure must be similar in certain respects to that of the territory it represents. The arrangement of the symbols, the dots, lines, etc., of the map must accord with the arrangement of the actual cities, roads, rivers, etc., of the territory. For example, if in the territory we find, from west to east, Denver, Omaha, Chicago, then on the map we must find these places correspondingly represented. If on the map they are represented in the order of Denver, Chicago, Omaha, the order or structure is faulty, the map is not coordinated with the territory, and the traveler who tries to follow such a map is likely to suffer consequences which may range from mere annoyance to utter calamity. Among other experiences, he will be likely to suffer shock more or less, depending upon the degree to which he maintains awareness of the difference between map and territory. If . . . he scarcely recognizes any difference at all between symbol and fact—map and territory—he will be gravely confused for some time after discovering that he is in Omaha instead of Chicago. If, however, like a scientist, he has practically no ten-

dency to identify symbol and fact, practically no readjustment at all will be required of him when he discovers that the map was wrong. He will merely change his map and go on his way.

The trouble with the more primitive traveler is that he would hardly understand what was wrong. Assuming as he does that map and territory are practically identical, he places undue confidence in the map and so he is not semantically prepared to handle his difficulty with the obvious (to us) solution of changing the map. Such a solution would occur only to a person to whom map and territory were distinctly different—and who understood that the usefulness of a map depends precisely on the degree to which it corresponds structurally with the territory. (Johnson, 1946, pp. 131–132)

As we listen to the words of a client telling his or her story, we must try to remember that we're hearing about the *map*. The words the client is speaking are *not* the events the client experienced. In response to "Tell me what happened," counselors usually hear very few words that simply describe events; generally, clients offer words *about* the events:

COUNSELOR: Tell me how the fight with your wife started last evening.

CLIENT: The usual way. She started nagging and I just blew up.

At this point, the map of the territory of last night's domestic event is pretty vague.

The client's map indicates that the fight started "the usual way. She started nagging, and I just blew up." How effectively do these words represent his experience? Does "the usual way" indicate that he and his wife were in the same room at the same time in the same proximity, and so on, as in the last "fight"? Did the client hear his wife say the same words while observing the same look on her face as she responded to the same event as their previous altercation? Or were there different circumstances, observations, and interpretations with which he can refine his map of "how fights start"? By "nagging," what did he observe? What did she say, in what tone of voice, accompanied by what collection of nonverbal actions? And "just blew up" involved what thoughts, feelings, and actions on his part? What was he saying to himself and what did these words respond to? Were they accompanied by any images or memories associated with other moments in his life? What did he experience in his body: Tension? Movement? Changes in breathing? How did he act as he "blew up"? How did he speak, move, change position? And how did these actions affect his thinking and feeling? What did he notice his wife doing in response to his actions?

The client's responses to these questions create a more vivid representation of "usual way," "nagging," "blew up." The map for how the fight started becomes a more effective tool for creating the map of how to stop the next fight, or prevent it from starting, or make it a fair and productive fight, depending on the client's goal.

As you listen to the words of a client, try to remember that the map at best will be incomplete because of these constraints:

1. More goes on than words can describe.
2. Experience is dynamic; words are static.
3. The client is the observer/reporter—from his or her own point of view.
4. Clients frequently confound *map* and *territory*.

Let's consider each of these limitations further.

1. More goes on in experience than words can describe, in part because a function of our brain is to limit the stimuli in our awareness. Language imposes additional constraints, further limiting awareness in many ways. There are more things to be spoken of than there are words to describe them. We use the same words for many different experiences. Anyone who has tried to write a love letter has experienced the inadequacy of words.

When doctors say, "Point to where it hurts," they're trying to enhance verbal maps with action. An attentive, imaginative counselor hears a client say, "I just can't say what I need to say to Dad; I've tried and tried." This counselor asks the client if she would be willing to act as if the counselor is Dad, and say one of the things she "can't say." Perhaps the client's enactment in the counseling setting can clarify what words to that point have left unclear.

2. Experience is dynamic; life is process. Awareness is a stream of ever-changing sensory interactions with ourselves and our context. Our language, however, is constructed to reflect certainty and stability. Language is not an apt tool for sharing dynamic personal experience, yet we rely on it. As a counselor, be aware that the static implications of language itself have confounded the developing map.

Counselors hear (and use) words like *can't*, *should*, *never*, and *always*, as people describe maps of their lives. Terms like these box us in; they present a situation as if set in stone.

> COUNSELOR: You could never tell your mother that you're not coming home for Christmas this year.
>
> CLIENT: I could never do that.

The client's map as constructed describes a situation with no options, no choices, no possibility for change. It must seem hopeless. Does the map fit the territory? The real world? The map is so "real" for the client that she hasn't questioned its accuracy. Maps are powerful, in part because we assume that our maps tell it like it is. But they're maps, not territory.

3. If you've played or watched basketball games, you know that when the referee's whistle blows, there are at least two different views of what actually happened moments before. All of us are observers from our own points of view. Television replays sometimes enable us to go back in time and, in slow motion,

see just what happened moment-to-moment—at least from the camera's perspective. Whether this second look changes the participants' perceptions, it does afford an opportunity for considering the event from a different vantage point. As a counselor, be aware that the client's map will be drawn from her or his own personal perspective. To the extent that a different perspective can be evoked (e.g., What would I have seen or heard if I had been there?), the validity of bits of the map can be examined. The most reliable maps are those that contain features that others agree on.

4. Clients, like the rest of us, frequently confuse *map* and *territory*. When we ask clients a question such as "What do you mean by 'trouble with procrastination'?" they usually respond with generalities, with a kind of composite description of how they miss performance deadlines one after another. What's missing in their response is a reasonably clear *report* describing their actions, thoughts, and feelings and the context in which these occurred that represents an example of a deadline missed and regretted. What one hears are generalized terms, abstractions that are usually loaded with negative valences, that basically say, "I wanted to do good, and I did bad, and I feel awful." Such a general map isn't much help in understanding just what happened in this person's world and how it might be improved. It is, at best, a map of value-laden thoughts and feelings *about* a map of the territory. It is a starting place, and counselors must start where their clients are.

Behavior as Hypothesis

As counselors, we need a way to think about behavior that helps us to help our clients make the changes they seek. We think that viewing behavior as hypothesis, and viewing people as scientists who create and test hypotheses, are useful points of departure for counselors.

A hypothesis is a statement predicting what one expects to observe in the future. Hypotheses are found everywhere. Las Vegas provides ready examples. When a blackjack player tells the dealer "Hit me," the player has formed a hypothesis, a prediction about the future. The player expects that the next card he receives will not raise the total of all his cards to more than 21. A bet is a hypothesis about what one expects to observe in the future.

Think of placing a bet as a behavior, made with expectations about what will follow. Now, think of all behaviors as "bets," placed with expectations or predictions about what will happen next. Behaviors can be viewed as hypotheses, predictions about what will follow. We place our behavioral bets and observe the consequences. If we "win," our hypothesis survives; if we "lose," our hypothesis is suspect. (Realize, however, that one or a dozen "wins" doesn't rule out other possible explanations.)

We owe a considerable debt here to psychologist George Kelly (1905–1967), particularly to his work on personal construct theory and his discussions of psychotherapy. His view of persons-as-scientists and human behavior as question or hypothesis (Kelly, 1966) has helped us think about how we do what we do, as people and as counselors, and how we can change.

Behavior can be viewed as a question: If I do X, what will follow? If I do X, will Y follow? Stated as a hypothesis, if I do X, then Y will follow, or if ABC occurs, then Y will follow. Our "expertise" as persons-scientists negotiating the world grows in part as our hypotheses become more frequently supported. To say it another way, we get along better in the world as we learn to behave in ways that reflect better hypotheses.

Having the same problems over and over can be seen as a result of doing "bad science." By bad science, we mean things like distorting the results of hypothesis testing, ignoring unpleasant side effects, and posing trivial questions. A father may say to his child, "If I've told you once I've told you a hundred times, don't touch my computer!" If the father can be believed, he must still hypothesize that saying "Don't touch my computer" will "work." Bad science exacts a toll of dissatisfaction for the "scientist" as well as for those in the scientist's vicinity—child, spouse, parent, neighbors, co-workers. Thus, generating effective "If-then" hypotheses is an important part of living effectively. From the perspective of person-as-scientist, the counselor becomes the client's co-researcher, seeking to understand, examine, and submit alternative hypotheses to experimental test and revision. A door to change is opened by entertaining the thought, "What if instead of . . . you did . . . ?"

The Client in Your Mind

As we strive to understand our client, what we see and hear contributes to creating an image of the client in our mind. Blocher (1966) says, "The counselor always responds to the 'real client' as though he were like the hypothetical model that exists only in the counselor's mind" (p. 130). We, as individuals, supply the words and images that create our "map" of the clients to whom we respond.

Verbal "maps" that are more consistent with experienced reality make for choices with more satisfactory—and more predictable—results. Suppose George lunches periodically with a friend, Jerry. Their weekly lunch date is for noon at La Indita, and Jerry usually arrives about 12:10—and George is beginning to steam because Jerry is "late." How is it that after dozens of experiences with Jerry arriving at 12:10, George is still able to get upset because Jerry is late? For whatever reasons, George's map of this set of experiences—lunches with Jerry—doesn't fit the actual experiences very well, and so George is able to be surprised, upset, and make "should" statements under his breath when Jerry does what Jerry does: arrive at his usual time, 12:10. If George could learn to *hear* "12:10" when Jerry says "noon," George's expectation for Jerry would more likely be met. George's map would better fit the territory of his relationship with Jerry.

Our behavior as individuals fits the facts as we know them. We operate from the verbal map we have. We believe that people who have accurate facts make good choices. People whose verbal maps tend to be more complete, to match the territory more accurately, also tend to navigate life's tasks with minimal distressing surprises. Some of our maps improve with experience; we're open to learning and we navigate some neighborhoods more easily as time passes. However, some of our maps seem fixed in spite of experience; like George, we hit the same potholes over and over in some of life's neighborhoods.

The Importance of Empathic Listening

At the risk of appearing simplistic and redundant, we think the skill that distinguishes good clinicians from the average is their ability as empathic listeners. We cannot overemphasize the importance of accurate listening.

As counselors, we bring much with us that gets in our way as listeners: our own agendas, expectations, assumptions, experience, habits of categorizing data and people (adult, woman, middle-class, bright, poor self-image, fat, drinker, in denial), our need to appear expert, to be helpful, to be comfortable. It is very difficult to leave these "distractors" behind and to bring what Suzuki (1970) calls "beginner's eyes"— eyes that start at the beginning with this person in this moment, putting aside assuming, interpreting, analyzing, categorizing, labeling, and other processing in favor of openness—to what is here and now. This attitude of intentional naivete is a powerful asset to counselors. Counselors may have a great deal of life experience, and experienced counselors may have seen many clients, but none of us knows the next person who walks through the door. Even if we saw the person yesterday, life has continued to happen, involving him or her in things we don't know about. For a counselor, to *be aware* that you don't know and that you need instruction from your client is a powerful tool in improving your understanding.

As individuals we like feeling sure, or fairly sure, about the world we experience. We want to nail things down and get on with it. These usually useful and comfortable habits carry a price. Zukav (1979) observes that to understand something is to give up other ways of conceiving it. Once we tell ourselves we understand, we tend to stop entertaining other possibilities. That sinking feeling you get when someone says to you, "I know just what you're going through," may be partly due to your realizing that she's not interested in any more understanding than she now has. Her "film" is exposed, printed, and in the album.

As counselors, however, our knowing or understanding of clients and their world needs to be as open as possible to revision. For example, compare the expectations you might have from being introduced to an adult identified as being in an abusive relationship and an adult identified as a batterer. We have strong tendencies as humans to see and hear what fits our understanding and to ignore the rest. We need constant reminders to preserve our "beginner's eyes" and to remind us that our understanding at this moment is always tentative and subject to revision. The two mechanisms we've described earlier help us keep our beginner's eyes. The map/territory metaphor reminds us that the map of verbal descriptions is only a map and needs continual validation against the territory of the client's world. Behavior as hypothesis provides a connotatively neutral way of examining and modifying behavior that clients tend to find useful. The good or bad, success or failure judgments are separated from the act. Morals are not out the window; rather, values and actions are differentiated, so that we can better consider both.

 ## SUGGESTIONS FOR INTEGRATING ACTIVITIES

1. Sometimes we seem stuck in some part of our life; clients sometimes describe themselves as stuck in a situation. (e.g., I hate to work overtime, but I just can't turn her down). Listen to yourself or others for two or three examples of verbal maps that include situations that sound as if set in stone. For each map, think of one or two ways the map might be validated as well as ways that open up other options.

2. Monitor yourself in several situations during the next day or two. Notice a time when you feel happy, or mad, or bad. What happened in the moment just before or just as you became aware of your feeling? What expectations can you identify as existing in the moment just before the "happening"? Can you chart your map of this micro-journey? How could you experience this feeling again?

3. We are all human, striving for perfection, but with a way to go. This chapter conveyed some ideals, and writing it reminded us of places we still fall short. As an example, all clients deserve our respect. There are occasional clients who inspire us to fall short of this ideal. We hope not to just pass it off, blaming them as beyond respect. After all, it is *our* ideal. What we'd like to do is use this experience to learn more about what we mean by "every client deserves our respect." There may be something we missed when we created the mental picture of this client to whom we responded disrespectfully.

   Before we can grow from an experience where a personal ideal was unrealized, we must recognize it. We think we notice a little tweak of bad feeling somewhere inside in the moment when we abandon an ideal. Monitor yourself during the coming week or two. See whether you are aware of a moment when one of your ideals gets shunted aside. In your journal, see what you find to say about how it happened, what it means to you, and what you want to take from the experience.

   Counselors, we think, are presented with many opportunities to sacrifice ideals for some apparently more expedient act. Sharpening our skills at recognizing our derelictions is a first step in learning to anticipate and deal more satisfactorily with the issues involved. This helps to reduce the diet of bad feelings, too.

REFERENCES

Blocher, D. H. (1966). *Developmental counseling.* New York: Ronald Press.
Johnson, W. (1946). *People in quandaries—The semantics of personal adjustment.* New York: Harper.

Kelly, G. (1966). Ontological acceleration. In B. Maher (Ed.), *Clinical psychology and personality*. New York: Wiley.

Suzuki, S. (1970). *Zen mind, beginner's mind*. New York: Weatherhill.

Zukav, G. (1979). *The dancing wu li masters*. New York: Morrow. *"To understand something is to give up some other way of conceiving it."*

SUGGESTED READING

Ellerbroek, W. C. (1978, Spring). Language, thought, and disease. *CoEvolution Quarterly*, pp. 30–38. *"We will constantly remind ourselves that our observations are subjective data, and are not to be confused with 'fact.'"*

Johnson, W., & Moeller, D. (1972). *Living with change: The semantics of coping*. New York: Harper & Row. *"I have seen individuals wasting their lives fighting phantoms that they make out of words. We create our world linguistically. How else? . . .Categorization can be seen, I think, as the mechanism of racial and religious and doctrinal prejudices. If we label a person, we . . . react to him as if he and all the other people so labeled were all the same."*

Sarason, S. B. (1985). *Caring and compassion in clinical practice*. San Francisco: Jossey-Bass. *"Professionals are not noted for their willingness to engage in self-scrutiny."*

Tyler, L. E. (1978). *Individuality: Human possibilities and personal choice in the psychological development of men and women*. San Francisco: Jossey-Bass.

CHAPTER 3

Underlying Assumptions and Beliefs

Reality is what we take to be true.
What we take to be true is what we believe.
What we believe is based upon our perceptions.
What we perceive depends upon what we look for.
What we look for depends upon what we think.
What we think depends upon what we perceive.
What we perceive determines what we believe.
What we believe determines what we take to be true.
What we take to be true is our reality. —Gary Zukav

In this chapter, we identify certain beliefs that are the basis for the view of professional counseling presented here. These assumptions establish points of reference you may find helpful as you examine the logic of the ideas described in this book. Other fundamental assumptions, as yet unarticulated, may become apparent to you as you read on.

Regarding Professional Counseling

Counseling as a Voluntary Relationship

In our opinion, professional counseling occurs within a voluntary relationship. The corollary is "If it's not voluntary, it's not counseling." We prefer this view for several reasons. First, as members of a society espousing democratic ideals, we believe that all of us have the right to decide for ourselves whether counseling is in our own best interests. Second, theories of counseling assume a help *seeker*, someone who is experiencing distress, wants change, and will try new ways of being to achieve the desired outcomes. The validity of such counseling theories seems threatened when client participation is mandated by someone else (such as a spouse or the court system) and not voluntary. Third, we think of counseling as a means of helping people find and exercise their own power and growth. This happens best when people take responsibility for their own behavior, including seeking counseling.

Even so, the person referred by a spouse, a parent, or a probation officer does have the potential to be a counselee. Many people who attend the initial meeting with a counselor are required to do so by someone else ("I'll get a divorce if you don't see a counselor" or "A condition of your probation is your involvement in counseling"). From our viewpoint, these individuals may or may not leave the initial session as clients in a counseling relationship. It is the counselor's task to initiate a counseling relationship and provide the potential—and sometimes reluctant—client with information about the possibilities, limitations, and responsibilities of both counselor and client within a voluntary counseling contract. The counselor's adherence to ethical professional practice standards and a client-centered process in the initial meeting and subsequent sessions allows the mandated candidate to become the voluntary consumer of counseling services. Some options to consider in working with mandated referrals are presented in Consultation Time sections (in Part 2, "The Counseling Process Model") found in Chapters 6 through 11.

Professional Counseling as a Master–Servant Relationship

We think of professional counseling as a master–servant relationship. More generically, all professional relationships are seen as master–servant relationships, with the client/patient as the master, and the professional as the servant, bound to serve the best interests of the master (client). We have received a great deal of well-intentioned feedback about the political incorrectness of master-servant language. Our risk of offending the reader is mitigated by the power of this metaphor. The adoption of a service commitment to the will of his or her client is the guarantor of the counselor's efficient, effective, and ethical practice.

In a democratic society, each individual is considered best able to determine what is in his or her own best interests. The master/client has the right to make informed choices regarding which outcomes are to be sought, what means will be employed, and what resources (time, energy) will be committed to pursuing a mutually agreeable counseling objective.

We use the term *servant* to emphasize the primacy of client rights of self-determination and the duty of the counselor to respect those rights. Counselors, of course, are not bound to support any and all possible client goals. The relationship is voluntary for both parties.

Counseling as an Ethical Relationship

Professional counselors are bound by guidelines for ethical behavior. A number of professional associations have formal statements of professional ethics that set out the rights and responsibilities of counselor and client. Probably most counselors refer to the American Counseling Association *Code of Ethics and Standards of Practice* (Appendix A) for ethical guidance. The important point is that you should be familiar with standards of ethical practice. In a nutshell, ethical practice means treating people with the respect you would expect in their place and delivering what you advertise.

One important ethical principle is "informed consent." The client must give informed consent to—or not to—attend and participate in the proposed "treatment," with the right to terminate the counseling relationship at will. Of course, professional counselors may decline to participate in the pursuit of a client goal they find objectionable. Ethical counselors will choose not to participate when they do not feel qualified or trained to assist a particular client in addressing an issue. A referral to a more qualified counselor would follow.

The client exerts considerable influence in the counselor's life. One immediate implication of client-as-master is that it's really important for the counselor to be clear about the client's identity. As counselors, we usually assume that the person seeking change is the person in front of us, but that's not always the case. Determining the person to whom the counselor-servant owes allegiance can be complicated when more than one individual is involved, such as couples, families, parents, court personnel, or referring persons. Every time we've been part of a discussion involving some ethical predicament, ours or others, one contributing factor has always been the counselor's failure to clarify some important condition that affected possible counseling outcomes. Frequently, the major error has been failure to reconcile conflicting expectations about who the counselor is working for. In our experience, time spent clarifying the identity of the "master" is time well spent.

Counseling as the Conduit for Change Desired by the Client

Successful professional counseling is associated with change desired by clients in their life outside the counseling hour. People seek counseling because something in their present situation is unacceptable or distressing and they desire change. Professional counseling advertises itself as a means of reducing distress and increasing life satisfaction. Consequently, the ultimate criterion for professional counselors is the extent to which the client's life outside the counselor's office has moved in the desired direction.

The Counselor's Responsibility for Client Progress

Counseling is not always successful; clients sometimes don't achieve what they hope for. Sometimes clients leave a counseling session with good intentions and return the following week to report no change. Clients say things like, "After I left, I thought about it and decided I just couldn't do it," or "I forgot," or "I was too busy," or whatever. What do we do when we become aware that clients aren't meeting our mutual expectations for progress or change?

As counselors, we prefer to assume that the first explanation for unsatisfactory client outcomes or lack of progress in counseling is our own ignorance or misperformance. Counseling may not be meeting expectations because the counselor was distracted from the counseling process model tasks presented in Chapters 6 through 11. Perhaps the counselor misunderstood or misconstrued client concerns. There are other ways of "explaining" lack of counseling progress that turn attention from the counselor to the client. Clients are sometimes described as "being resistant," "being defensive," or "being in denial," for example. Rather than attributing lack of progress to our clients, we prefer to attribute it to faulty counselor performance for several reasons:

• By attributing lack of progress to counselor performance rather than to the client, we're still in the game and the next step is up to us. My behavior as a counselor is something I can change; my misperformance is something within my power to remedy—perhaps by listening more sensitively and accurately to the counselee or perhaps through seeking consultation or supervision.

• Counseling is a young profession, and there is much we don't know about how people grow, learn, and change. It would be amazing if we didn't reach the limits of our knowledge at times. Lack of counseling progress implies a need and an opportunity to acknowledge and repair our ignorance, if possible.

• We really believe the client *will* make progress if we do a better job of helping him or her articulate a desirable counseling objective and discover a means of moving toward it. If we as counselors don't really believe counseling can help this client, chances are we'll be proven right.

• And finally, "accepting responsibility for lack of progress" is a skill that we are willing to *model* for clients. Yes, clients' acknowledgment of their own responsibility for progress, or lack of it, is important within a collaborative helping relationship as well as in the achievement of desired outcomes in the clients' future. We believe that clients' responsibility for their behavior is developed more effectively within a nonjudgmental, caring relationship in which there is less need to *resist, defend,* or *deny*.

Counseling, like other team efforts, works when both counselor and client behave as if they share a common understanding of the *purpose* of counseling, their *roles* (helper, help seeker), the *focus* of counseling (a mutually desired outcome), and the *limits* that control the relationship (such as time, cost, confidentiality, behavior taboos). Counseling has its best chance of success when participants commit to a common purpose, achievable within their resources, and meet each other's expectations within the rules that apply.

Regarding Professional Counselors

We see the counselor (that is, the counselor's behavior) and the counseling process as a *catalyst* for changes in client awareness, perspective, and behavior. Counselors participate by being expert followers, collaborators, and communicators.

Following the Client's Lead

Through careful seeing and hearing, the counselor follows the client's lead, reflecting the clarity/confusion and accuracy/inaccuracy of the counselee's perception of his or her world. High-fidelity following by the counselor provides a mirror that allows the client to view his or her own thoughts, feelings, and actions more clearly.

The preemptive counselor interest in counseling is in identifying the client's purpose in seeking counseling and achieving mutually agreed-on outcomes. Any other interest (for example, building my caseload, filling my Anger Management Skills Group, preserving this marriage regardless) is a potential conflict of interest relative to counseling effectiveness.

Sometimes, for myriad reasons, counselors find themselves "counseling" faster than their clients can keep up. Counselors who get ahead of their clients may find themselves all alone.

Building a Collaborative Counselor/Client Relationship

The effective counselor brings an attitude of striving toward establishing a collaborative relationship with the client. The effectiveness of the collaboration is directly related to the following:

- The mutuality of the counseling goal
- The shared understanding of the counseling process
- The definition and division of roles and functions of counselor and client
- Effective use of an array of available tools

Effective counselors attend to client strengths and resources. The counseling process works best when clients become more aware of their own resources and capabilities in reaching desired outcomes.

Acknowledging and Penetrating Cultural Biases

Our own culture distorts our ability as individuals to accurately mirror, or empathically understand, counselees. The issue is not *whether* we are biased but *how* we are biased. To be an acculturated human is to be biased (Becker, 1971). Furthermore, as counselors, our cultural heritage as individuals becomes overlaid by another cultural system, that of professional counseling. As counselors, we are unwittingly enmeshed in a counselor culture, created through training and work setting, and marked by a proliferation of counseling theories, constructs, and strategies as well as by professionalization through certification, licensure, registries, third-party reimbursement processes, and other professional elements (Holiman & Lauver, 1987).

The counselor culture, like any other, invisibly influences our work as counselors, shaping what is attended to and what is ignored in our observing and understanding the client. The professional language within the counselor culture serves as a barrier to counselors attempting to understand clients on their own terms, apart from the professional rhetoric (Lauver, Holiman, & Kazama, 1982). As counselors we are challenged to acknowledge, recognize, and penetrate this culturally created and maintained zone of abstraction if we are to realize the ideal of empathic understanding and effective collaboration with our clients.

Regarding Clients

Our fundamental assumption about counselees is this: Don't assume anything beyond the obvious, that each counselee is a unique individual. Having said that, we do offer some observations about clients. Counseling seems to go best, and counselors function most effectively, when clients can and do learn to use their counselors well. We've identified some attributes of successful clients and present these under three headings below. We hasten to add that we believe counselors have a responsibility, as a part of informed choice, to help clients be successful. When these attributes are expressed as counselor assumptions, it is incumbent on us as counselors to check them out.

Informed Consent and Voluntary Participation

For new clients, we assume they may have questions about who the counselor is, how the counselor works, and what the counselor may expect of them. The better informed clients are, the better prepared they are to get what they need from the counselor. One way some counselors deal with this is by putting information in the hands of clients before the first session. Examples of two such handouts are included in Appendixes B and C.

We assume the person is here voluntarily, and we acknowledge the corollary, that the client has the right to stop the counseling at any time. We're interested in

---

how clients come to counseling, in part to identify their volition and also because their expectations have a lot to do with what can happen.

Desire for Change

Further, we assume that something in the person's life is no longer tolerable and that the person is seeking change. The change may be simply finding someone to listen; the change may be more profound.

All clients need to feel better about themselves. It's tough to admit personal insufficiency and to ask for help. Clients tend to underestimate their own abilities, resources, and options, discounting their past and present achievements as real evidence of personal power. Client maps tend to be full of "never" and "always" and "not really" as they describe themselves, their resources, and their achievements.

Strengths and Resources

Clients know their world better than you or I. They know what's possible, realistic, satisfying, and appropriate in the context of their world. This is not to say that their ideas and perceptions are fixed and not subject to change, but it serves as a reminder that counselors who assume they know how it is for their clients are setting themselves up for surprises.

Self-Determination and Choice

We assume clients will disclose to counselors only what they wish. What they choose to disclose may change—for better or for worse—as the relationship moves along.

Clients will always do and say what seems best to them in the moment, just as you and I do. This may create some confusion for the counselor over time as apparent inconsistencies may appear. As counselor, I need to recognize that the inconsistency and confusion I'm aware of are *my* reactions. I may need to seek help from the client in clarifying my confusion (for example, "Today I heard you say this, and I was surprised to hear it, because last week I thought I heard you say that, and I can't understand how both could be").

Issues of Respect, Trust, and Encouragement

All clients deserve my respect and trust. I'll take what they say at face value. As I become aware of feeling skeptical, unclear, or confused, I'll put my data on the table and ask for client help with my reservations or my confusion. And, as a counselor, I want to respect the client's resources of time, energy, money, and confidence; none of us have resources to waste.

Clients need to leave the first session, and every session, with something encouraging—not a counselor pep talk, but some portable resource that helps them through part of the week ahead. Many clients come to only one counseling session.

Responsibility as Consumers of Services

We assume clients will put their own interests first, without feeling pressed to please or protect their counselor. Clients may do and say some things to meet my expectations, to please, to protect, to impress, or otherwise to affect me. This possibility makes it really important for counselors to stay focused on working toward goals *clients* have chosen.

We assume every client has the right to ask about anything the counselor does, says, or suggests. Further, the client has a right to the best possible informative response. Sometimes this means the counselor needs to dig out more information about the possible effects of a suggested intervention.

Faulty Assumptions as Barriers to Effective Counseling

The assumptions we make about who we are, what our role is, and with whom we can work have a lot to do with what we can accomplish. Assumptions are ways of describing what we believe to be true of our experiences with counseling in the past and what constitutes our starting place with the next client.

Faulty or inappropriate assumptions are possible. Paying attention to how your clients behave with you can provide some clues to the appropriateness of the assumptions you're starting from. Faulty assumptions can lead to confusion and frustration, and if they are unexamined, they can cause counselor burnout.

For example, one of us took a job as a high school counselor. Part of the job description was to "counsel" with each student who appeared on the Failure List (an F in a subject for the reporting period). The counselor's procedure was to send out call slips to study hall and request the student to appear in the counselor's office. The sessions started off something like this:

STUDENT: Are you the counselor?

COUNSELOR: Yes, come in. How are things going?

STUDENT: Why did I get this call slip?

COUNSELOR: I wondered how things were going for you in school this grading period.

STUDENT: Fine.

COUNSELOR: Having any trouble in any of your classes?

STUDENT: I think I'm doing OK.

COUNSELOR: Things are going OK for you in all your classes?

STUDENT: Yeah.

COUNSELOR: (*Pause*) Well, thanks for coming in.

STUDENT: Will you sign my pass so I can get back to study hall?

Isn't this awful? Apparently the counselor is seeing a "client" where no client exists. Wherever the counselor is starting from, it's not appropriate to the situation at hand. This counselor badly needed to take a look at the territory and revise his map. A good starting place in a relationship is to pay attention to the assumptions of each participant.

❖ SUGGESTIONS FOR INTEGRATING ACTIVITIES

In the preceding section describing our assumptions, there are a number of statements of belief with which you may or may not agree. Some of these statements are listed below. For each, indicate A if you agree, AR if you agree with reservations, or D if you disagree. Then, where you have reservations or disagreement, rewrite the statement in a form you can live with, at least for now.

It might be worthwhile to find a classmate with whom you can review and discuss each other's statements.

A	AR	D	
___	___	___	1. If it's not voluntary, it's not counseling.
___	___	___	2. Professional relationships are master-servant relationships with the client as master.
___	___	___	3. The client must give informed consent to any proposed treatment.
___	___	___	4. Counselors may decline to participate in pursuit of a client goal they find objectionable.
___	___	___	5. The first explanation for unsatisfactory client progress is counselor misperformance.
___	___	___	6. The preemptive counselor interest in counseling is achievement of mutually agreed-on outcomes.
___	___	___	7. The issue is not whether counselors are biased but how they are biased.
___	___	___	8. Clients handle most parts of their lives as well as most counselors handle theirs.

			9. Clients know their own world better than you or I know it.
____	____	____	10. Clients will do and say what seems best to them in the moment.
____	____	____	11. All clients deserve the counselor's respect and trust.
____	____	____	12. Our assumptions may need to be changed as a result of experience.

REFERENCES

Becker, E. (1971). *The birth and death of meaning* (2nd ed.). New York: Free Press.

Holiman, M., & Lauver, P. J. (1987). The counselor culture and client-centered practice. *Counselor Education and Supervision, 26,* 184–191.

Lauver, P. J., Holiman, M., & Kazama, S. (1982). Counseling as battleground: Client as enemy. *Personnel and Guidance Journal, 61,* 99–101.

SUGGESTED READING

American Association for Marriage and Family Therapy. (1991). *AAMFT code of ethics*. Washington, DC: Author.

American Counseling Association. (1995). *Code of ethics and standards of practice*. Washington, DC: Author.

American Psychological Association. (1987). *Casebook on ethical principles of psychologists*. Washington, DC: Author.

London, P. (1971). *Behavior control* (Perennial Library edition). New York: Harper & Row. *"The proper use of power is seldom obvious to thoughtful men, especially if they lack religious revelations or "natural" ethics for deciding what is just."*

National Association of Social Workers. (1990). *Code of ethics* (rev. ed.). Silver Spring, MD: Author.

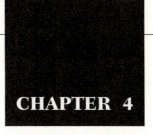

CHAPTER 4

Counselor Intentions

*The modern Indian Health Service hospital in Chinle,
in the heart of the Navajo Nation, has a hogan room so
medicine men can perform healing ceremonies. The eight-
sided room has wood walls and a wood-burning stove in
the center, similar to the traditional Navajo hogans where
healing takes place.*

*It was built out of respect for Navajo ways and to
encourage traditional believers . . . to come to the hospital. A
well-kept attractive room, it is a monument to good
intentions.*

*Yet the room is rarely used, says Dr. Carol Baase,
clinical director at the hospital. She said she thought it
may have to do with the Navajo belief that spirits linger
after death.*   —L. Myers

The preceding paragraphs appeared in a feature story entitled "Healing
Ways in the Navajo Nation." The author (Myers, 1991) was interested in
the encounter between Western medicine and ancient Navajo traditions.

It seems to us that the unused room described in the article exemplifies
too much of what counselors do with clients. Too often, we're afraid that
we listen just long enough to convince ourselves that we understand the
client's situation, and then we begin "counseling." And our clients leave.

What we're wondering now is how many of our clients leave with "empty hogans." I wonder how often our help appears reasonable and logical to us as counselors but is useless to our clients because of our ignorance of their world.

It is truly difficult to work *with* people whose world is different and to be effective in building something in *their* world that is of use to them. Perhaps if the hospital personnel in Chinle had set out to build a hogan *with* the people they hoped to serve, rather than *for* those people, the hogan might have served its intended purpose. The world of hospital realities provided a room, with wood walls and a wood-burning stove, but in a building where people die; in traditional Navajo belief, a building where a person dies is not used again. The world of hospital realities doesn't include dirt floors as an option, and a hogan without a dirt floor is not a good place for ceremonies intended to connect participants to Mother Earth.

The empty hogan story strongly suggests that those who wish to be of service to others need to be guided by the realities of the other's world. If we wish to serve others, we need to consciously put ourselves in the role of learner, seeking instruction and guidance in how useful hogans are built in their country, and by whom, and under what circumstances.

Role and Function in Counselor Behavior

The empty hogan news story caught our attention for two reasons. For one, it involves skilled professional caregivers with good intentions. Their good intentions were consistent with one of their acknowledged roles as healers: to provide a place for healing. In their function of providing a healing place, however, their performance misfired. Another reason the empty hogan caught our eye is because we have each had our share of similar experiences—good intentions consistent with our roles as child, friend, parent, or counselor that have not achieved the desired results.

The purpose of this chapter is to suggest some ways to think about counselor role and function that are intended to reduce our tendencies as "helpful" human beings to build empty hogans. What professional counselors do with clients is shaped by the requirements of counselor role and counselor function. Let's clarify what we mean by the terms *role* and *function*.

- *Counselor role*—the *whither* of counseling: Where are we going? What does the counselee want or need from counseling? What outcomes will the counselee experience if he or she deems counseling successful?
- *Counselor function*—the *how* of counseling: How can we get there? How can the client's goal be achieved? What techniques will make the most efficient use of this client's resources in achieving the desired outcomes?

Notice that both the role and the function of counselor are expressed totally in terms of the client: the *client's* needs, experiences, outcomes. If the counseling is to

TABLE 4.1 ■ Interaction of Client Needs and Client Awareness

Domains of Client Awareness	Nature of Client Need			
	Support	Clarify	Decide	Change
Think	"I need help."	"I don't know what to do."	"Should I or not?"	"I want to be respected."
Feel	Scared, alone	Confused, frustrated	Puzzled	Angry, determined
Act	Sit alone, weep	Start more things than I finish	Ask for opinions	Fight with partner

be successful, the counselor must help the client to articulate the needs that have brought him or her to counseling. Often clients are aware of their needs in different ways, on different levels. The counselor must be sensitive to these varied types of awareness as he or she helps the client move to a realization of the counseling goals. Next we examine client needs and awareness in relation to the counselor's functions.

Functions Implicit in the Counselor Role

Gilmore (1973) has defined the purpose of counseling in language with which many would agree: The purpose of counseling "is to help people of all ages in a variety of settings cope constructively with the business of being human" (pp. 4–5). An important function of the counselor is to help clients delineate the kinds of change the clients seek (their needs) in the process of coping with the business of being human. The matrix shown in Table 4.1 assumes a universe of possibilities defined by four categories of human need (after Tyler, 1969) and three domains of human awareness. Within this matrix are examples of what clients might report for each category of awareness and need.

Understanding Client Needs

The kinds of things for which people seek help from counselors can be considered in four general categories: support, clarification, decision making, and change. Sometimes the focus moves from area to area; sometimes several areas seem mixed together.

1. *Support.* All people seeking help, say Frank and Frank (1991), are alike in that they are to some extent demoralized; their confidence in their own abilities is shaken. Thus, everyone seeking counseling needs support, and there are times of

crisis in everyone's life when support makes a rough spot easier to handle. Synonyms for support might be attention, caring, or love.

2. *Clarification*. Sometimes a part of life seems too complicated to sort out. Confused thoughts and feelings make it hard to know just how things stand. Events that seem positive reveal negative aspects that leave us uncertain; words carry double messages that create a kind of internal fog. We begin to mistrust our ability to think straight. "I don't know what to think. I don't know how I really feel. It's like being on a roller coaster."

3. *Decision making*. People seek help around "crossroads" issues, such as which career to pursue or whether or not to marry, to leave a job, to ask for a raise, to leave home. Sometimes people are stuck because their options are not clear, or because the options raise critical issues of personal values, or because the consequences seem large and uncertain. Sometimes people simply don't seem to know how to make a decision.

4. *Change*. In a sense, everyone seeking counseling wants change in some part of his or her life outside the counseling relationship. Something about the present is distressing or unsatisfactory. Maybe the person wants to manage money or time better or find a different way of dealing with a relationship; maybe it's a more pervasive issue, like becoming more assertive.

In summary, counselees are viewed as people seeking the four kinds of help noted above: *support, clarification, decision making*, and *change*. With any one counselee, of course, one or more of these areas might be involved at any point in time. The counselor needs to know which of these areas is most important to the counselee at the moment in order to be an effective and efficient helper.

Interpreting Needs through Client Awareness

One factor in understanding a counselee's needs is observing how the counselee reports awareness of his or her experience. People differ in the aspects of their behavior of which they are most aware. Some counselees "tell their stories" in terms of their *thoughts*; others may report *feelings* or *actions*. For a given individual, the salient aspect of experience (thoughts, feelings, actions) can change from situation to situation. One client may say, "I'm more aware of *thoughts* while I'm listening to a lecture, or planning my day." Another may report "I'm more aware of *feelings* while hugging my spouse, or watching a sunset." And for still another, "I'm more aware of *actions* while building a cabinet, or paddling a canoe." *Thoughts, feelings*, and *actions* can all be quite vivid at the same time, as when I'm driving along on the freeway and someone crosses lanes right under my front bumper! (This can bring a surge of *feeling* . . . angry *thoughts* . . . foot *hits* brake!!!!)

Although people experience thoughts, feelings, and actions concurrently, they sometimes are much more aware of one domain than of others. And there are situations in which people seem unable to report awareness of what they were feeling, or thinking, or doing. We think about such situations as ones that are incompletely "mapped" and thus difficult to comprehend and change. Counselors who attend to all three domains of client experience—*actions, thoughts,* and *feelings*—are best equipped to build high-fidelity "maps" of their counselee's experiences.

We're fairly sure that other domains of experience exist. People refer to spiritual, transcendental, ethereal, mystical, and other realms of being. Actions, thoughts, and feelings, however, represent the domains we usually find ourselves involved in as counselors. These three domains are the central focus of an array of counseling theories that are briefly examined in the next section.

Helping Clients Achieve Their Goals

One traditional source of ideas about how change can be effected through counseling has been counseling theory. There are many theories or models of counseling. Corsini (1981) presented 64 of what he called "major innovative approaches" in one book. One way counseling theories differ is in which domain of behavior each accords most prominence. If counseling theories wore T-shirts, most theories might wear one of the following messages:

> *Think* Right, Be Right (cognitive theories)
> *Feel* Right, Be Right (affective theories)
> *Do* Right, Be Right (action theories)

We know of no major counseling theory that, even though emphasizing one, does not recognize the importance of *each* of these aspects of human experience.

Theories can be described as having a range and focus of convenience (Kelley, 1958). They are originated by individuals who have observed a particular set of phenomena through a particular set of beliefs and have created an explanation that fits their observations. The *range of convenience* of a theory is the range of circumstances/individuals/phenomena that a theory explains most effectively, whereas the *focus* of a theory is the nature of the events/phenomena the theory addresses. Thus, cognitive theories focus primarily on *thoughts*; they include techniques helpful in elucidating thoughts and offer strategies incorporating thoughts as a mechanism of change. Affective theories similarly have a range and focus of convenience centering on *feelings*, and action theories center on *actions*.

Where do we as counselors look for resources when faced with a client whose need is support and whose primary awareness is of feeling, or lack of feeling? The *affective* theorists are most likely to have the concepts and tools needed to work with this person, at this time. With the same client, later on, thoughts may be more salient than feelings, and concepts and techniques from *cognitive* theorists are likely to be the most appropriate. Still later, if life changes become desirable, *action* techniques may be most helpful. At the end of this chapter we have included a partial list of theory references we have found useful.

In our view, a professional counselor's choice of tools—concepts, strategies, techniques—is more appropriately determined by the needs, resources, and context of the immediate client than by commitment to a theoretical model of human behavior. The counselor's value is in her or his ability to identify the most efficient and effective tool for the work to be done by this client in the client's world. The counselor's ability as "expert consultant" is enhanced by a number of conditions:

- *The counselor's attention to the counselee's own resources and experience with particular tools*—If posting a list of goals on the car dashboard worked in the past, maybe we should select an adaptation of this approach. If it wasn't the right tool for the job with a previous counselee, will trying it again be a waste of time and effort?

- *The counselor's willingness to stock her or his professional toolbox with a variety of information and skills to increase the options available to address counselee concerns and goals*—The best counselors we know review books and journals, take classes and workshops, get regular clinical supervision, make audio- and videotapes, and otherwise regularly expand their toolboxes.

- *The counselor's ongoing evaluation of the effectiveness of each tool when applied in particular contexts*—The counselor who is willing to learn from his or her own experience, and the experience of each counselee, will realize that certain approaches and techniques work very well in some contexts and not as well in others. The counselor who evaluates her or his efforts with integrity will, from time to time, realize—sometimes painfully—that a particular "tool," which may have cost time, money, and commitment to a set of values, is a piece of counseling *junk*.

- *The counselor's involvement in a professional situation that offers her or him the opportunity to reorganize and refamiliarize herself or himself with the toolbox from time to time*—It's easy to be "on automatic" in the midst of a schedule filled with hourly appointments and other demands of public and private counseling settings. When we're reacting to our clients rather than responding to their specific needs we tend to use the same tools time and again rather than selecting the approach or technique that is most responsive to *this* person with her or his specific needs.

It seems to us, then, that counselor behavior is influenced by these elements:

- Expectations the counselor brings to his or her role as counselor
- The counselor's view of the counselee and the nature of the counselee's needs
- Counselor commitment to serve the best interests of the counselee as mutually agreed on
- The counselor's adherence to a counseling process that can result in the counselee's needs being met
- The skills the counselor has learned to use

SUGGESTIONS FOR INTEGRATING ACTIVITIES

1. Apply for membership in a state and/or national professional organization for counselors. Most have special rates for students. Your membership should bring you a copy of the association's guidelines for ethical practice, a periodic newsletter, and at least one periodic professional journal. Each of these presents information with implications for appropriate, effective counselor behavior. The addresses for four associations are given here:

American Association for Marriage
and Family Therapy
1100 17th Street, N.W., 10th
Floor Washington, DC 20036-4601

American Counseling Association
5999 Stevenson Avenue
Alexandria, VA 22304-3300

American Psychological Association
1200 Seventeenth St., N.W.
Washington, DC 20036

National Association for Social
Workers
7981 Eastern Ave.
Silver Spring, MD 20910

2. Begin building familiarity with the range of counseling theories and approaches to be found in the professional literature. You might start with examples of cognitive, affective, and action-based models presented in one of the books listed in the "Surveys" section of the Suggested Reading at the end of this chapter. You might organize your impressions of each model with questions like these:

What accounts for human problems?
How do people change?
For whom is this approach appropriate?
What is expected of the counselees?
What is the role of the counselor?
How is the counseling process described?
What special techniques are involved in the process?
What is the outcome of successful counseling?

REFERENCES

Corsini, R. J. (Ed.). (1981). *Handbook of innovative psychotherapies*. New York: Wiley.

Frank, J. D., & Frank, J. B. (1991). *Persuasion and healing* (3rd ed.). Baltimore: Johns Hopkins University Press.

Gilmore, S. (1973). *The counselor-in-training*. New York: Appleton-Century-Crofts.

Kelley, G. A. (1958). Man's construction of his alternatives. In G. Lindzey (Ed.), *The assessment of human motives*. New York: Rinehart.

Myers, L. (1991, January 6). Healing ways. *Arizona Daily Star* (from *Chicago Tribune*), pp. E1, E9.

Tyler, L. (1969). *The work of the counselor* (3rd ed.). New York: Appleton-Century-Crofts.

SUGGESTED READING

Surveys of counseling theories/models

Corsini, R. (Ed.). (1981). *Current psychotherapies*. Itasca, IL: F. E. Peacock.

Patterson, C. H. (1986). *Theories of counseling and psychotherapy*. New York: Harper & Row.

Prochaska, J. (1979). *Systems of psychotherapy: A transtheoretical analysis*. Pacific Grove, CA: Brooks/Cole.

Stefflre, B. (1972). *Theories of counseling*. New York: McGraw-Hill.

Tosi, D. J., Leclair, S., Peters, H. J., & Murphy, M. (1987). *Theories and applications of counseling*. Springfield, IL: Charles C Thomas.

Cognitive models

Adler, A. (1968). *The practice and theory of individual psychology*. Totowa, NJ: Littlefield, Adams.

Berne, E. (1961). *Transactional analysis in psychotherapy*. New York: Grove Press.

Berne, E. (1964). *Games people play*. New York: Grove Press.

Dinkmeyer, D. C., Pew, W. L., & Dinkmeyer, D. C., Jr. (1979). *Adlerian counseling and psychotherapy*. Pacific Grove, CA: Brooks/Cole.

Harris, T. A. (1969). *I'm OK—You're OK*. New York: Harper & Row.

Manaster, G. J., & Corsini, R. (1982). *Individual psychology*. Itasca, IL: F. E. Peacock.

Affective models

Rogers, C. R. (1951). *Client-centered therapy*. Boston: Houghton Mifflin.

Rogers, C. R. (1961). *On becoming a person*. Boston: Houghton Mifflin.

Perls, F. S. (1969). *Ego, hunger, and aggression: The beginning of gestalt therapy*. New York: Random House.

Action/behavioral models

Kanfer, F. H., & Goldstein, A. P. (Eds). (1986). *Helping people change* (3rd ed. rev.). New York: Pergamon Press.

Krumboltz, J. D., & Thoresen, C. E. (Eds.). (1969). *Behavioral counseling—Cases and techniques*. New York: Holt, Rinehart & Winston.

Meichenbaum, D. (1985). *Stress inoculation training*. New York: Pergamon Press.

Stuart, R. B. (Ed.). (1977). *Behavioral self-management*. New York: Brunner/Mazel.

CHAPTER 5

The Counseling Process Model

The map must fit the territory if we are to get where we think we are going. —Wendell Johnson

In this chapter, we describe a counseling process model that is consistent with the assumptions and beliefs about the nature of professional counseling discussed earlier. A process model is a kind of cognitive map that suggests a direct and immediate guide for action. It supplies a way to answer the counselor's question, "What should I be trying to achieve right now?"

The model presented here describes the counseling process as a series of six *counselor* functions or tasks. Although the counseling process could be described in terms of client tasks, emphasizing the counselor tasks better suits our purposes here. This book is designed as a guide for *counselors*; therefore, presenting the model from the counselor's perspective encourages the reader to focus on the helper's thoughts, feelings, and actions.

Evolution of the Six-Function Model

The model discussed here is built around six functions, but there is nothing magical about that number. The steps evolved naturally through our experience as counselors.

The senior author began professional life with a one-function model: Emulate Carl Rogers (one of the two most influential counselors of this century). That model evolved—through collaboration with a colleague,

Dr. Tom Froehle—to a three-function model of counselor tasks: Understand, Do, Evaluate (Froehle & Lauver, 1970). The one- and three-function models provided some focus on counselor tasks, but important aspects of the counseling relationship were lumped together and thus tended to be overlooked and poorly understood. In retrospect, the three-step model represented an important attitude shift—from concern about counselor performance to focus on counselor purpose: achieving client goals.

In 1970, we encountered Robert Mager's (1962) groundbreaking book, *Preparing Instructional Objectives*, in which he articulates a three-question basic guide to the problem-solving process: Where are we going? How can we get there? How will we know we've arrived? Mager's three guiding questions represent a process committed to collaborative, goal-oriented thought and action, a very appropriate perspective for counselors. These three questions are benchmarks or guides for problem solvers. These guiding questions orient our efforts and keep us on track as counselors. When we're confused, it's probably because we haven't paid sufficient attention to one of these questions—and it's usually the first one!

The next generation was a 10-step process model, elaborating each of Mager's questions to better reflect the details of counseling, but 10 steps were a lot to keep in mind. The present 6-step process model has proved the most useful to date. It's simple enough to remember as a functional map of the counseling process, and it seems to highlight the critical tasks in helping clients.

The primary point of this historical aside is that a process model is intended to be a practical personal guide for the counselor. Use the one presented in this book as a starting place and let your experience with counselees teach you how to adapt it to your capabilities. If you're interested in other versions of process models, several are listed at the end of this chapter. However your personal model develops, though, we believe that Mager's three questions are still fundamental to any professional helping process. You will see how they work with the Counseling Process Model, discussed next.

The Six Counselor Tasks
of the Counseling Process Model

The Counseling Process Model presented in this handbook is anchored in the premise that counseling (a) is a collaborative *relationship* between counselor and counselee, (b) is guided by the counselee's goals, and (c) follows a process committed to achieving those goals. The success or lack of success of the counseling process is gauged by the client's experience—his or her thinking, feeling, and doing—outside the counseling hour, relative to the goals established within the counseling relationship. Thus, client goals not only drive the counseling process—that is, whatever occurs in counseling must serve counselee goals—but they also create the yardstick for measuring the effectiveness of the counseling enterprise.

Counselors' function is to help clients cope with problems in living and to achieve more satisfactory lives. The ultimate test of a counseling process model, then, is client outcome. We believe that counselors who perform the tasks named in the present model will deliver what they have advertised—namely, helping counselees achieve the changes they desire in their lives.

Each of the six steps or tasks of the Counseling Process Model is briefly described below. The steps are headed by the "Guiding Question" they address. Each task statement begins with a *verb* indicating that action is required from the counselor to advance the process.

Guiding Question 1: Where Are We Going?

STEP 1: INITIATE COUNSELING RELATIONSHIP

Counselors must create a relationship within which clients can share their most intimate and personal concerns. Further, the client's expectation that counseling can be helpful is a critical determinant of counseling outcome (Frank, 1973). Maintaining and enhancing clients' positive expectations is a crucial counselor task throughout the relationship (Kirsch, 1990). The initiation phase of the relationship usually progresses smoothly when consensus is reached on the purpose and focus of counseling, the roles of the counselor and the client, and the limits of the relationship.

STEP 2: UNDERSTAND COUNSELEE CONCERNS EMPATHICALLY

The success of counseling depends heavily on the client's belief that the counselor understands and accepts him or her. The counselor's ability to exhibit genuineness, warmth, and accurate empathic understanding has systematically been shown to affect client outcome (Truax & Mitchell, 1971). Counselors need to be clear about what is unsatisfactory in the client's life and what changes are desired.

STEP 3: NEGOTIATE COUNSELING OBJECTIVES

Clients and counselors need to agree on clear and specific desired outcomes to ensure mutuality of purpose and efficiency of effort. Helping counselees achieve their desired objectives is the counselor's reason for being in the relationship.

We have found one study of the accuracy with which counselors understand client goals (Thompson & Zimmerman, 1969). At a university counseling center, 315 clients and their 27 counselors were given a goal checklist at several points during counseling, including after the first and the final sessions. Each was asked to check the goals clients wanted to reach. The researchers found a marked discrepancy between goals of clients and their counselors, with no convergence of goals over time. This is not encouraging.

We can't overemphasize the importance to counselors and clients of keeping Mager's first question in mind: *Where are we going?* The answer to this always needs to represent an outcome of importance to the client. And what clients believe is important can change during the counseling process for a number of reasons: new experience, new insights, greater trust in the counselor, and others. Don't assume that the counseling objective will not change.

Guiding Question 2: How Can We Get There?

STEP 4: IDENTIFY PLAN TO MEET OBJECTIVES/ACHIEVE OUTCOMES

An effective plan is a sequence of actions that can lead to the desired outcome. The model here involves an outcome-oriented, collaborative planning process that takes advantage of the client's present skills, knowledge, and resources. Efficient counselors will attend to the counselee from the first moment, noting human relationships, skills, information, and achievements that represent potential client resources during the planning stage. Further, efficient counselors continually build a repertoire of techniques that may serve as a basis for planning with counselees. (Examples can be found in the Erikka transcripts that begin in Chapter 6.)

Guiding Question 3: How Will We Know We've Arrived?

STEP 5: SUPPORT THE PLAN

Plans by themselves don't change things; action does. The challenge is to help clients act on their intentions in *their* world, outside the counseling office. Some counselors call this "doing the homework" (and some clients find the "homework" metaphor objectionable). When homework is not done, the counselor must analyze performance problems to learn how the expected performance is being side-tracked.

STEP 6: EVALUATE COUNSELING

The effectiveness of the plan, and of the process, is observable ultimately in the form of desired change in the client's world. Specifically, counseling is successful when the negotiated objective is met. But every day is a new day, and every day we are different people. Circumstances change, as do our ideas of what's good for us. Clients are entitled to change their priorities; counselors need to be prepared to renegotiate objectives in midstream. Change is the nature of the universe; nothing else is constant.

The Importance of Communication Skills

This model is presented in terms of counselor actions, and that focus may convey the impression that counseling is something done *to* counselees. However, as you become familiar with these materials, you will see that counseling is a process done *with* counselees. The more the counselor can engage the client as a co-worker, the more the counselor can empower the client's informed choices at decision points, the more powerful will be the counseling process.

The success of counseling depends heavily on the client's belief that the counselor understands and accepts him or her (Frank, 1973). The counselor's ability to exhibit genuineness, warmth, and accurate, empathic understanding has systematically been shown to relate to client outcome (Truax & Mitchell, 1971). Table 5.1 outlines the Counseling Process Model and indicates basic interpersonal counselor skills that contribute to each task. The tasks identified in this model and the skills required to perform them are the subject of the rest of the book.

The Process Model as a Map for Counseling

The Counseling Process Model itself is a map we have adopted as a useful way of thinking about and guiding ourselves through the territory of counseling relationships. Our experience has been that when we follow this map we stay on track in counseling; we tend to arrive at our desired destination: client goal achievement.

The Counseling Process Model is thus both a map describing our past experiences as counselors, and a map or plan we will use to guide us through our next counseling encounters. As we work with clients using the model, we are interested in learning about their past maps reflecting problematic territory for them as we work toward understanding the problem, and their possible future maps reflecting the territory we hope to help clients reach as we consider where we are going.

We think of the first three tasks, Steps 1–3, as the process of learning about the client's map in the neighborhood of the distressing experiences that have brought the person to counseling. As clients begin telling their stories, we usually get the equivalent of aerial photos, sometimes from quite a distance. By *aerial photo* we mean general images: "We've been fighting a lot more lately," or "Now that she's earning her own money she's more independent."

The process of initiating the relationship (Step 1), understanding client concerns (Step 2), and negotiating the counseling objective (Step 3) involves creating a collegial partnership to consider which parts of the aerial photo are important and to get closer to those parts, toward creating a high-fidelity map of the areas of interest. The emerging details are useful in resolving the issue, Where are we going? Map study also yields information about resources that may help us with the next

TABLE 5.1 ■ COUNSELING PROCESS MODEL AND BASIC COMMUNICATIONS SKILLS

Guiding Question	Counselor Tasks	Interpersonal Skills
Where are we going?	Step 1. Initiate counseling relationship	*Attending* Attend Accept Use open leads
	Step 2. Understand client concerns empathically	*Following* Restate Paraphrase Reflect
	Step 3. Define desired outcomes	*Focusing* Pinpoint actions, thoughts, and feelings State specific objectives
How can we get there?	Step 4. Identify plan to achieve desired outcomes	All the above
	Step 5. Support the plan	All the above
How will we know we've arrived?	Step 6. Evaluate counseling	All the above

question—How can we get there?—and that will support the client's proposed journey into more satisfactory territory.

We think of the skills in Step 1 as a means of manifesting the counselor's commitment to helping. The skills in Step 2 encourage clients to explore their problematic territory and keep counselors on track with their clients. The pinpointing skills in Step 3 help to create the most high-fidelity maps possible of past and present client experience and hoped-for future experience. As a desirable future territory comes into focus, still another map-related operation begins: How can we get there? This implies planning the journey that likely will lead into the desired territory. Our purpose as counselors at this point is to support clients as they try out their new maps. Finally, in Step 6 the counselor verifies continually that the process is on track for this client and is progressing toward achievement of the agreed-on client objective.

In using the map metaphor as we work with clients, we sometimes talk in terms of *inside world* and *outside world*. Your inside world is the world as you experience it. Your outside world is the world you share with others. Maps that are effective for you represent a good fit between inside world and outside world. Conversely, we often find it useful to think of maps that don't work well as inside world/outside world mismatches. As an example, if the inside world of the dieter says, "I can drink all the light beer I want and still lose weight," the outside world of scales and belt sizes may contain some unpleasant surprises.

A key part of recognizing and repairing map/territory differences is the ability to discriminate between inside world and outside world. We try to keep this in mind as we work with clients in two ways. Obviously, we're concerned about inside world/outside world confusion among clients. To resolve these issues, we find pinpointing procedures helpful. More challenging for counselors themselves is keeping a high level of agreement between *their* inside map of the client and the outside territory of the client who is actually there. This technique is demonstrated in the transcripts of the counseling interview with Erikka, presented at the end of each chapter, beginning with Chapter 6. Notice how the counselor continually uses pinpointing and following responses. These tools contribute substantially to ensuring the highest possible agreement between the counselor's map of the client and the territory of the client, as represented by Erikka's behavior during the session.

SUGGESTIONS FOR INTEGRATING ACTIVITIES

1. Read Winborn's (1977) excellent discussion of the need for better consumer education by counselors. He includes a model counselor "advertisement" for potential clients.

2. Write a draft of a one-page "advertisement" of your opening practice as a counselor. Your intended audience is your potential counselees. Describe the purpose and focus of counseling as you offer it, counselor and client roles in counseling, and limits or conditions under which your services are offered.

Of course, you will be limited in how specific you can be right now by how clear you are on whom you want to serve, and where. Just go ahead and make whatever assumptions you want to make at this point in order to get a draft written. Because people have a range of ideas about who counselors are and what they do, you should be as clear as possible in your own mind about what your role and function as a counselor will be.

References

Frank, J. D. (1973). *Persuasion and healing* (rev. ed.). Baltimore: Johns Hopkins University Press.

Froehle, T. C., & Lauver, P. J. (Eds.). (1970). *Perspectives on counseling: Understanding, doing and evaluating*. New York: Selected Academic Readings, Simon & Schuster.

Kirsch, I. (1990). *Changing expectations: A key to effective psychotherapy.* Pacific Grove, CA: Brooks/Cole.

Mager, R. F. (1962). *Preparing instructional objectives.* Belmont, CA: Fearon.

Thompson, A., & Zimmerman, R. (1969). Goals of counseling: Whose? When? *Journal of Counseling Psychology, 16*, 121–125.

Truax, C. B., & Mitchell, K. M. (1971). Research on certain therapist interpersonal skills in relation to process and outcome. In A. E. Bergin & S. Garfield

(Eds.), *Handbook of psychotherapy and behavior change: An empirical analysis* (pp. 299–344). New York: Wiley.

Winborn, B. B. (1977). Honest labeling and other procedures for the protection of consumers of counseling. *Personnel and Guidance Journal, 56,* 206–208.

Suggested Reading

Brown, J. H., & Brown, C. S. (1977). *Systematic counseling: A guide for the practitioner.* Champaign, IL: Research Press.

Corrigan, R. E., & Kaufman, R. A. (1966). *Why systems engineering?* (2nd ed.). Palo Alto, CA: Fearon.

Silvern, L. C. (1972). *Systems engineering applied to training.* Houston, TX: Gulf Publications.

Stewart, N. R. et al. (1978). *Systematic counseling.* Englewood Cliffs, NJ: Prentice Hall.

P A R T

The Counseling Process Model

Where Are We Going?

An Overview of Steps 1 through 3

This first of the three guiding questions seeks to set the purpose of the relationship. In each relationship, the destination will be uniquely personal to each counselee. The first three steps of the Counseling Process Model are intended to result in a sharply focused and individually unique response to the question of purpose.

Step 1, *Initiate the Relationship*, and Step 2, *Understand Counselee Concerns Empathically*, usually seem to happen together, the relationship beginning and developing as the counselor seeks to understand how this person came to counseling and what the client hopes for as a result.

As the client's "story" emerges, the guiding question "Where are we going?" impels the counselor to listen especially for two kinds of information: *expressions of distress*, which may be indicators of the locus and nature of problematic aspects of the counselee's life, and *hopes, wishes*, and *aspirations*, which may be indicators of possible counseling objectives.

Concurrently, the skilled counselor, anticipating "How can we get there?" begins an inventory of client assets. As the client self-discloses, the counselor begins compiling a mental inventory of client achievements, information, skills, and resources—human, physical, and psychic—that may be tapped to support client efforts to change.

As the counselor senses that the "story" has been told, at least for now, and the inventory of distresses and aspirations seems complete, it may be time to move toward the next level, Step 3, *Negotiate Counseling Objectives*. One way to begin this phase is for the counselor to reiterate the problematic events and the counselee's hopes and wishes arising from them. In cases of multiple issues, some counselors ask clients which they prefer to work on, or which would be the best first step for them to take. The task is to examine possible objectives and to agree on which will be addressed initially. This process of setting the first objective may come quickly, as some clients have pretty clear ideas from the outset. Setting objectives may take considerable time, however, with lots of cycling back to Step 2 as additional information is needed in considering options and arriving at an objective that's important to the counselee, is worth some effort, is achievable, and promises a more satisfactory future.

CHAPTER 6

Step 1:
Initiate Counseling
Relationship

Learn your theories as well as you can, but put them aside
when you touch the miracle of the living soul.
—C. G. Jung

A primary factor in determining success for counselors as well as for anyone else who lives or works with human beings is accurate communication. Lack of communication or faulty communication is the diagnosis we hear of many kinds of human problems—from faltering marital relationships to getting the wrong dressing on the salad we ordered. "We're not communicating" is a frequently heard complaint. "You don't understand" is the way too many dialogues come to an end.

To be effective, counselors must be able to create a relationship within which counselees can share their most intimate and personal concerns. Clients who like, respect, and trust their counselors are most able to explore themselves and their life situations fruitfully. It is not enough for counselors simply to want and expect the liking, trust, and respect of their clients; counselors must *earn* it.

Initiate Counseling Relationship is identified as the first task in the counseling process because client expectation is so important from the first moments. We believe the primary determinant of counseling outcome for clients is their expectation that counseling can be helpful (Kirsch, 1990). To the extent that the counselor can maintain and enhance positive expectations, good things can happen in clients' lives. Counselees have long been known to value their counselors' understanding, acceptance, and respect (Fiedler, 1950).

The materials presented in this chapter focus on how counselors can set the stage for a successful joint venture. They were developed to help beginning counselors acquire the communications skills needed to earn the liking, trust, and respect of their counselees. These same materials have been used with students in business, teaching, law, health care, and other areas where skilled listening is important. The skills themselves are also useful between friends, parents and children, co-workers, and with any others when accurate, empathic understanding is intended and valued.

Counselor Communication Skills and Client Expectations

Think of communications skills as tools. Tools can be used well or poorly, depending on the competence and attitudes of the user. The tools themselves don't determine the quality of the result. Rather, effective use of tools requires the *user* to have a clear purpose in mind and a genuine commitment to achieving it as well as a measure of skill. Just as it takes more than paints and technical skill to create a work of art, so it takes more than words to create a feeling in a speaker that he or she is being understood. Any power in the listening skills discussed here rests primarily on the assumption that you *want* to be an accurate and effective listener, that you sincerely want to understand the other person as accurately and completely as possible. Technical competence with communications skills alone is insufficient; effective communication occurs when skills become a genuine expression of your sincere desire to enter and understand the world of the other person.

The Power of Clear Intentions

Intending to be an accurate and effective listener, being clear and consistent about your intention to understand, is important in three ways: really intending to listen builds trust, reduces confusion, and leads to better listening skills.

1. *Intending* to understand builds trust, because the other person senses a *consistency* of purpose in your nonverbal and verbal messages.

2. *Intending* to understand reduces the confusion that can come from conflicting counselor goals that may cycle in and out of the relationship. If, instead of wanting to appear an expert, you concentrate on wanting to understand, you will not confuse the client.

3. Consistently *intending* to understand leads to improved skills as you get feedback about how others respond to your efforts. A person who feels understood lets you know it, and that lets *you* know which listening tools are most effective with this particular client.

Each of these three points is important enough for us to examine it in greater detail.

INTENTIONS AND TRUST

Trust in a relationship is essential. Trust means that one's behavior is dependable, predictable, and consistent. We tend to be wary of people who send conflicting messages about the real focus of their attention. The waitress who takes your order while looking out the window, the cashier who makes your change while talking to someone on the phone, or the person who answers your question while looking at the newspaper all make you wonder whether you can trust their response. Contrast this with someone who asks you, "Where is the nearest restroom?" You have that person's whole attention; he or she really wants to hear and understand your response.

We communicate both verbally and nonverbally. We send messages with our words as well as by our posture, gestures, tone of voice, facial movements, and body position—our whole selves. We tend to *trust* people when their nonverbal messages seem consistent with the words they utter. On the other hand, we are wary of people whose words say one thing while their faces, tone of voice, or gestures say something else; their words register as insincere.

Trust is built when words and nonverbal signals are in harmony. In counseling, as in other relationships, trust grows when both verbal and nonverbal messages are consistent. Consistency of these messages is produced by clarity and constancy of intent. If you don't really *mean* to listen, you can't fake it very long. "People do quite readily understand the true meaning when the verbal and implicit nonverbal parts of a message are inconsistent—they rely on the implicit part and make their judgment accordingly" (Mehrabian, 1981, p. 86). If you do advertise your intention to understand someone, and if you maintain this intention throughout the relationship, the speaker will find that your words and your nonverbal messages create a harmonious whole, and the person will come to trust you over time as someone who really does what you say you will.

INTENTIONS AND REDUCTION OF CONFUSION

Confusion in a relationship arises when expectations are upset. In counseling, as in other relationships, people become confused when we act in an unexpected way. If you have advertised your willingness to listen and understand, expectations are set up about how you will behave. For example, clients will expect the flow of information to be from them to you, not the reverse.

In a relationship, many roles are possible: adviser, teacher, judge, entertainer, rescuer, consoler, attacker, master, expert, to name a few. In the process of listening and understanding, it is easy for us to be distracted from the *listener* role. We hear someone's "mistake" and want to correct it. We hear someone's pain and want to relieve it. We hear someone's lapse and want to judge the person. Our clients become confused when we abandon our advertised intention to listen and understand and instead assume other roles.

When you find yourself involved with someone and confusing things seem to be happening, check your intentions. You may have abandoned your initial role without being aware of it. Get back to your advertised intention, and do it to the best of your ability.

If for some reason your original intention is no longer appropriate, discuss the situation with the other person. Whatever you do, *do not* unilaterally "bail out" on your original contract! Maintaining awareness of your intention to understand empathically provides a solid answer when you find yourself asking, "Why am I here? Where are we going? What should I be doing to find out?" Listen!

INTENTIONS AND SKILL BUILDING

Practice alone does not bring perfection. It is intentional practice guided by observed results that produces competence. Becoming a more skilled listener, becoming better at understanding people, starts with intending to understand. Learning the skills described on the following pages will help you become a better listener; but practicing these skills while really *intending* to understand what the other person is describing will move you farther and faster along the road to competence. You will move faster because your nonverbal behavior will be more consistent with your verbal behavior. When you say "Tell me more about that," you will *look, act,* and *sound* as though you really want to know. You will move further because you will find yourself modifying these skills and creating new ones as you encourage and facilitate the responses of your clients. Necessity is the mother of invention; when you know you need more information, you will find ways to elicit it.

Your experience in attempting to understand another person can be a powerful teacher, if you can recognize the clues. The moment-to-moment actions, thoughts, and feelings that bombard your awareness during an interchange with another person represent your best attempts to listen and understand. Observing your own performance on audiotape or videotape is an excellent way to track how your performance matches your intentions. After-the-fact recollections aren't much help for this purpose; they are inevitably biased and incomplete accounts of how things went. Similar to the verbal replays of Monday morning quarterbacks, your undocumented recollections of your earlier performances serve needs at work in the present moment. One picture or videotape is worth a thousand words because words, especially recollections, simply cannot capture experience.

Clarity of intention is a powerful ally in consistent, effective performance. Confusions arise when intentions are unclear or change without warning or notice. Just as you set yourself to practice the skills in the following pages, make it a habit to tell yourself very explicitly your immediate intentions, perhaps something like this: "For the next five minutes, I want to use attending and following skills to listen and understand as completely as possible whatever this person wants to share with me; and for the next five minutes I will ignore other goals and pursue just this one."

This point is so important we can't leave without reiterating it: *Clarity of intention is a powerful ally in consistent, effective performance.* As we watched the recent Winter Olympics, performer after performer talked about the importance of being focused. We watched clips of skiers at the top of the hill, standing crouched, eyes closed, as they went down the hill in their minds, arms and hands moving as they focused on each piece of their anticipated performance. We heard athletes disappointed in their performance talk about being distracted from their tasks, about losing focus. When you are experiencing confusion and uncertainty, when things seem to be out of control, getting in touch with your intentions and regaining your focus can help clarify the best direction and the means to achieve it.

Attending Skills

Clients must experience you as really interested in them and as really caring before they will be willing to participate fully in counseling. You need skills that communicate your attention and interest and caring to your counselee. Using attending skills appropriately is an effective way of expressing your willingness to develop a counseling relationship.

Earlier, we said that trust develops over a sequence of interactions in which the nonverbal messages fit the words. Your use of attending skills to build trust with each individual counselee must be guided by the understanding and acceptance of cultural variations in nonverbal signals. For instance, you cannot assume that eye contact always "signals" interest, respect, and concern. For the counselee whose culture has taught that eye contact signals *dis*respect, a counselor who consistently attempts to use this signal is out of harmony with his or her expressed intention to understand empathically the counselee's world.

The following section on nonverbal attending and accepting responses provides clues about the signaling variations associated with some cultures. We suggest that you view every counselor-counselee interaction as a cross-cultural one that requires modification of your attending skills to create a consistent message regarding your willingness to develop a helping relationship.

Our experience has taught us that the four major skills involved in attending are these:

1. Setting your focus on the task of attending
2. Using nonverbal attending and accepting responses
3. Using verbal accepting responses
4. Using brief, on-topic, open leads

The four skills are explained and discussed in detail in the following sections. Suggestions for building and strengthening these skills are offered at the end of the chapter.

Setting Your Focus on the Task of Attending

Earlier we stressed the importance of intention as a determinant of performance. Our intentions to watch our diet produce only frustration unless we're aware of our intentions while we're scanning the menu. With intentions, timing is everything. If you watch basketball, you've seen players "set" themselves before attempting a free throw. They appear to focus, to concentrate on the immediate task, no matter how distracting the opponents and the crowd behind the basket may be. When a player misses 8 of 10 tries, commentators say things like, "He lost his concentration; shooting free throws is all mental."

Effective attending, like shooting free throws, requires setting the focus on the task at hand, withdrawing attention to distractors, and physically and mentally positioning yourself to do what you intend.

How do we position ourselves for effective performance in the moment of need, under game conditions? We think of it as running a prerecorded set of self-instructions on a tape recorder in our head. For a counselor, it might go something like this: "Now it's time for me to pay attention to this person. I'll start by breathing in a relaxed way, and do the things I know how to do to let this person know I'm really paying attention. Nothing else matters right now except concentrating on this person, letting her know nothing else matters to me at this moment."

We suggest that before your first practice performance you take time to put into words whatever best expresses your intentions at the moment performance begins. Actually write out whatever words will help you position yourself to achieve your intentions. Then, just as you actually begin to attend, set yourself by playing your mental "time to attend" tape. With experience, the words of the message may change, but there will never come a time while you are a counselor when setting yourself to attend will be unimportant to your client.

Using Nonverbal Attending and Accepting Responses

Eye contact, space, body position, and body movement carry nonverbal meaning between individuals. Each of these is considered below.

EYE CONTACT

Eyes are probably the single most powerful nonverbal communicators. Just how eyes are used varies with individuals and cultures. Among *Anglos*, eye contact is often actively sought as a way of ensuring attention: "Look me in the eye!" The comfort level of eye contact varies with persons and with the situation. *Guideline*: When working with Anglos, offer just a bit *more* eye contact than is accepted. Eye contact usually increases as the relationship matures.

For other cultures, eye contact may be quite different. Traditional Navajos are among those to whom eye contact may connote *disrespect* (Isaac, 1975). The same connotation may hold for some Hispanic individuals (LeVine & Padilla, 1980). *Guideline*: For non-Anglo cultures, don't push to maintain eye contact with a person who seems to avoid it.

SPACE

The *distance* between two people affects their perceptions of each other (Mehrabian, 1981). Comfort levels vary with cultures (Hall, 1966). With Hispanics, closer is more comfortable (LeVine & Padilla, 1980). With Navajos, farther away is generally better (Isaac, 1975). *Guideline*: Start at a distance of about four feet. Respect the other person's movement toward or away from you.

BODY POSITION

Mehrabian (1981) has observed that exhibiting relaxation conveys power; in excess, it proclaims arrogance. Exhibiting tension suggests attention; in excess, it conveys submission. Thus, body position can suggest *power* and *attentiveness*, two attributes that most clients would find attractive in a helper. *Guideline*: Start with an uncomplicated body position: comfortable, but not lounging; alert, but not tense.

BODY MOVEMENT

Body movements signal our approach-avoidance impulses. Moving back or moving into position to rise from a chair are signals of avoidance. Leaning forward and moving forward signal approach. Approach movements nourish the development of relationships; avoidance movements chill relationships. The affirmative head nod and the nonverbal "Um-hmm" are also actions that convey attentiveness and acceptance—but beware of seeming mechanical. Approach movements, head nodding, and um-hmms are fairly consistent indicators of attention and interest across cultures (Isaac, 1975). *Guideline*: Even minimal approach movements, head nodding, and um-hmms convey your caring, acceptance, and desire to understand.

Using Verbal Accepting Responses

Feeling accepted contributes to clients' willingness to talk about their personal concerns, doubts, and private trepidations. Counselors must be able to create and maintain an atmosphere in which clients feel accepted. Utterances that are brief and neutral can serve to enhance the communication of acceptance. Such statements as "Yes" or "I see" or "Go on" tell speakers that you hear and accept and want them to go on speaking.

The *brevity* of the statements means that they can be uttered while the other person is speaking—like spurts of verbal "oil" easing the process along.

The *neutrality* of the statements is equally important. Statements such as "That's good" or "Too bad" or "What a terrible thing!" impose the *listener's* judgments and conclusions on the *client's* experience. Judgments threaten developing feelings of acceptance. *Guideline*: Use brief, neutral utterances such as "Yes" and "I see" to show speakers that you hear and accept them and what they are saying. Don't try to fake acceptance by using these comments if you do not sincerely *intend* to hear and accept the other person. You will sound like a phony mechanical parrot if your words are saying "Yes" while your body language says "No."

Using Brief, On-Topic, Open Responses

Brief, open responses that reflect the client's topic are effective ways of encouraging the client to share his or her concerns. Such responses indicate your interest in learning more about the client's situation; it helps him or her tell the story. Each of the three types of responses is examined.

BRIEF RESPONSES

Two common errors counselors make are to ask long, rambling questions (that are usually speeches in disguise) and to ask a string of three or four questions at a time. Being brief gives the client more time to speak. *Guideline*: Confine yourself to one simple sentence when you are in the *attending* mode.

ON-TOPIC RESPONSES

When your purpose is to help the client tell his or her story, for you to introduce a new topic or to talk about yourself confuses the purpose and focus of the interview. Let your response flow from content already introduced. By staying on the client's topic you show that you *are* listening and *are* interested in hearing more. *Guideline*: *Listen* to your clients so your comments will relate to *their* story.

OPEN RESPONSES

An *open* response or question invites more than a one- or two-word answer. Open responses invite clients to speak at length on the topic, in their own words. *Closed* responses—questions that ask for yes/no responses—invite only one or two predetermined words. The examples in the following chart should show you the differences between open and closed statements.

Open	*Closed*
How is that important to you?	Is that important to you?
What are your reasons for deciding against college?	Did you decide to get a job instead of going to college?
Tell me about your family.	How many brothers and sisters do you have?

Open responses invite counselees to describe their own experience in their own words and tend to elicit material previously unmentioned and unknown to the counselor. *Guideline*: Avoid closed responses except in those rare instances where a one- or two-word response is *exactly* what is needed, such as "Would you like to make another appointment?"

Here are four ways to help yourself make more open responses:

1. Use the imperative form of response. *Examples*: "Tell me how you felt." "Describe what happened next."
2. Share your thinking out loud. *Example*: "I wonder what was going through your mind at that moment."
3. Use incomplete sentences. *Examples*: "So the day after the big fight you were walking toward the Union, saw her coming toward you, and said to yourself . . ." "And the next thing you were aware of was . . ."
4. Start your response with how, what, or (if you must) why. Examples: "How did you . . . ?" "What happened after . . . ?"

We caution against asking "Why?" because it can be aversive. Some people hear a "Why" question ("Why did you do that?") as a negative message ("That was a dumb thing to do!") and feel that they are being asked to defend themselves rather than describe themselves. But, more important, when behavior change is the issue, knowing the *why* of a behavior may not be as useful as knowing *how* it happens. As an experiment, the next few times you find yourself asking "Why?" change the *why* to *how* and see what happens.

Setting the Stage for the Initial Client Contact

There are several other issues regarding the counseling environment and counselor behavior that you should consider in an initial encounter with the counselee. Before the client sits down to begin the first session, he or she has been involved in a number of activities related to initiating counseling. These include thinking about and deciding to see a counselor, sorting through information about counselor experience, selecting a counselor to see (if there's a choice), costs of service, availability, making an appointment, locating a baby-sitter, finding transportation, finding the way to the counselor's office, and in some cases, doing some paperwork. We believe it is important for counseling professionals to put themselves in the clients' shoes as they go through these initiating activities before the actual face-to-face encounter. From this perspective, counselors can then ask, "What could happen when I call for information about a counselor that would maximize my level of comfort? Of informed consent? Of trust that my concerns are important?" For example, I might have a more satisfactory experience if the counselor's receptionist asks me whether I have any questions, or offers me the option of speaking with the counselor over the telephone prior to scheduling my first appointment.

Counselors can do a number of things to convey their intentions and attitudes of empathic understanding in their particular counseling environment. Providing counselees with good directions to the office, information about the fee payment process, a friendly greeting, and a comfortable place to wait before the session are all ways of reducing clients' anxiety and increasing their readiness to address the concerns that prompt them to seek counseling.

Introducing the Erikka Interview Transcript

Several years ago, we videotaped Dave conducting a demonstration counseling session in a counseling techniques class of which the counselee, Erikka, was a member. With her permission, throughout the book we present dialogue excerpts transcribed from Dave's interview with Erikka (not her real name) to exemplify attending skills and accepting responses as they happened within the flow of one counselee-counselor interaction.

We also present the counselor's "self-talk" at intervals throughout the interview. Counselor self-talk helps the counselor become ready to meet and work with the counselee throughout the counseling session. As we follow through the Counseling Process Model, task by task, we return to Erikka and her counselor to see how these steps fit together within an ongoing counseling relationship.

Nonlinearity of Counseling

As we reviewed the Erikka transcript, we were not surprised to notice that it represents a nonlinear explication of our apparently linear (Step 1 → Step 2 → Step 3 → . . .) Counseling Process Model. The transcript does *not* convey a counseling process in which the counselor "completes" one step, such as Understand Counselor Concerns Empathically, then moves to the next step, Negotiate Counseling Objectives, never to return to Understand Counselor Concerns for the remainder of the session (or the relationship). On the contrary, counselor and client appear to cycle back and forth through these steps as concerns, objectives, plans, and outcome evaluations are defined, reconsidered, and refined. This cycling among tasks is the norm; it's the way the process usually goes with our clients.

Counseling Process Model as Map;
Erikka Transcript as Territory

We've previously discussed our belief that our verbal map cannot accurately reflect the territory of our experience. We intend this transcription of one counseling session as an example of the territory that our six-step Counseling Process Model map is describing. We hope that, in combination, the transcript and the chapters on each step of the model will enhance your understanding of the relationship between map and territory in the role of professional counselor.

 ERIKKA TRANSCRIPT

A segment of the Erikka transcript follows each chapter/step in the Counseling Process Model, beginning with this one. Each segment includes comments and Dave's responses to questions from the audience of class members.

Counselor Readiness

Counselor "self-talk" prior to and in the early stages of a relationship with a counselee can create a readiness in the counselor to behave in a caring, collaborative, and client-centered manner. We referred to this earlier as setting focus on the task. The counselor who assumes that a "true professional" is just naturally cognitively and emotionally ready to address the needs of the next counselee is, no doubt, unprofessionally oblivious of the competing demands of appointment calendars, financial considerations, requests by co-workers, and the myriad little things that fill a workday—"Now, how many copies of this form am I supposed to sign?"

Each segment of the Erikka transcript is preceded by examples of counselor self-talk, setting the counselor's focus on the task ahead.

> It's time to set aside what I'm doing and get ready to see Erikka for her first session. The phone calls, paperwork, thoughts about my previous session, and other matters will wait so they won't distract me. Right now I want to focus on Erikka.
>
> I'm going to recall our telephone conversation and any other information that helps me to be attuned to the reason Erikka has made this counseling appointment. I want her to know that I am attentive to her individual concerns and goals.
>
> I'm going to stop myself from making assumptions about this person and the problems she brings to counseling. I will do

my best not to let my biases distract me from attending to and accepting her experiences in her world.

I'm ready to meet Erikka and convey a positive, caring, confident demeanor. I want my nonverbal and verbal signals to communicate consistently that I am totally committed to understanding, accepting, and respecting her as a person.

The Interview

(Throughout this transcript, CO refers to the counselor, Dave, and CL refers to the client, Erikka. Each question/statement by the counselor and response by the client are numbered as a set—CO1, CL1; CO2, CL2—so that particular question/response sets can be referenced easily in the subsequent comment or discussion.)

CO1: What is it that brought you up here to be a client?

CL1: I'm becoming very concerned. A lot of tensions come up from here to here (moves hands from stomach to forehead), and I'm getting terrible, terrible headaches that I've not gotten in the past. I've never been one to take aspirin and it seems I'm just popping them like, um, Pop-Tarts. I find I'm getting a large amount of headaches nearly all day. I didn't have one today and I was congratulating myself and I've been leaning my head against the back wall ever since class started.

CO2: Do you have a headache right now?

CL2: Um-hmm.

CO3: And so it sounds like one thing you're saying is that you feel there's some relationship between these headaches you're getting and you're *not*, what, putting something out?

CL3: I don't know what it is. I'm very aware that in the last month or so things have been going real good. Things have been coming together for me. . . . When I returned to Tucson from the summer I had a lot of *ifs* and *buts* about getting back into the program and now everything's clicked. I'm feeling really good about people I'm associating with. Everything seems to fit in, where, say, a month ago it wouldn't have. A month ago was technically when I should have been getting the headaches, but *now* I'm getting them, and what has been coming out is that everything's going real good, and what I'm getting kind of frightened about is that my headaches are telling me something. And I'm very aware of my physical well-being and I've always considered myself lucky that I've been in excellent physical health. And that's why the headaches are really disturbing me, more than they would someone else who has had them frequently.

CO4: So it sounds like part of what's going on is it's hard to make *sense* [CL: Exactly. Right, right.] of your headaches. You also sound like someone who's pretty good about paying attention to what you're feeling, what's going on with you physically [CL: Yeah, I am. Very much so.] And that somehow all those resources that usually work for you in terms of paying attention to those kinds of things aren't really working for you right now.

CL4: Um-hmm. Sometimes I've gotten a nervous stomach in the past when things are going on or there's something I'm anticipating. My stomach will tell me that. Never has it been the head. We were joking at dinner last night because I was seeing, like, darts, like flashing lights, and my roommate had just been to some seminar and they had talked about migraines. And I just said "No." I can't even stand the thought that that might be happening. So, it's like I would joke last night, but it's really disturbing me.

CO5: And, if we were going to use counseling as a way to address this concern, what is it that you'd like? Do you have some idea of what you'd like us to do or do you have some idea of what you'd like the outcome to be?

Comment: In CO1, Dave implies the purpose of this new relationship by inviting Erikka to talk about how she decided to seek counseling. Erikka, more knowledgeable than many who initiate counseling, responds with some detail to Dave's invitation. CO3, CO4, and CO5 show Dave's intent to listen and to understand Erikka's expectations for counseling.

Debriefing

After a demonstration, observers frequently have questions about the counseling they have seen. The following questions are from students who have observed the Erikka counseling demonstration, either in person or on videotape. The counselor's response follows each question.

OBSERVER: Did this session fit the norm in the way that it began? Can we expect other counselees to present their concerns in the same way as Erikka?

COUNSELOR: The most difficult part of thinking like a counselor as I begin a counseling relationship with a client is what I *don't think*: that everyone I work with grew up in the same neighborhood. If I assume that working with Erikka will be like working with other graduate students—or other women, other blonde-haired, blue-eyed people, other people with headaches—I am already interfering with my ability as a counselor to understand my client's world through his or her personal map. In other words, the counselor who acknowledges and appreciates the diversity of people who come for counseling brings new eyes and new ears to the concerns and aspirations of every counselee unimpeded by assumptions and expectations of what "should happen" in the counseling session.

OBSERVER: Is there anything the counselor didn't do that he would usually do in the beginning of a counseling session?

COUNSELOR: This session was a videotaped demonstration in a classroom setting. If the session had been scheduled at my office, I would have taken time to discuss Erikka's expectations of the counselor and the counseling process, my responsibilities regarding maintenance of Erikka's confidentiality, scheduling and fee arrangements, and other issues. In Appendixes B and C, a copy of a colleague's client orientation and (a) contract format are provided as one example of how to initiate a consumer-driven counseling relationship in the initial interview.

OBSERVER: What is the counselor thinking as he listens to Erikka?

COUNSELOR: "Active" listening involves a great deal of mental activity by the counselor, and most of my thinking is committed to observing Erikka and organizing what I hear and see in an attempt to create a clear picture of what she is experiencing. I am not committing energy to another type of thinking—interpreting my observations of Erikka. I'm not creating a diagnostic impression of Erikka, deciding how I can best intervene to address the headache complaint, and so on. I am, instead, noticing what Erikka is saying and doing and organizing my observations of her concerns, desired outcomes, and discomfort as if I were tacking things up on a mental bulletin board.

 ## SUGGESTIONS FOR INTEGRATING ACTIVITIES

Some Thoughts about Skill Practice

In Chapter 1, we discussed the experience of learning to be a counselor. Specifically, we examined the awkwardness or discomfort that many of us feel in states of conscious incompetence and conscious competence that are part of almost everyone's journey toward skilled professional counselor status. We are more likely to experience this discomfort when we are practicing our skills in front of our peers; reviewing audiotaped and videotaped demonstrations; and discussing our choices, questions, opinions, and feelings about what to do in counseling sessions and how to do it.

We want to mention four guidelines that we find personally useful when we are involved in skill practice discussion or supervision. We think these guidelines are helpful reminders for observers providing feedback, whether of their own performance or of others. We believe that using these guidelines mitigates the potential for discomfort in public practice and enhances the opportunities for counselor growth.

1. *Discriminate between observation and inference.* Read the following responses and decide whether they demonstrate observation or inference.

INSTRUCTOR TO CLASS:	What comments do you have for Joe about his performance?
RESPONSE 1:	Joe seemed to be really listening.
RESPONSE 2:	Joe showed a lot of warmth.
RESPONSE 3:	Joe maintained good eye contact.
RESPONSE 4:	Joe used three brief, open leads.

These are typical comments after a decent practice demonstration. Each of the four speakers above thought he or she was talking about Joe. That's what makes inferences so treacherous. Just because Joe is the subject of each sentence does not mean that each statement is about Joe. In fact, the first two speakers were describing themselves, their inferences about the meaning of some bits of Joe's behavior. Only the last two comments are *observations* of Joe's work.

Observations report publicly verifiable events. Our two observers are reporting aspects of Joe's performance—eye contact; brief, open leads—that you or I might have seen had we been there. With observations we are all experiencing the same information because it's public. We can all see it or hear it if it's there.

With inferences we have someone's idea about the *meaning* of some observations. "Warmth" and "really listening" are in the eyes of the beholder; they are not publicly verifiable. We don't and can't know what someone's inference means without asking the person who made the comment some questions. What do you mean by "warmth"? What did you see and hear that seemed warm to you?

Observations are generally about the outside world unless they are my reports about my inner world. Inferences are always about the inside world of the person who makes them. You can't look at Joe to discover "warm"; only the speaker knows what "warm" means in this context.

When you have done a demonstration and you're getting feedback, it's good to be able to listen and sort out the observations (reports of your performance) from the inferences (how an observer interpreted it). We suggest that when you hear a judgment/inference about your work or someone else's, you might ask something like this: "What did you *see* or *hear* that made you think Joe was listening?" "What did Joe do or say that seemed 'warm' to you?"

2. *Use Encouragement.* We believe that people build on strengths. Competence is achieved through successive approximations of helping skills, built on past

achievement. In-class exercises and practice assignments are most effective when participants recognize and celebrate achievement rather than take it for granted.

One of the many things counseling students, experienced counselors, and their clients have in common is the need for *encouragement* and its by-products—motivation, self-esteem, and creativity. The counselor education setting offers counseling students firsthand experience in creating conditions that foster encouragement:

- Set up bite-size objectives, making sure that the skills to achieve the task are available. For example, competence in the step, Initiate Relationship, seems more achievable if we're practicing only one or two attending skills at first.
- Structure your skills demonstration to make achievement highly probable; have a quiet space, appropriate "client" behavior, and so on. We never ask anyone to do anything he or she cannot do.
- Document the achievement of objectives by tape recording or by using live observers. Public evidence and validation of competence is invaluable.

After the performance, pay attention first to what went right. Confirm whatever achievements were noted. It's not very encouraging to talk about objectives and performance in terms of success or failure, good or bad. As in hypothesis testing, things are observed or not observed. We try our best, applaud effort, and what happens, happens. We credit ourselves for our achievements, learn what we can about *how* we help ourselves achieve objectives—what made it hard; what made it easy—and try again.

3. *Be aware of doing it right versus being effective.* Somewhere we heard someone say that the difference between leaders and managers is that leaders do the right thing while managers do things right. Our observation is that some counselors-in-training work hard to do it by the book. Mastering skills is worth the effort, but skills are only important as they serve client interests.

Counseling students ask questions about counselor behaviors. "Is it OK to ask a closed question?" or "Is it OK to answer a personal question from a client?" or "Is it a good thing to let a client know you've had the same problem?" The answer is almost always, "It depends." That's the nature of professional service. The efficacy of any professional behavior is measured on the yardstick of the client's best interests. Isn't that the way you would want it if you were the client?

So, work hard to master an array of knowledge and skills. But counseling is not about doing the right things, it's about helping clients achieve what they need to achieve to live more satisfactory lives.

4. *Remember that giving good feedback is similar to good counseling.* Feedback is an important source of information about our performance and its consequences. In the movie *Hoop Dreams,* Coach Pingatore was an important source of feedback for the players on the St. Joe basketball team. His feedback seemed to focus primarily on perceived deficits and consisted mainly of derogatory comments. Our somewhat limited experience leads us to believe this is not an uncommon style of feedback.

We prefer to think of giving good feedback as being similar to how good counselors operate in the Support the Plan phase of counseling. As you may have gathered by now, our "set" for feedback is like a counselor supporting a client's determination to pursue a planned change. We want to be clear about our client's purpose, we want to be able to gather the pertinent data about client performance, and we want to share our observations in a way that focuses on achievement. We particularly share observations that document achievement of intended results. We help in analyzing the performance by attempting to discover what facilitates performance and what impedes it. We seek and share information, not judgments.

Practice in Attending and Acceptance

1. Identify at least once each day this week a moment when at least one of your intentions is to understand what someone is telling you. Set yourself to use attending and accepting skills, and then use them. Observe the other person as you do so. Note whether your responses seem to be experienced as attentive and accepting by the other person.

Record in your journal your experiences with attending and accepting. Comment on what you're aware of in being attentive and accepting. Equally important, note instances when you as a person find it difficult to attend, to accept.

2. Increase your awareness of your and others' nonverbal behaviors. Notice your reactions as a receiver of eye contact, body positioning, and body movement messages. Notice your tendency to reciprocate the message you receive. Test this out by nodding and smiling at the next three people you pass on the street.

3. Sometimes you feel ignored, rejected, or judged. Make note of how you observe people signaling you or others that they do *not* wish to attend or to accept. How do people let you know that they're ready to end a conversation? How do you convey this to others?

Practice in Using Brief, On-Topic, Open Leads

4. Increase your awareness of open versus closed questions by listening for them in others' speech and in your own. Someone defined a question as an honest request for information.

- Notice questions in the next conversation you're part of. How many are open? Closed? Seem to be "honest requests for information"?
- When you notice someone addressing you with closed questions, try using just the words required to respond to the question. Observe the effects on the questioner. (Closed questions sometimes evoke lengthier responses because of the powerful nonverbal accompaniment.)

5. When you find yourself in conversations or trying to start a conversation when you are really interested in hearing the "story," try using brief, open questions. As a topic emerges, stay with it. See where it takes you, if you have the time.

6. Set up brief practice sessions with fellow students. Structure them as slices of counseling life that give you opportunities to perform attending skills and receive feedback that encourages the enhancement of these skills. One skill-building format is a triad exercise involving three counselors-in-training. One person takes the role of counselor, another is the counselee, and the third is the observer.

First, set up a scenario that approximates a counseling setting—limited distractions; counselor and counselee seated facing each other, approximately four feet apart; counselee and counselor roles sincerely adopted in verbal and nonverbal behavior. The observer sits off to the side with attention focused on the counselor's performance of attending skills and the counselee's response to the counselor's behavior.

Next, complete a 5-minute demonstration of a counseling interaction. The observer may want to take notes as a memory aid. At the completion of the 5 minutes, review this slice of the counseling process and its demonstration of counselor attending skills.

In this review, or feedback process, we suggest that you follow a format designed to make skill demonstration as safe, encouraging, and skill-profitable as possible. The feedback will focus on each of the four attending skills:

A. Setting your focus on the task of attending
B. Using nonverbal attending and accepting responses
C. Using verbal accepting responses
D. Using brief, on-topic, open leads

The first person to provide feedback to the counselor is the counselor, who begins by reviewing what he or she did and did not do in each of the skill areas. Remember: These are self-*observations*, not value judgments. "I maintained eye contact with my client" and "I felt nervous about being observed" are observations. "I should have been more focused on attending before we started" is a value judgment. In general, the self-observation process works best if the counselor attends to effective skill performance first before acknowledging the skills that seemed to be left out.

After the counselor reviews this performance, the client shares observations on counselor attending skills and how this behavior affected the counselee's experience. For example, "When you leaned forward, I felt like you were really interested in what I was saying." "When you raised your eyebrows I was wondering if you believed me." Finally, the observer reports his or her perceptions of counselor attending skills and counselee responses. We like it when those who observe us start out by saying, "One thing you did that really seemed effective was . . ." It's helpful when the observer ends by saying, "One thing you might try next time is . . ."

Triad members should each have a turn at each role. With 5-minute sessions and 10 minutes of feedback, a triad can complete a cycle in less than an hour. We think triads work best when the same three people complete only one cycle; then the triad should be reconstituted with different participants. Working with different triad members will be a more realistic experience because it is more like actual practice.

CONSULTATION TIME

At the conclusion of this and the remaining chapters, we present a series of counseling scenarios under the heading Consultation Time. The scenarios are typical of situations students have brought up during weekly internship seminar sessions. Typically, a student-intern working in a counseling setting would describe or enact a predicament he or she had encountered and ask seminar members to suggest options for handling the situation.

Our purpose in including Consultation Time throughout our discussion of the process model is to help you integrate your ongoing understanding of the Counseling Process Model with the questions, choices, and occasional confusion experienced by practicing counselors in their work settings.

Scenario 1

COUNSELOR: What do you want to get out of counseling?

CLIENT: I don't know.

COUNSELOR: If counseling works for you, how will your life be different?

CLIENT: I don't know.

What options does the counselor have at this point?

- "I can't help you if you don't tell me what you want to work on."
- "You say you don't know what you want to get out of counseling, but you came to see me for some reason. I wonder why you came."
- "How did you happen to get here today? Who made the appointment for you?"
- What might you say?

Scenario 2

COUNSELOR: What do you want to get out of counseling?

CLIENT: My wife told me that I had to see a counselor or she would divorce me.

COUNSELOR: So your wife said she would divorce you if you didn't see a counselor.

CLIENT: Right.

What options does the counselor have at this point?

- "I don't see people unless they want to see me. Do *you* want to see me?"

- "I wonder how your wife decided it was so important for you to see a counselor."
- "Your wife wants you to see a counselor. And I see you here so you must want to stay married. Does anything else need to happen?"
- "I wonder what your wife meant by 'see a counselor.' I wonder how she thought that would help you two stay together."
- How might you respond?

Scenario 3

This counselor, who has no experience in working with families, is on the phone:

VOICE: My wife and I need help. Our two boys, age 7 and 9, are driving us nuts. A friend of my wife's said we ought to get family counseling. I'd like to make an appointment for us to come see you.

COUNSELOR: I see. (*Pause*)

What are the counselor's options?

- "I don't do family counseling but I would be glad to give you the names of three people with experience in working with families. OK?"
- "Tell me a little more about why you're concerned. What happened that made you think you needed to find some help?" (I want to find out whether kids are likely to be safe until the family gets counseling.)
- "Sure. Let's find a time when you and your wife can come in and we can talk about what you need help with." (I'll just work with the parents. I can do that.)
- How might you respond?

REFERENCES

Fiedler, F. E. (1950). A comparison of therapeutic relationships in psychoanalytic therapy, non-directive and Adlerian. *Journal of Consulting Psychology, 14*, 436–455.

Hall, E. T. (1966). *The hidden dimension*. Garden City, NY: Doubleday.

Isaac, Lawrence. (1975). *Cross-cultural differences in helping interviews*. Unpublished paper, Department of Counseling and Guidance, University of Arizona, Tucson.

Kirsch, Irving. (1990). *Changing expectations: A key to effective psychotherapy*. Pacific Grove, CA: Brooks/Cole.

LeVine, E., & Padilla, A. (1980). *Crossing cultures in therapy: Pluralistic counseling for the Hispanic*. Pacific Grove, CA: Brooks/Cole.

Mehrabian, Albert. (1981). *Silent messages: Implicit communication of emotions and attitudes* (2nd ed.). Belmont, CA: Wadsworth.

Suggested Reading

Benjamin, A. (1981). *The helping interview* (3rd ed.). Boston: Houghton Mifflin.

Carkhuff, R., & Berenson, B. (1967). *Beyond counseling and therapy*. New York: Holt, Rinehart & Winston.

Evans, E. R., Hearn, M. T., Uhlemann, M. R., & Ivey, A. G. (1993). *Essential interviewing: A programmed approach to effective communication* (4th ed.). Pacific Grove, CA: Brooks/Cole.

Okun, B. F. (1992). *Effective helping: Interviewing and counseling techniques* (4th ed.). Pacific Grove, CA: Brooks/Cole.

Rogers, C. R. (1951). *Client-centered therapy*. Boston: Houghton Mifflin.

CHAPTER 7

Step 2: Understand Counselee Concerns Empathically

If you don't understand my silences you won't understand my words. —from a letter to Dear Abby

To want *to understand implies a commitment to action whose boundaries are necessarily unclear until one has reached the point where one feels that one understands. If we resist that process, it is in part because we intuitively know that the commitment to action may involve pain or inconvenience or self-sacrifice on our part; that is, we resist the changes within us that understanding and a commitment to action imply.* —S. B. Sarason

Developing an effective counseling relationship requires the counselor to understand as clearly as possible the client's world. *Rapport* and *empathy* are words used to refer to the extent to which you are successful, not only in putting yourself in the client's shoes but also in demonstrating to the client your desire and ability to understand empathically. Out of this "under-standing" will emerge the counselee's belief that you know what's distressing him or her and that you can help sort it out.

Following Skills, Intentions, and Responses

Two elements crucial to being an effective listener are *following skills* and *intentions*. Neither, by itself, is enough. Having following skills is not sufficient. If you don't sincerely want to understand empathically, you're only going through the motions. Just using the right words usually comes across as phony and insincere. Your sincere *intention* to understand is a private desire. Using following responses skillfully, as manifestations of your sincere intention to share someone's experience, lets that person see you as genuinely striving to understand.

Verbal following responses are counselor utterances that contain the words, meanings, and/or feelings conveyed by client communications. Following responses may be categorized as *restatements*, *paraphrases*, or *reflections*.

> *Restatement*: The counselor restates all or nearly all that the client said using the client's own words.

> CLIENT: I just don't know what to do next.

> COUNSELOR: You just don't know what to do next.

> *Paraphrase*: The counselor rephrases what the client said using the counselor's own words.

> CLIENT: I just don't know what to do next.

> COUNSELOR: The future isn't at all clear to you right now.

> *Reflection*: The counselor responds in a way that not only acknowledges the *words* spoken by the client, but also recognizes the *feelings* that are implicit in the client's words, tone of voice, facial expression, gestures, or body position.

> CLIENT: I just don't know what to do next.

> COUNSELOR: You're feeling puzzled and perhaps a little scared because the future isn't very clear now, and your next move isn't at all clear to you.

Reflections are the following responses that generally come closest to attending all three domains of experience—actions, thoughts, and feelings.

Check Out the Concept

Restatement, paraphrase, or reflection—which is it? Let's see whether we've made the concept clear. For each counselor response, check the following response you think it best represents.

			CLIENT:	It's a long story. I can't get on with people. If there is any criticism or anyone says anything about me I just can't take it.
___	___	___	COUNSELOR 1:	You can't get on with people; if there is any criticism, you just can't take it.
			CLIENT:	Well, it doesn't even need to be meant as criticism. It goes back a way. In grammar school I never felt that I belonged. Oh, sometimes I would try to feel superior, but then I'd be way down.
___	___	___	COUNSELOR 2:	Other things people say bother you, too. Even back in grammar school there were ups and downs in the way you got along with others.
			CLIENT:	Lately it's been worse. I even feel that I ought to be in a sanitarium. There must be something awfully wrong with me.
___	___	___	COUNSELOR 3:	You sound hurt and scared because things have been so bad lately that you wonder if you are normal.
			CLIENT:	Yes. Of course, in school I used to get high grades. I know I studied all the time. I didn't go out with anybody. I sort of shut myself away because I was hurt so much.
___	___	___	COUNSELOR 4:	You shut yourself away because you hurt so much.
			CLIENT:	Yes, because when I was with people I just didn't feel comfortable. I felt so left out of social things and things of that sort. When I studied, it was sort of an escape for me and I tried to forget. I sort of made it like it was a different world, my studying. I sort of secluded myself. Know what I mean?
___	___	___	COUNSELOR 5:	You felt awkward and unhappy around people, left out; and just studying in your own world was a less painful way of living. Studying let you close out the rest of the world.

			CLIENT:	Mm-hmm. That's right. And I—and that wasn't the right attitude; I know it wasn't. Because it was supposed to integrate you with life but it didn't—I made it an escape.
___	___	___	COUNSELOR 6:	The studying just closed you off from others instead of preparing you to be with others—and you feel bad for hiding in your books.
			CLIENT:	That's right. And everybody else wondered why I liked to do homework and I just enjoyed it. I seemed to enjoy it— and, well, it gave me something—it sort of stood me up a little, but I don't seem to have learned very much from it because, well, my memory doesn't seem to be good at all now. It's all such a muddle.
___	___	___	COUNSELOR 7:	Burying yourself in homework seemed a good idea at the time, and it did give you something to be proud of, but nothing much came of it that is any help now. You can't remember much and it's all so confused.
			CLIENT:	Um-hmm. It's such an effort for me to just go around living and thinking these things and something will have to be done. It's an effort for me to walk down the street sometimes. It's a crazy thing, really.
___	___	___	COUNSELOR 8:	It takes almost all you have just to get along these days. You are confused and tired because of the effort required simply to live, and you really want life to be different.

Review Your Answers

Counselors 1 and 4 essentially *restate* the client's message using the client's words. Counselors 2 and 7 *paraphrase* the client's verbal message in the counselor's words. The counselor does not explicitly acknowledge counselee feelings.

Counselors 3, 5, 6, and 8 *reflect* the counselor's understanding of both the *content* of the client's message and the client's *feelings* as well.

Now, practice forming your own following responses to these items to see how well we've gotten this across. For each of the statements given, compose and write a response that would indicate to the speaker that you are "following" and understanding.

SPEAKER: School is even more boring this year than it was last year. I'm really getting burned out.

YOU: _____

_____

_____

SPEAKER: I'm having quite a bit of trouble talking in class and it seems like I—well, I want to talk in class but I can't. I, I, oh, I get scared and freeze up.

YOU: _____

_____

_____

SPEAKER: Well, you talk about mixed up! My mother is coming down from Oregon for spring break. I really want her to meet Luis—and she wants to meet him—but I don't know what's going to happen when she learns we've been living together this semester.

YOU: _____

_____

_____

SPEAKER: It's really great! You get out there with those kids who have never spent a night of their lives outdoors, and by the end of the week they are different people. Oh, the first couple of days on the trail present some problems, but the kids are so hooked on the adventure and all that everyone is sad when it's all over.

YOU: _____

_____

_____

Now, review the responses you just composed. Check for the following:

1. Does the response contain the *ideas* in the speaker's statement?
2. Does the response mention the feelings stated or implied by the speaker?

If you could say "Yes" to each question for each of your responses, you are ready for live practice, with a real person—but only if you really want to listen!

Counselor's Vocabulary for Following Responses

Now that we have defined *paraphrase* and *reflection* as following responses, we want to comment on the counselor's choice of words in making these responses. In general, we find ourselves using the client's words in our following responses, but there are times when it may be quite important for the counselee's story to unfold only in the words he or she chooses. Two instances come to mind.

In the first instance, you may be working with a counselee who seems to be in the process of recalling an experience from a much earlier time, such as childhood. Here, it may be important to stay with the words that emerge as part of the childhood experience. The counselor who attempts to facilitate recall by supplying language to a client groping for expression may contaminate the client's "map" with adult concepts, alien to childhood experience. To stay with the client's words is to stay closer to the client's world.

In another instance, you may be focusing on the specific problematic experiences of the client, and in identifying the specific outcomes the client is seeking in counseling. In this case, staying with the client's words rather than interjecting counselor language helps ensure that the focus in counseling will be on an aspect of importance in the client's world as she or he construes it. Staying with the client's words is a way of reducing potential cross-cultural confusion. If you're hearing words you don't understand, it's consistent with your intent to understand to ask their meaning.

How and Where to Practice

It's not practice that makes perfect; it is *intentional* practice that makes perfect. Start by being clear with yourself that you intend to listen and understand other people's messages. You must really want to understand, to walk in their shoes, to share their experience and their perspective. Your sincere wish to understand is crucial to being experienced as an accurate and empathic listener.

Look for everyday situations in which you *really want* to listen and understand what's being said to you. Conversations with your children, spouse, friends, partner, associates, and others can provide excellent opportunities for practice. (*Note*: Those who know you well may notice if you change your style of listening with them. Be prepared to respond honestly that you are working at becoming a better and more accurate listener.)

Does practicing following responses feel awkward? The first steps in learning anything can feel awkward. As you consciously attempt to use following responses, some of your attention will be drawn away from the person you are listening to and become focused on yourself as you try to make a good response. (Mom used to call this listening with half an ear.)

Avoid splitting your attention between the other person and thinking about how you will respond while he or she is speaking. You can learn to do it! First, put all your attention on the other person while that person speaks. Then, focus on what you have heard, and express it as a following response. Learning to cycle your focus of attention—first concentrating on the speaker, and then, when he or she has finished, on yourself—can help you become a skillful and accurate listener.

Old Habits and Personal Needs as Barriers to Empathic Understanding

Listening sounds simple, but real effort is required to do it consistently and well. Two powerful forces interfere with accurate, perceptive listening: habits and needs. Let's consider needs first.

Needs

We may start out meaning to listen, but the emergence of some other personal need—to defend a point of view, to be "expert," to correct, to help, to escape pain—can confuse and change our purpose from listener to something else without our even noticing it. We find ourselves assuming we understand, and acting as if *our* experience was the speaker's.

To become aware of the needs that tend to pull you out of the listener role, try this: Notice others in conversation. See how often someone in the "listener" role shifts away from listening before the "teller" has finished the story. Wendell Johnson (1972) says we grow up learning to be defensive listeners, alert and responsive to potential threats to our self-esteem and to opportunities for self-enhancement. These self-protective listening habits are difficult to give up; stay focused on your intent to understand.

Habits

Now about habits. As mature individuals, we bring an established array of social habits to the counseling relationship. These habits have served us well in many situations. They are not bad things in themselves. Many of these habits, however, are barriers to empathic listening. We offer 10 examples of problematic habits.

1. *Questioning.* We are habitual "askers." We seem to believe that the way to learn most about the other person's experience is to ask questions. As Edward Bordin (1968) observed,

---

The inexperienced counselor is often impatient with the necessarily slow process of accumulating understanding by constantly attentive listening and observing. Sometimes he foolishly rushes ahead, assuming he can more efficiently extract the information he wants through direct questioning or by indirectly (or "subtly" as he hopes) guiding the conversation. (pp. 221–222)

Think about it. How can you conduct the tour of the unknown territory of the other person's experience? Try, instead, to be a persistent and dogged and sensitive follower—relentlessly naive!

2. *Judgments.* Listen to others; listen to yourself. Are you like those who, while listening, emit utterances like "Great," or "Too bad," or "What a mess," or "How wonderful"? This kind of judgmental scorekeeping is not appropriate when the goal is being an accepting, empathic listener.

3. *"If you think that's something, let me tell you about my operation."* Sometimes conversations seem to degenerate into a kind of "Can You Top This?" situation, with participants taking turns trotting out their war stories. It can be tempting to tell *your* story, but it's not often helpful when your goal is to understand the other person.

4. *"Me, too!"* or *"That same thing happened to me last year,"* or *"I'm separated from my wife, too."* So what! This type of response moves the focus away from the client—and confuses the issue. Who is learning about whom? Some folks argue that "me-tooing" can be a rapport builder. We think it mostly strokes the counselor's ego at the client's expense.

5. *"You're OK"* or *"That didn't hurt, did it?"* We have lots of ways of responding to expressions of pain that are alike in that they do not acknowledge the pain. Be sensitive to expressions of pain; it's easy to minimize it or exaggerate it. Both distortions have the effect of closing us out of the situation.

6. *"Silence is poison."* That's not the maxim we've all heard, but it is the one we Anglos tend to live by. Don't speak just to fill a silent moment. Stay with your role as empathic listener, respond to a silent (introspective? confused? uncertain? grieving? remembering?) counselee empathically, and strive to understand the speechless moments for what they may be.

7. *Expert.* "I know *just* how you feel." Did anyone ever answer you that way? Did you believe that person? Neither do we. Furthermore, there seems to be a put-down in this response. Are you not a unique individual? Has anyone other than you lived *your* experience? Never! "I know just how you feel" seems to come from the speaker's needs for assurance or status. It's no help to clients; if anything, it seems to shift the focus away from their experience. And it leaves them feeling even less understood.

8a. *Robo-Counselor I:* "You feel . . . You feel . . . You feel . . . You feel . . ."

8b. *Robo-Counselor II:* "How do you feel when . . . How do you feel when . . . How do you feel when . . . How do you feel when . . ."

9. *Stone face*. This listener shows all the expressiveness of the Sphinx. Use your normal human tools of expression in listening and following the other person and in conveying your intention to understand.

10. *Word factory*. Some folks speak in sentences, some talk in paragraphs, and some just go on and on and on . . . Occasionally we get the impression that the client is afraid to stop talking for some reason. And sometimes the client is engaged in a kind of cathartic outpouring; let it come, and get what you can. If, however, you think you need to understand specifics and you're getting confused and overwhelmed with information, say so. Talk about it. You might try something like, "You've given me a lot to keep track of. Let me see if I've got this straight so far. You said . . ."

Bailing Out

We use a general term for any of the dozens of ways we have of quickly, almost reflexively, shifting the focus from a painful or awkward moment to some other topic: *bailing out*. As counselors, we, too, have needs, values, and areas of vulnerability that can become activated and energized as we listen to the client's story. Areas of our vulnerability can include the death of someone close, a painful relationship, an abusive partner, or other bad experiences. So, we bail out of potentially distressing situations by laughing, by looking away, by asking a question, by challenging, by any means that gets *us* on safer, more comfortable ground.

In social conversations, bailing out is a useful maneuver; it often saves us and sometimes others grief. Bailing out, however, is definitely out of place in the role of empathic listener. When our clients have the courage to share a difficult, painful moment, the least we can do is to hang in there with them.

Good listening sometimes calls forth some pretty powerful personal sharing involving intense and painful feelings. When this happens to you, please remember that your agreement with the other person was to listen and try to understand. And that's *all* you're responsible for right now. At this point, your license does not include problem solving, rescuing, or bailing out. Just be with the other person, where he or she is, to the best of your ability. That was your intention and your agreement; it is still your responsibility until some other, mutually acceptable, explicit agreement is worked out. Following responses are powerful tools that let another person know you want to understand as completely and accurately as possible. The tools come across as phony if your wanting to understand is not sincere. It takes discipline to honor your intention, to stay in the role of listener rather than become parent, teacher, advocate, rescuer, guru, expert, clown, or whatever when listening gets uncomfortable.

Perceived Discrepancies in Client Stories

Most of us don't listen to other people talk about their troubles very long without noticing a couple of kinds of behaviors. One is that people—and not just politi-

---

cians—say one thing and then do something else. Another is that some people assert things that seem to us to be utter nonsense—unrealistic, "crazy." These situations are alike in that they challenge our expectations: We expect words to fit deeds, usually, and we expect people to be "realistic," "smart," and commonsensical.

Sometimes we confront apparent discrepancies: "If this is vegetarian chili, what are these meatballs doing in here?" Sometimes we label as nonsense things that seem to us stupid or unrealistic: "You can't get to India by sailing west. That's silly."

These two habits—confrontation and spotting nonsense—are very useful defensive listening maneuvers. Talk shows and political debates, for example, would come to a standstill without them. We believe, however, that they aren't very good strategies for counselors. We prefer a counselor stance that furthers rather than impedes empathic understanding, and that maintains a collegial relationship rather than creating an adversarial one. We prefer what we think of as collegial confrontation.

Collegial Confrontation

Part of the counselor culture (Holiman & Lauver, 1987) is the concept of *confrontation*. The idea is that counselors may find confrontation helpful in "identifying discrepancies between (a) what a client has said in the past and is saying now, (b) what a client says versus what she or he does, or (c) what a client describes about herself or himself and what you actually observe" (Kottler & Brown, 1985, pp. 154–155). Counselors sometimes describe themselves as confronting clients "in denial" in order to help clients face their "avoidance" of a problem or their "inconsistencies" in behavior (Nugent, 1990). A counselor-perceived *discrepancy* in client behavior is the cue for counselor confrontation.

More forceful, vigorous confrontation is advocated by some Gestalt and substance abuse counselors, actively challenging counselees to acknowledge and share the counselor's perceptions and to resolve the perceived contradictory behaviors. Counselor confrontation, however, is also seen as potentially damaging. Many authorities suggest that counselors be cautious, diplomatic, and careful in inviting counselees to consider behaviors the counselors see as contradictory. Confrontation is thus available as a tool to the counselor perceiving discrepancies in counselee behavior, although its injudicious use has the potential of driving the client from the relationship.

Corey (1996) suggests that at its best, "authentic confrontation is basically an invitation to the client to consider some dimension of self that is preventing positive behavioral or attitudinal change" (p. 307). However, one of the few empirical examinations of confrontation (Kaul, Kaul, & Bednar, 1973) found little support for the hypothesis that confrontation encourages self-exploration on the part of clients.

We believe that a more effective way for counselors to confront perceived discrepant client behavior and respond to it is with *collegial confrontation*. Collegial confrontation rests on several assumptions:

1. Counseling is a client-centered process, and whatever benefit is to be gained will occur in the world of the counselee.

2. Any behavior is logical in the moment and context of the actor.
3. To the extent the counselor empathically understands the counselee, the "logic" of apparently discrepant behaviors in the moment of their occurrence can be articulated.
4. To the extent the "logic" can be articulated, it is available for consideration, verification, and modification.

Collegial confrontation, as we construe it, is *self-confrontation* by the counselor. What needs to be confronted in those instances when we perceive discrepant counselee behavior is our own ignorance. Given our assumption that all human behavior is logical in the moment, what we are ignorant of, as outsiders looking in, is the logic in the counselee's world supporting the two behaviors we view as discrepant. The counselee, as colleague, is our best source of information about the logic supporting his or her own behaviors.

Confrontation in the traditional form is triggered by our response to something *we* perceive as "nonsense" ("That's not realistic!") or an up-ended expectation ("How can you say you love her and then spend your anniversary on a fishing trip?"). *Nonsense* and *expectations* are in the eyes of the beholder; they are conclusions drawn by the counselor about relationships between events.

Nonsense and Discrepancies as Opportunities

We must recognize our "nonsense" responses, our "unrealistic" responses, our sense of facts being discrepant as indicators that *we* have reached a limit of *our* understanding. When our intent is empathic understanding of the other's world, we must acknowledge our naivete about that world. What must be confronted is our inability to make sense of what we're hearing and seeing.

At moments when we're aware that we've heard two things that don't seem to fit, some form of the following response can be most helpful: "A few minutes ago, I understood you to say that you hoped to practice law some day, and now you are talking about doing a sheet metal apprenticeship. These careers seem to lead in different directions. I wonder how these two goals fit together."

Collegial confrontation has several important characteristics. First, this response is a genuine expression of listener confusion caused by ignorance of the other's world; it involves confronting the *listener's* ignorance by acknowledging a desire for more information. Second, the collegial confrontation response reiterates the "facts" at issue for the counselor and provides an opportunity for the client to correct the data. Third, the form of the confrontation response makes explicit the counselor's awareness that it is the counselor's perceptions of the data that are being examined. The counselee's behavior is not being challenged; rather, the counselor is seeking to improve his or her understanding of the counselee's world. The counselor's self- confrontation is emphasized by such qualifiers as "I understood you to say . . ." and ". . . seem to lead in different directions."

Peter Falk's Columbo is a model for collegial confrontation. Columbo, when confounded by criminal circumstances, owns his confusion and takes responsibility for it. "I'm stuck. I'm just wondering how in the world . . . Do *you* have any idea . . . ?" There is tremendous power in asking for help from counselees, as in the following example.

> COUNSELOR: I'm trying to sort out my confusion about what I'm hearing you say and what you tell me you're doing. I'm wondering what it must feel like to say that you're not going to support your husband's drinking while you call his boss and make up a story that he's too sick to work.

The "logic" of the apparently discrepant behaviors in this example refers to the function of the thoughts, feelings, and actions that some professionals might describe as "denial" or "resistance." The collegial confrontation process provides the client and counselor with opportunities to articulate, accept, and understand the behavior and how it has worked for the counselee in the moment.

But suppose the counselee really does appear unrealistic or inconsistent? It would be amazing if we didn't encounter inconsistencies in our counselees' lives. Each of us could find any number in our own lives. For example, we know someone who says she's on a strict diet but somehow hasn't lost any weight. We know a counselor who has chronic asthma and smokes a pack of cigarettes a day. Each one of us has "maps" like these that don't fit a particular territory very well: The empirical link between caloric intake and weight is well established, as is the link between smoking and respiratory problems.

How can apparently unrealistic or inconsistent maps be addressed and revised? *Awareness* seems to be the first requirement if seeming inconsistencies are to be examined. All the apparently inconsistent elements need to be on top of the table, in awareness, available to the counselor and the client at the same time. One way we hang on to our inconsistencies is by keeping the parts separate in our awareness.

Descriptively accurate naming is another piece of the process. Whatever we call it—treat, reward, energy booster, snack, a taste, a nibble, a bite—one ounce of milk chocolate contains 150 calories at least. Effective maps give things more appropriate names for the purpose of more effective navigation. Naming is a tremendously powerful act; who controls names controls the world (Orwell, 1954).

Valuing is another part of the process. This involves a consideration of the value attached to each option: What is important to me, and what am I willing to do to achieve it? Or, in more familiar terms, of the choices open to me, where do I really want to go? How can I get there?

Collegial confrontation sets the stage for a collaborative examination of the map and the territory. Counselees tend to be willing to talk about the issues, move in the direction of more accurate naming, and consider how various options relate to their ideals when the counselor participates as a mutual explorer rather than as an adversary.

Collegial confrontation, relative to more traditional confrontation, seems more in harmony with the ideals of the helping relationship. Conventional counselor confrontations might look something like this:

- "You say you want her to grow up, but you don't let her assume any responsibility around the house."
- "How can you say you won't support your husband's drinking when you turn around and call his boss with a story that he's sick?"

Conventional confrontation assumes the superior authority of the counselor's view. The counselor's version of truth or reality is seen as ultimately valid, the criterion against which the counselee is measured. The counselor's view is counterposed against that of the counselee in an adversarial process. The implied counselor task is one of winning counselee compliance to the counselor's worldview and bringing the counselee to a more valid way of being. If you were the client, wouldn't this strike you as a bit presumptuous, if not downright arrogant?

Our experiences on the receiving end of confrontation, even by well-meaning friends, relatives, parents, and spouses, have rarely left us feeling stronger, more responsible, or more empowered. Cormier and Cormier (1991) acknowledge the possibility that counselees may feel counselor confrontation as an attack by listing five ways counselors can anticipate that clients will defend themselves. All this rhetoric about attack and defense sounds more like warfare than counseling. We believe that relative to the usual approach, *collegial confrontation* as described here is a confusion- reduction process that is in harmony with the avowed purpose of counseling: helping people find better ways of being.

Counselee Strengths and Resources

As you listen attentively to counselees telling their story, it is all too easy to focus primarily on the distress, the confusion, the frustration as you seek to learn why they sought counseling—and to determine "Where are we going?" Although this is a primary counselor goal, you also need to be attentive to the strengths, resources, and capabilities in the counselee's situation. An awareness and an inventory of counselee assets can be most useful, both at the moment and when the time comes to plan for achieving counselee objectives ("How can we get there?").

Jerome Frank (1973) observes that if one characteristic holds true across all counselees, it is that they are, to some degree, demoralized. Their faith in themselves is shaken. Many counselees seem to be experiencing a kind of tunnel vision regarding themselves and their world. They see the pitfalls, the dark side; their talk is of failures and inabilities; their arsenal of resources seems empty; past achievements count for little. The counselor who can maintain perspective and not be caught up in the counselee's tunnel vision can recognize cues to counselee assets amid the talk of problems.

What are counselee assets? First, let's remind ourselves that most people function very well most of the time in most parts of their lives. This competence in living constitutes an impressive pool of information, skills, experience, and achievements. Surviving in today's world is not easy. Respect the counseling clients you encounter as competent human beings. They, like most of us at one time or another, have found themselves in a predicament with which they want help.

Problems can seem discouraging and overwhelming because of the way we think and talk about them. Moment-to-moment experiences are lumped together and reported as "a depressing evening" or "a total mess" or "a bad week"; all are overgeneralizations that darken the skies from horizon to horizon. Such global terms obscure counselees' awareness of their moments of competence, which are genuine current assets. The following questions frequently highlight potentially useful client resources.

1. "Has this sort of situation come up in the past? How did it go?" In the process of hearing the counselee's story, the issues as presented may suggest similarities to previous situations the client has successfully encountered, such as relationships, conflicts, decisions, or ambivalence. The common thread may be one of process, such as making a decision or ending a relationship, or it may involve common content, such as dealing with anger or stress.

2. "What parts of the present predicament involve skills and behaviors that can also be part of the solution?" Although the problematic situation might be unsatisfactory, it's likely that some parts of it are going all right. For example, a young man who was distressed about his inability to establish a long-term relationship and feared he was doomed to loneliness was quite skilled in meeting people and in initiating relationships, two elements that would be real assets in a sequence of experiences leading to his goal, a lasting relationship. Noting existing skills can help counselees reestablish contact with their competencies and bolster their self-esteem.

3. "How did you decide to come for counseling now?" As individuals, our self-esteem is enhanced by coping responses and eroded by avoidance. Counselors can help build client self-esteem by overtly recognizing as coping responses their decision to seek counseling and their willingness to tell their story. Those who seek counseling can be recognized as having made an active effort to cope with an ongoing predicament rather than avoid it or continue to tolerate it. Counselees, in seeking the help of counselors, can walk a little taller because they have made the effort in their own behalf.

The counselor culture, more often than not, encourages practitioners to focus on deficits and shortcomings, label them, and get paid for addressing them. We hope these suggestions argue persuasively for the importance of attending to client strengths and resources as well.

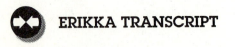 **ERIKKA TRANSCRIPT**

Counselor Readiness

Your self-talk can handicap or enhance your performance, as you have probably learned through earlier experiences. Your self-talk in the counselor role is critical to your ability to experience and convey empathic understanding with each counselee. You can keep yourself focused and on task by giving yourself reminders of what to do. The following are representative of Dave's self-talk at about this point with Erikka:

> I need to focus on Erikka's experience. I can best do that by following her intently and using my listening skills to develop a progressively clearer picture of her experience, of her thoughts, feelings, and actions.

> I will maintain my awareness of my own nonverbal and verbal behavior to be sure that I'm signaling my intention to understand this client's experience.

When appropriate, remind yourself of what *not* to do as well:

> Whoa! I'm paying more attention to what I think and feel is going on with Erikka than I am to *her* experience. I need to stop creating interpretations and get back to being an active, accurate listener.

> I'm already jumping in with suggestions of how to solve the problem. It's not my responsibility to rescue Erikka (or myself) from experiencing her pain. It *is* my responsibility to keep us both focused on understanding everything we can about her experience before we set goals and explore solutions.

In the dialogue that follows, notice how consistently the counselor uses following responses along with pinpointing responses, discussed in the next chapter, to clarify the action, thought, and feeling components of Erikka's problematic situation.

The Interview

CL5:　It's my belief that I pretty much control how my body reacts. I think that I'm somewhere losing control. I really don't feel that I have something organically going wrong with me that I'm having these headaches. [CO: OK.] I'm letting the inside things stack up in a way that they're all coming up right to here (*points to forehead*). So I'm not addressing something, and I guess that's what I reached up here (*points to forehead*) for.

CO6:　All right. So, one thing you're saying is that you want to re-establish more control over your . . .

CL6:　Yeah. I feel like I'm losing control by having headaches and by having them control me, like I have the urge to lie down. They're stopping my flow of energy.

CO7: OK. And you're feeling like somehow if the flow of energy were different, if you had a different kind of experience in terms of your flow of energy, we'd know that something had changed and you'd be more in control.

CL7: Yeah, yeah.

CO8: And where is it, how is it you know your flow of energy is on track or not on track?

CL8: I guess the thing that's coming to my mind right now is that I've been very aware during the last year of having schedules and lists of things to do and staying on track with all that. And lately, I'm taking a whole lot more time and realizing I haven't done a whole lot of things. I'm getting panicked because I'm sitting in class now and realizing I haven't made any plans to make tapes. I feel like I'm moving toward another extreme in that I was so very structured and putting the energy out to get these five things done. . . . I feel that in the last couple of weeks I'm going the other way. . . . I'm just getting things done, but I'm not really moving after them. The lists keep getting smaller and smaller, but the things to do are still there; they're not any less.

CO9: So part of what happens in your life, you interpret your flow of energy according to the length and number of lists in your life, how much structure you impose?

CL9: Yeah, and how much of that structure I get accomplished.

CO10: What do you do? Check off things on your list?

CL10: Um-hmm.

CO11: So it sounds like you've got a couple of real good indicators now that let you know whether or not things are changing in your life in a direction that you like.

CL11: Right, right. And I see a change taking place now, and it's upsetting me, the direction it's taking. I'm looking at myself and thinking, "I'm pretty lackadaisical in how I've been putting out my energy in the last week or two weeks."

CO12: OK. Is that what you say to yourself, "I'm being pretty lackadaisical"?

CL12: Pretty lazy.

CO13: Lazy?

CL13: It's not me. I'm looking at myself and saying, who's that?

CO14: It's not you. You feel like you're sort of alienated from yourself or whoever it is you want to be.

CL14: Yeah.

CO15: And when you say those things to yourself, what happens in terms of how you feel?

CL15: (*sighs*) I get upset. I find myself getting more nervous about the things I'm not attending to. I feel disappointed because I wonder why I'm letting myself down and not doing those things.

CO16: Upset, disappointed. [CL: Yeah.] Concerned about what's going on with you.

CL16: Yeah, very much so.

CO17: Obviously one place where you're having a very intense experience it sounds like is your head. [CL: Yeah.] We'll pay more attention to that in just a minute. Are there other places in your body that sort of tell you that you're being concerned or upset or . . .

CL17: Yeah. I guess the next would be my stomach. Sort of grindy noises will come out when I'm not even hungry. There's something churning in there.

CO18: And is that related to what's happening in your head? Do you notice there's more activity in your stomach when you're having headaches?

CL18: Not really. Not really. I find it's still kind of minimal as far as the stomach's concerned. It really all seems to go up here (*points to head*).

CO19: You've made that motion (*moves hands from stomach to head*) a couple of times, to go up here. [CL: Um-hmm.] What is it that's going up here?

CL19: The turmoil, the tension. I don't know; it's such a weird feeling to try to describe this. It's pounding, it's *circulating* (*moves hands from stomach to head*). It's like it's coming up here and then a dam breaks and it's all just . . . disturbing.

CO20: It comes on as a lot of pressure (*hands to head*); can you show me on your head where you feel that?

CL20: Right here (*points to forehead*), and sometimes right here (*points to back of head*). Today it's up here, but yesterday it was here (*points to back*).

CO21: And then you said, "and the dam breaks." What happens when the dam breaks?

CL21: I run around at 11 o'clock at night and try to get all the things done I didn't get done earlier. And I don't get to bed until 2:00 and I wake up and I'm tired and I have a headache. It's just a vicious cycle, really.

CO22: I see. You aren't as efficient, you aren't as productive as you want to be. [CL: "Efficient" is a good word.] "Efficient" is a good word. [CL:

That fits, completely.] And a lot of pressure builds up as you say those things to yourself: "I've been pretty lackadaisical; I've got all those things to do and gee, I just feel lazy and" [CL: Yes, yes.] "and then as I'm doing that I feel a lot of pressure building up; maybe I have that experience in my stomach." [CL: Yeah, but not a whole lot.] Not a whole lot. And then it builds up, and then all of a sudden it's what? The dam breaks.

CL22: Yeah, yeah . . . and it's not even a lazy thing, not like I'm doing nothing. I find that I'm doing things, but they're not necessarily productive things. I've joined Nautilus and I spend so much time there now. Yesterday was a typical example. I went to aerobics, spent a couple of hours at Nautilus, came home and did my ironing, and before I knew it, it was 9 o'clock at night and I hadn't done any of the so-called productive things, and in the meantime during the course of that day I started to get a terrible headache about 4 o'clock.

CO23: Um-hmm. So it sounds to me that you've taken this concern pretty seriously and you've started to mobilize some things to address it and there's something about that that's not feeling so successful.

CL23: Not at all. 'Cause I was feeling this way last week.

CO24: OK. I guess I want to come up with what it is that we're gonna be shooting for so that you'll be back where you want to be. Sounds like "back," because you have plenty of experience that tells you where you want to be, and this is a departure. Is that right?

CL24: Yes, yes. Exactly.

We'll interrupt right here, a somewhat arbitrary place, and not because the counselor suddenly ceases Understanding and shifts to Negotiating. Rather, counselor emphasis now begins to shift from Step 2, Understanding, to Step 3, Negotiating Objectives, but the processes are mutually supportive, each contributing clarity to the other.

Counselor responses 6, 7, 9, 11, 22, and 23 look most like the following responses presented in this chapter.

Counselor responses 8–22 work as focusing tools, to clarify the nature of the counselee's concern. We refer to this as Pinpointing in Step 3.

In C022, the counselor tries to pull it all together, toward establishing consensus that both parties share a common understanding of the client's immediate concern. In map-territory terms, the counselor is verifying that he and Erikka are using the same map. Dave is also verifying the relationship between the emerging map and the territory of Erikka's actions, thoughts, and feelings.

Debriefing

OBSERVER: Is this really such a serious problem for the counselor to put so much energy into? Why doesn't he just refer Erikka to a stress management class?

COUNSELOR: One of our colleagues speaks of the metaphorical "ticket" that each client holds to get himself or herself in to see a counselor. For one client, the ticket is what is acceptable to her as the reason she's seeing a counselor. For another, it is the choice of which of the many issues he's facing in his life is the one he believes he can actually do something about. Another ticket is the problem a client can pose to determine if this counselor is someone who can help her.

As counselor, I am not labeling the problem as serious or minor. To do so would be to project my values and beliefs regarding Erikka's situation. Erikka is indicating that the problem is serious to her and this is where I begin with her. Following her lead will determine whether other concerns come into focus.

OBSERVER: Why is the counselor being so methodical? Is it really that necessary to determine when Erikka has her headaches and whether she differentiates "lazy" from "unproductive"?

COUNSELOR: When Erikka says she gets headaches or feels "lazy," she sounds like a million other people. This counselor wants to understand how Erikka *experiences* these generic descriptions of her concerns. My effort to translate conceptual and interpretive language into thinking, feeling, and acting domains of experience not only helps me be empathic with Erikka's concerns but also facilitates Erikka's ability to represent the territory of her concern with more precision and validity. This precision and validity require considerable time and effort to achieve.

OBSERVER: Erikka says she wants to be in control of her life. Is the counselor thinking of ways to help her do that?

COUNSELOR: Until Erikka—and this counselor—have answered the question "Where are we going?" to Erikka's satisfaction, "How do we get there?" is not very relevant. I am open to the possibility that Erikka may know how to be in control of her life. She indicates that she has a number of skills and substantial experience at being in control. I will be more successful in encouraging her to select and use the tools she is capable of and comfortable with using if I am learning about her toolbox instead of searching through my own.

SUGGESTIONS FOR INTEGRATING ACTIVITIES

1. In a series of conversations or interactions with five different people, pick a moment and try out a *following* response. Record the *person's* statement and your following response in the format suggested below. In the *effect* column, note what you observed after your following response. Find a classmate and share your experiences.

Person: (words he or she spoke to you)   Effect:

You: (your following response)   Effect:

2. After you've tried activity 1 in an extended conversation with someone who has something to share, practice using a series of following responses, using reflections in particular. Tape the conversation if possible. From your tape, memory, or notes, transcribe five consecutive exchanges of your best following responses, and bring the transcript to class.

A. In a small group of fellow students, circulate your transcripts and, as a group, select the best example you find of a restatement, a paraphrase, and a reflection. Write each on the chalkboard, including the person's statement and the exemplary following response.
B. Is there consensus about whether following responses are accurately labeled? It's sometimes hard to tell from just the words.
C. Ask participants to share one thing they noticed about themselves in the process of doing this assignment: What made the assignment hard to do? Easy to do? Ask participants to indicate their observations of the effects of the following responses on the other person.

3. Conduct at least one experiment in collegial confrontation, preferably with someone who knows you. The opportunity to use this strategy occurs when you find yourself ready to respond to someone with confrontation or with a "nonsense"-type comment. Instead, assume that from the other person's perspective, what you've observed *is* logical and *does* make sense. Set yourself to discover just how the other person's perceptions and logic make sense of the situation you find puzzling. Pay attention to the collegial part; set yourself as a co-seeker of enlightenment, not as judge and jury.

 # CONSULTATION TIME

Scenario 1

COUNSELOR: So, tell me why you decided to see a counselor.

CLIENT: Well, it really wasn't my idea. My parole officer told me she thought I ought to get counseling for anger management, and she told me to make an appointment with you.

COUNSELOR: So you need to improve your anger management skills, is that it?

CLIENT: No. *I* don't have a problem with anger.

What options does the counselor have at this point?

- "So the reason you came in today to see me was to get your parole officer off your back. I wonder how much you know about what counselors do."
- "You've done at least part of what your parole officer asked; you've come to see a counselor. Is there anything you'd like to ask or anything you'd like to talk about the rest of this hour?"
- "You don't think you need any work on anger management; anger isn't a problem for you. I wonder why your parole officer thought that working on anger management might be a good idea for you. Can you give me any insight into what your parole officer might have been thinking?"
- "Your parole officer thought you needed to work on anger management, but anger isn't a problem for you. I wonder why you're here?"
- How might you respond toward learning "Where are we going?"

Scenario 2

CLIENT: (*appears at office for scheduled session with two small children in tow*) "My baby-sitting arrangements fell through at the last minute so I just brought the kids along. They'll play on the floor while we talk. That's OK, isn't it?"

What are the counselor's options?

- "It's frustrating when plans don't work out and you have to make last-minute changes. It seems you did the best you could."
- "I wonder how well you and I will be able to concentrate on the issues with your children in the room."
- "I would be willing to try it this time, but I'd rather not after today."
- "My office isn't childproof; I'm concerned that your children might hurt themselves on something."
- How might you respond?

REFERENCES

Bordin, E. S. (1968). *Psychological counseling* (2nd ed.). New York: Appleton-Century-Crofts.

Corey, G. (1996). *Theory and practice of counseling and psychotherapy* (5th ed.). Pacific Grove, CA: Brooks/Cole.

Cormier, W. H., & Cormier, L. S. (1991). *Interviewing strategies for helpers* (3rd ed.). Pacific Grove, CA: Brooks/Cole.

Frank, J. D. (1973). *Persuasion and healing* (rev. ed.). Baltimore, MD: Johns Hopkins University Press.

Holiman, M., & Lauver, P. J. (1987). The counselor culture and client-centered practice. *Counselor Education and Supervision, 26,* 184–191.

Johnson, W., with D. Moeller. (1972). *Living with change: The semantics of coping.* New York: Harper & Row.

Kottler, J. A., & Brown, R. W. (1985). *Introduction to therapeutic counseling.* Pacific Grove, CA: Brooks/Cole.

Kaul, T. J., Kaul, M. A., & Bednar, R. L. (1973). Counselor confrontation and client depth of self-exploration. *Journal of Counseling Psychology, 20,* 132–136.

Nugent, F. (1990). *An introduction to the profession of counseling.* Columbus, OH: Charles E. Merrill.

Orwell, George. (1954). Politics and the English language. In G. Orwell, *A collection of essays by George Orwell.* New York: Doubleday /Anchor.

Sarason, S. B. (1985). *Caring and compassion in clinical practice.* San Francisco: Jossey-Bass.

SUGGESTED READING

d'Ardenne, P., & Mahtani, A. (1989). *Transcultural counseling in action.* Newbury Park, CA: Sage. (Transcultural counseling is *not* about being an expert on any given culture, nor does it adhere to a particular school of counseling. Rather, it is a way of thinking about clients, where culture is acknowledged and valued.)

Egan, G. (1994). *Exercises in helping skills* (5th ed.). Pacific Grove, CA: Brooks/Cole.

Egan, G. (1994). *The skilled helper* (5th ed.). Pacific Grove, CA: Brooks/Cole. (Especially Chapter 9, "Skills and Guidelines for Effective Challenging," pp. 177–198. This is the best discussion of confrontation we have found published.)

CHAPTER 8

Step 3: Negotiate Counseling Objectives

Who wills certain things also wills their consequences; if he does not like the consequences he should oppose the things from which they originate. —Paul Henri Spaak

We have all heard people ask, "But what's the *real* problem?" or say, "But that's not the *real* problem." People act as though there are two categories: problems and *real* problems. They seem to have a kind of intuitive understanding that situations don't get better unless real problems are addressed. The purpose of this chapter is to suggest how real problems differ from problems, and to describe a process whereby real problems can be identified and articulated, thus increasing the likelihood that problematic situations can be improved.

The term *real problem* is being used here to refer to the sensory experiences that are the immediate and actual parts of a problematic episode. The territory of the real problem contains the individual's actions, thoughts, and feelings experienced as elements of the problem situation in the moments of its occurrence—what was real versus what was imagined, ideas about its meaning and value, memory, myth, and so on. An individual's description of the real problem would be a very accurate and detailed map of the problem situation. Obviously, the more finely tuned individuals can be in using awareness and language to describe to themselves and others elements of the real problem, the more clearly they will designate the route from problem identification to problem improvement to problem resolution. We believe that when people have accurate maps, they probably don't often need counselors. Conversely, when the map doesn't fit the territory, people have more difficulty finding satisfactory ways to resolve problems.

Distinguishing between Problems
and *Real* Problems

CONNIE: I have a problem with a relationship.

COUNSELOR: Tell me about it.

CONNIE: I'm having some conflict. I'm, uh, starting a business with a personal friend of mine. And I'm having a little conflict on business boundaries and friendship boundaries. The business stuff gets over into the friendship and the personal friends thing gets into the business.

The terms *problem* and *conflict* are generalized names for the actions, thoughts, and feelings people experience as unsatisfactory or problematic. *Problem* statements usually are expressed in such general terms that they could fit any number of people as well as the speaker. Problem statements usually lump a whole series of experiences together and refer to them as if they were identical: "I always freeze on an exam," or "She never gives me credit for my help." When Connie says she has a problem with conflict in a relationship, we are hearing a generalized statement, a conclusion about what may be a whole series of distressing experiences with a partner. At this point in the problem identification process, Connie's map describes her territory no more clearly than a U.S. map describes the backroads of southeastern Arizona.

How does a problem continue to be a problem over time? One reason problems persist is because they are discussed at such generalized, abstract levels that only broad, general responses are possible. In an attempt to clarify how Connie experiences her problem, the interaction between Connie and her counselor might go something like this:

COUNSELOR: Tell me about the last time your relationship problem came up.

CONNIE: The last time that I felt bad about business and friendship getting all mixed up was last weekend when Maria and I were going to meet our friend for her birthday. . . . I bought this nice gift to give to our friend, and when I showed it to Maria, she gave me a really hard time.

COUNSELOR: A really hard time?

CONNIE: Yes, she asked me how much the gift had cost and said that she was surprised that I could afford to be so generous when I was just starting a business.

COUNSELOR: And how did you feel when she said that?

CONNIE: Like, "What right does she have to tell me how to spend my money?"

COUNSELOR: So that's one *thought* that went through your mind. What were you *feeling* when you said to yourself, "What right does she have . . . ?"

CONNIE: I was feeling bad about the change in our relationship since we started working together.

COUNSELOR: You were feeling bad—what kind of bad feeling? Can you be more specific?

CONNIE: Judged, criticized. It just seems like Maria is always on my case these days.

COUNSELOR: Did it seem to you that Maria was "on your case" when she was talking with you last weekend about how much your friend's gift cost?

CONNIE: Well, I think so . . . but it was kind of hard to tell.

COUNSELOR: It was hard to tell if she was really on your case?

CONNIE: Well, she was kind of laughing when she said it—like she was teasing me.

COUNSELOR: So, when Maria asked you about your ability to afford the cost of the gift, she was laughing and you thought to yourself, "What right does she have to tell me how to spend my money?"

CONNIE: Yes.

COUNSELOR: And you felt judged and criticized at that moment?

CONNIE: Well, I did, but now I'm wondering if Maria meant what she said in that way.

One way problems stay alive, or escalate to the blow-up stage, is for the *real* problem never to be addressed. The real, actually experienced actions, thoughts, and feelings of the specific person or persons involved in the problematic incident are rarely identified and considered. Instead, we get into blame and counterblame.

What can be done to ease the problem with Connie and her partner? It is very difficult to arrive at an effective response for a specific individual to a problem that is stated in general terms. We would like to understand the situation better. We would like to know about the real problem, about what is actually happening, what she experiences with her partner that she objects to. Although problem statements convey very little information other than that someone is unhappy, they can suggest where to look for examples of the real problem as it is experienced in real life.

To reiterate, the term *real problem* is being used here quite literally to refer to the sensory experiences that are the immediate elements of a problematic episode. Part of every problematic episode is at least one unpleasant feeling—mad, bad, sad. Without unpleasant feelings, the episode would not be felt as problematic. *Real problems* are described in terms of the individual's *actions*, *thoughts*, and *feelings* experienced as elements of the episode in the moments of its occurrence in real life.

Describing the Real Problem

In Connie's situation, lack of agreement about the terms *business* and *friendship* seems to block progress in dealing with the problem. It is important to learn what Connie has experienced (the actual actions, thoughts, and problematic feelings) that she refers to as mixing friendship and business. The key question to clarify generalizations and general problem statements is "What do you mean by that?" We can help Connie move from generalization to the specific by asking, "What do you mean by *mixing business and friendship*? Can you give me an example? Tell me about the last time you thought business and friendship were mixed up." The counselor responses, "What do you mean by . . . ?" "Give me an example of . . ." "Tell me about the last time . . ." are fairly standard opening moves in the process of pinpointing. These and other pinpointing tools are presented in the next section.

The Pinpointing Process

There are times when we think pinpointing is at the core of empathic understanding. When we're in the middle of this process with someone, it often seems to us that we are jointly considering aspects of their personal experience that are very private, very personal. Furthermore, we will frequently find ourselves uncovering some previously unmarked action or thought or feeling that the client acknowledges as important and authentic but which he or she has been unaware of to this point. In this sense, pinpointing sometimes brings to light important but hitherto unattended parts of ourselves. Times like these provide us with the nearest sense we'll have of what this part of the other's world is like.

What Is Pinpointing?

Pinpointing is the process of producing a high-fidelity description (verbal map) of an episode of human experience (territory as it was/is/might become). High-fidelity descriptions of the counselee's thoughts, feelings, and actions provide the foundation for both accurate problem identification—finding the real problem—and problem resolution. Pinpointing is a way to bring a single moment of experience into focus in our present awareness. Pinpointing is the "slow-motion replay" that discloses the specific actions, thoughts, and feelings of a critical incident of life. Pinpointing also functions to create a clear and specific description of a desired outcome—the thoughts, feelings, and actions the counselee would like to experience in future versions of the critical incident that prompted him or her to seek counseling.

Pinpointing is a powerful tool for further clarifying and understanding the *what* and the *how* of an instance of human behavior. As *what* and *how* come into clearer and more precise focus, counselee concerns about *why* are often addressed as well. Pinpointing is a process that can help to reduce confusion between map and territory. Pinpointing recalls and describes the territory so the validity of the map can be examined, and a more accurate map of the territory can be constructed.

Why Is Pinpointing Important?

Pinpointing the specific actions, thoughts, and feelings of a critical incident in the client's life is important because it gives both client and counselor a clearer view of the real problem. Pinpointing can result in a more focused picture of the actual elements of experience—the actions, thoughts, feelings—in the sequence in which they occurred in the target incident. Pinpointing, in eliciting the elements of experience, helps discriminate map (my *ideas* or *opinions* about what is) and territory (what is).

For many clients, pinpointing produces new information and new self-understanding that they need to set and achieve objectives that matter to them in their lives. For example, clients may hear themselves articulate guidelines for action ("Accept authority!" "Trust no one") they've been following habitually, without conscious awareness, perhaps for years. Pinpointing is an empowering process, equipping people with the information they need to make informed, considered choices about *how* they are, and thus *who* they are. As their actions, thoughts, and feelings in a particular situation emerge, clients have opportunities to challenge and change old patterns of behavior, bringing them into congruence with present values and ideals.

Effective pinpointing enhances the client's self-efficacy in a number of ways:

- It increases the amount of "behavioral information" the client has about his or her experience in the problem situation. For example, pinpointing a problem event like "blowing off my diet" can help the client identify how he or she thought, acted, and felt to achieve a self-defeating dietary lapse.

- As the specific action, thought, and feeling components of an event are identified, the counselee's territory of self-responsibility, accountability, and informed freedom of choice are expanded. The pinpointing process can "blow the cover" on apparently immutable personal attributes like "I just have no will power," or "Everyone on my father's side has an eating problem."

- Through pinpointing, habits of perception and expression like "will power" and "everyone has it" and "blow it off" are demystified. Counselees can begin to think of themselves and others less as people who have tempers or who lack will power and more as people who act and think and feel. Thus, they learn that they can do differently if they so choose.

- Pinpointing can help develop menus of functional behavioral options for anticipated challenging situations. An inventory of thoughts, feelings, and actions working for the counselee in situation A may suggest a basis for coping with situation B.

- Clients sometimes say about a possible plan, "I tried that and it didn't work." Pinpointing can help identify gaps in thinking, expressing feelings, and doing skills in a problematic episode, leading to an array of new skills and techniques. This discovery can counter a tendency to throw away a piece of machinery because one or two parts don't work. Sometimes when it's "broke," the smartest course is to use what's still usable and fix what needs fixing.

Subskills in Pinpointing

Successful pinpointing involves several different abilities: (a) distinguishing "fuzzies" (comments *about* behavior) from specifics (reports *describing* behavior); (b) attending to three domains of awareness: actions, thoughts, and feelings; (c) focusing on actual experience in a single event rather than on impressions (personal myth/map) of many events; and (d) discovering the temporal sequence of elements in the critical incident. Let us consider each of these abilities in turn.

Distinguishing "Fuzzies" from "Specifics"

Fuzzies (Mager, 1972) are abstractions—ideas or opinions we have about what a group of objects or events seem to have in common, or how a group of objects or events may be alike. Words like *reckless, lazy, energetic, lonely, courteous,* and *appreciate* are abstractions or thoughts *about* performances or events, inferences drawn by an observer. These words are verbal projections, opinions that arise out of mental processing of observed or imagined experiences; they are "fuzzies" because they contain little information about the objects or events they seem to describe.

Fuzzies, especially when uttered in a loud, clear voice, can sound authoritative: "Chester is lazy." Well, we know what the speaker thinks, but what have we learned about Chester? Fuzzies convey information about the *meanings*—usually goodness or badness—of events to the person who makes the statement. Fuzzies tell us about the mind, the values or expectations, of the observer/reporter, not about what happened. Fuzzies are fuzzy because we cannot see into each other's minds to observe just how a particular fuzzy was created. When Mom says, "Chester is lazy," *lazy* is a fuzzy; *lazy* doesn't tell us what Chester did or did not do. *Lazy* is Mom's idea about the *meaning* of what she has seen Chester do or not do relative to her expectations of him. Mom's map of Chester doesn't contain much information about the territory, about Chester; Mom's map seems to be about Chester, but it's actually about Mom's view of him.

Here is another example:

CLIENT: My friends have *rejected* me. (*rejected* is a fuzzy)

COUNSELOR: (*pinpointing*) Give me an example of what you mean by rejected.

CLIENT: Tim *gave a party* Friday night and I was *not invited*. (*gave a party* and *not invited* are *actions*)

Rejected is fuzzy because it could refer to many different kinds of actions, thoughts, and feelings. It could mean that "my friends did not invite me to the party on Friday," or "they told me to go home," or "they slammed the door in my face," or "they do not speak to me when we meet." Let's see how we're doing about getting the difference between fuzzies and specifics across to you. In the checklist below, circle your choice as either fuzzy (F) or specific (S). Then check your responses against the explanation that follows.

F	S	1.	Looked at me and smiled
F	S	2.	Appreciated her help
F	S	3.	Wanted to be here
F	S	4.	Said "I will help"
F	S	5.	Walking toward the library
F	S	6.	Spoke with three people
F	S	7.	Enjoyed your company
F	S	8.	Become better acquainted with
F	S	9.	Developed increased awareness
F	S	10.	Felt a pain in my chest

The specifics above are 1, *looked at, smiled*; 4, *said*; 5, *walking*; 6, *spoke*; and 10, *felt*. These are words that describe things that people do; they are *actions*. The terms in the other items are fuzzies. The fuzzy terms and one example of a specific performance suggested by each are given below. For each fuzzy, read the example and then write another example of a specific, an action. In the first item, for *appreciated*, ask yourself what action you might perform that could indicate *appreciation* to someone.

2. Appreciated her help   Example: Gave her a check for $20.00.
                                    or: _____

3. Wanted to be here   Example: Put the date on her calendar.
                                    or: _____

7. Enjoyed your company   Example: Asked for a date for next
                                                 Friday.
                                    or: _____

8. Become better acquainted with Example: Learn her name and phone
                                                 number.
                                    or: _____

9. Developed increased awareness Example: Read a book about it.
                                    or: _____

Differentiating among Actions, Thoughts, and Feelings

It's easier *not* to be aware of every little thing, and it's certainly easier not to remember each one. We learn to live efficiently by lumping small things together. A result, however, is that our awarenesses are *lumpy*; we lump experience together and think and talk about the lumps as if *they* were our experience. We forget that we created the lumps.

We experience ourselves as *actors, thinkers,* and *feelers*. Without denying other possible manifestations of life, actions, thoughts, and feelings are the usual dimensions of our own self-awareness.

> *Thoughts*: I am aware of thinking—saying words to myself, using symbols and images in my mental processing of experience.
>
> *Feelings*: I am aware of internal states—warmth in my cheeks, a quavering in my chest, a heaviness in my arms, an ache in the pit of my stomach, a wetness in my eyes.
>
> *Actions*: I am aware of writing, speaking, tasting, seeing, walking, glancing, hearing, sighing, smelling, smiling, stroking, inhaling, driving . . .

Individuals seem to be largely unaware of their specific moment-to-moment behavior; much of what we do seems automatic. When we need to refer to our activities, we tend to think in terms of lumps of behaviors and report our experiences in fuzzies.

Gaining awareness of the actual experience behind the fuzzy can be challenging. Accurately pinpointing a moment's experience calls for *awareness* of the three domains of human experience and *clarity* in reporting the experience, using descriptive, nonjudgmental language.

Actions seem the easiest to pinpoint. They are the most public, most observable element of human experience. Ask questions like these to help yourself pinpoint actions: "What did you do?" "Show me what you did." "What would I have seen if I had been there?"

Feelings can be more difficult to pinpoint because they are largely private, internal events. To pinpoint feelings, ask questions such as "How were/are you feeling?" "Where in your body do you feel it?" "Have you felt that way in other situations?" "What is it like (pressure? cold? heat? pain? waves?) for you to feel _____ ?" Metaphors can be a very useful way to represent aspects of feelings.

Thoughts seem to be the most difficult to pinpoint accurately. One reason may be that we usually are not aware of or clear about the specific words we say to ourselves in critical situations. Some of our responses are so well practiced they seem automatic ("I didn't think anything; I just did it"). The next exchange is an example of how to pinpoint thoughts:

> COUNSELOR: Just what words went through your mind when you saw her coming up the walk?

CLIENT: I thought I'd die.

COUNSELOR: What did you say to yourself at that moment?

CLIENT: I said, "Oh, my God. There's Mom and this place is still a mess."

The specific words, "I thought I'd die," did not go through the client's mind at the moment he saw his mom. Note that the counselor asks for *those* words.

The Erikka transcript segment at the end of this chapter contains a number of examples of pinpointing that occur during the flow of a counseling session. Some of these are extracted here. For example of a counselor beginning the pinpointing process, look at CO25.

CO25:   What are some things we would be shooting for to make things right again? These might include the way you think about yourself, feelings, or something that you do that would be desired outcomes.

In CO30, Dave focuses on pinpointing actions to clarify the client's fuzzy mention of "stuff coming up."

CO30:   And then you said you didn't want this stuff, whatever it is, to be coming up (*gestures with hands moving up from stomach to head*) [CL: Um-hmm.] What would be happening instead of that?

An example of the counselor's pinpointing Erikka's feelings and then thoughts follows next.

CO68:   That's about it? OK. How're you feeling?

CL68:   (*head comes up, chuckles*) I want to go to Nautilus and work out! . . . I'm feeling really bogged down.

CO69:   Bogged down?

CL69:   Very much so.

CO70:   And where do you notice that in your body right now?

CL70:   A lot of stress right across here (*touches forehead*), and my stomach's starting to get a little worse. More than it was . . .

CO71:   OK. Stomach's a little "grindy"?

CL71:   Um-hmm. Nervous, it's a nervous stomach.

CO72:   OK. And the tension's where, right here? (*CO hands around CL forehead*) [CL: Um-hmm, Um-hmm.] And the pressure's what, like that? (*CO hands to frontal part of CL head*)

CL72:   More on the side, on the side. [*CO moves hands: "Like that?"*] Yeah, yeah. Right, that's right, right there. That's it.

CO73:   And (*walks around to stand just behind CL on left side and says, in "voice" of CL*) as I'm sort of paying attention to all this pressure in my head and I've got all these things stacked up, and my stomach's getting "grindy," what am I saying to myself?

CL73: I'm saying, "God, you need to take care of things. You need to get things sorted out," and, uh . . .

CO74: (*continues for CL*) This isn't like you. [CL: No.] How'd you get yourself in this fix? [CL: Right!] Does that fit?

CL74: Right. You screwed up. (*head down*)

For the counselor, simply using pinpointing responses does not automatically bring awareness and clarity to the emerging map of actions, thoughts, and feelings. It's not unusual for clients to respond to pinpointing with more fuzzies. Counselors need to recognize when they are hearing descriptions of experience and when they are hearing more fuzzies. There can be several sources of confusion for the unwary pinpointer. Some of these have to do with the meaning a client gives to words.

As one example, just because a client says "I feel" or "I felt" does not always mean you will hear about *feelings*. "*I feel*" is frequently used instead of "*I think*" or "*I believe*." Thoughts and beliefs are not feelings, although they can seem very closely related at times.

Avoiding this potential confusion is possible. If the word *that* can be inserted after "I feel," then what follows is more likely a thought than a feeling. For example, "I feel (that) it's time to go" is really about a thought, not a feeling.

Here is another way the pinpointer can be confused by the meaning a client gives to words. Just because a client says "I thought" does not always mean that actual thoughts will be reported. You may hear *about* thoughts and not the thoughts themselves. "I thought I'd die" is *about* whatever thoughts and feelings occurred in that moment.

When your best pinpointing intentions seem to produce one fuzzy after another, you might try some of the following tactics that have worked for us.

- Ask clients to replay "the tape recorder in their brain," which contains what they actually said to themselves during the incident.
- Ask clients to report using the present tense, as though the event were happening right now.
- Ask clients to reenact the incident, and ask them to think out loud as they go through it.
- Ask "If you could know (recall) what you were saying to yourself at that moment, what would it be?"

When you are pinpointing thoughts, remember that some thoughts become automatic through repetition over the years. We don't remember these thoughts easily because it's been so long since we were aware of them. One way to get at them is to ask clients to take a mental videotape of the incident the next time it occurs so the "tape" can be replayed at the next session.

Focusing on a Single Event

Clients frequently seek help with some recurring problematic aspect of their lives. Procrastination is an example of a recurring problem. To know just what a person means who complains of procrastination, we ask for examples. To discover *how* a person procrastinates, we begin by focusing on one single event: "Tell me about the last time you missed a deadline."

Pinpointing the actions, thoughts, and feelings of a single incident permits us to identify the moment-to-moment events, the chain of responses from beginning to end, that constitute a complete episode of the real problem. When clients speak about their "problem," they tend to report fuzzies. Holding clients to the task of describing their moment-to-moment experience during one incident increases the likelihood that actual actions, thoughts, and feelings will be reported, and in the sequence in which they occurred. How the person procrastinates is then more apparent.

When a single incident has been pinpointed as completely and clearly as possible, it may be a good idea to see how typical it is of similar events. You might ask, "How does the incident we have been discussing compare with other times when you have seen yourself as procrastinating?"

The mental videotape assignment is a good tool for validating the accuracy of pinpointing based on recollection of earlier events. Ask clients to "record" the next episode that occurs that is similar to the remembered event and bring the "tape" to the next session. No two events will be identical, but expect structural similarities between recurring similar events.

In the next section, there is a diagram to be filled in when you are pinpointing a problematic episode. The form represents a general framework of information you need to describe and understand an episode of experience. When you are working with clients, the diagram can be the framework you use to develop your mutual understanding of the real problem. Occasionally, we will recruit the client's help in actually filling in the blanks. Remember that the more clients know about what you are trying to accomplish, the more help they can be.

Describing Single Incidents of Real Problems

Behavioral events have beginnings and endings, occur across a span of time, and happen in a context involving a place and perhaps other people.

The diagram in this section can help you describe self-awareness, life events, and problematic incidents as occurring (1) across time, with a beginning, an ending, and a sequence; (2) in three domains of awareness—actions, thoughts, and feelings; and (3) in an environment or context, including place, time of day, and other people present.

Completing the diagram on the following page helps you see that pinpointing a fuzzy involves filling in the blanks in five areas: actions, thoughts, feelings, time span, and environment.

TIME ——➤

A
W
A
R
E
N
E
S
S

    Actions ——————————————————————————————————➤

    Thoughts —————————————————————————————————➤

    Feelings ——————————————————————————————————➤

CONTEXT of experience being pinpointed ————————————————➤

The following example of pinpointing a real problem comes from the Erikka transcript at the end of Chapter 7, beginning with the response at CL8 and continuing through CO22. The counselor has heard Erikka say she feels like she's "losing control," is "having these headaches," and so on. Erikka says in CL8, "I'm getting panicked because . . ." and continues describing her current experience. The counselor wants to understand as clearly as possible just what the client means by "panicked" and how it is reasonable or logical for the client to experience panic (which, for now, becomes a target feeling). The counselor is very interested in learning what sequence of client actions and thoughts make panicky feelings logical for Erikka at this time. In counseling, we refer to problematic feelings as "target feelings" because these are usually the targets of efforts to understand and to change.

From information gleaned from Erikka's statements between CL8 and CL22, the following sequence of actions and thoughts has been constructed. Some are Erikka's direct report; some are inferences that could and should be verified. Think of the sequence here as a hypothesis about how Erikka is likely to begin panicking.

Example: Target feeling = panic

Context? ". . . sitting in class"

How it begins? Becoming aware of uncompleted task and saying to myself, "I haven't made *plans* to make tapes [assignment for class]." Then, saying to myself, "I'm getting less and less structured. I'm being pretty lazy. I'm looking at myself and saying, 'Who's that?'"

Unstated expectation/ideal: I'm structured. I get things done on time. I'm energetic.

Unstated conclusion: I'm not being me. I'm letting myself down. I'm not being good, as I should.

Feeling (target feelings):

"upset . . . getting more nervous . . . panicked"; pounding headache

How it (usually) ends:

"dam breaks—running around at 11:30 at night . . . wake up tired and have a headache."

We'd like to comment on several aspects of this example. It's fairly typical in that the counselor, working from what the client says, must sort out fuzzies and descriptions and make guesses about what fits and where if he or she is to build a "logical sequence of events." The counselor's guesses, of course, need to be verified by the client.

Erikka, like most clients, reports what she is aware of. Some parts of the sequence the counselor infers from context. We find that our expectations for ourselves and others, our ideals, and our "shoulds" often operate out of awareness. Examples of inferences about some of Erikka's ideals are included and identified in the example. These inferences should be checked out with Erikka. Examples of the counselor's verifying his inferences are in CO12 and CO21, when he seems to be reading between the lines.

Ellerbroek (1978) commented on the importance these expectations, ideals, and "shoulds" can have in shaping what we feel. "*Every* unpleasant emotion is associated with either a thought, verbal or nonverbal, or a verbal statement which is contrary to reality *as perceived by the person having the emotion*" (p. 32). For Erikka, a statement contrary to reality as she observes herself might be, "I'm a person who meets her responsibilities." According to Ellerbroek, when the expectation doesn't match reality as observed, distress results. And Erikka is distressed.

Using pinpointing to identify the sequence of actions and thoughts preceding the distress, counselors can help clients (1) identify the elements, (2) examine their validity, and (3) consider more desirable, less distressing options. As the session continues, the counselor and Erikka use this information as a basis for setting a mutually agreeable counseling objective that focuses on Erikka's distressing experience.

Setting Goals and Objectives

Goals and objectives are ways of expressing the wishes, hopes, and aspirations that reflect our ideas about how we would like something to be, a desired status. As used here, goals and objectives differ in specificity and utility. *Goals* are generalized expressions, indicating in broad, fuzzy terms whatever it is we would like to achieve. Goal statements can fit everyone! *Objectives* differ from goals in that objectives are *specific* to one individual. Objectives are what an individual experiences when that individual's goal is met. An example of a goal is, "I want to get in shape." This is a *fuzzy* statement. An objective might be, "I want to be able to walk 6 miles in 90 minutes." This is *specific* for me. For you, the objective might require 75 minutes.

Just as there cannot be a precise answer for a vague question, there cannot be a specific plan with much success of achieving a vague, general goal. We have unmet goals in part because we don't know what we need to do about them. With a specific objective comes the opportunity to create, and test, specific plans or hypotheses about the sequence of particular activities performed under certain conditions that will most likely lead to the desired result.

Why Are Goals and Objectives Important?

Counselee objectives are the counselor's raison d'être. In our opinion, we have no right to pursue an outcome except one desired by the counselee. Our bias is to specify as clearly and accurately as possible the outcome that is being sought in counseling. Goals and objectives are important to *counselees* in several related ways:

- Goals are verbal expressions of what a client hopes to achieve. For some clients, merely expressing an intention of achieving something may be an important forward step on their own behalf. Sometimes this is all they need.
- Being clear about goals is very helpful in making decisions about allocating resources such as time, effort, and money.
- Being clear about goals is crucial if clients are to gauge their own progress and to recognize their own success in achieving these goals.

Our self-esteem is directly related to our sense of achievement. Without goals, successes are easy to overlook and our sense of achievement may be severely undernourished.

Goals are important to *counselors* because they serve as a focus for counselor effort. How can a counselor help a client achieve his or her purpose in coming to counseling without discussing and setting objectives? A clearly stated and agreed-on counseling objective helps the counselor participate more effectively in identifying the most likely means of assisting the client to achieve the hoped-for success.

Goals and objectives are benchmarks that keep the counseling process on track. Ethical practice requires that whatever happens within the counseling process be validated in terms of its relationship to client goals and objectives, that the process be client-centered.

Implications of the Client-Centered, Goal-Setting Approach

Commitment to a "client-centered" perspective on goal setting through facilitating the counselee's development of functional, accountable, attainable, and relevant goals and objectives leaves little room for satisfaction of some of the counselor's own value judgments and aspirations. When you follow a client-centered approach to developing goals and objectives, you may well arrive with clients at places where their values, priorities, and expectations differ from those you have for yourself—and those you might wish you could prescribe for the counselee.

Of course, if you were the counselee, you might expect to set your own agenda! Isn't that what we mean by respecting personal freedom?

We would be remiss if we didn't share another observation and caveat with you. Counselors do not receive consistent support from their professional peers to be effective pinpointers. Some of our colleagues prefer to translate specific counselee behaviors *into* fuzzies, and then incorporate the fuzzies in their clinical descriptions and discussions. Sometimes a counselor hears or uses maps of counselee territory containing fuzzies like these: "enabling their spouse's addiction," "in denial about their drinking," "being codependent in the relationship," or "exhibiting the tendencies of a borderline personality." When this happens, counselors may well be distracting themselves and perhaps their counselees from pinpointing an awareness of the client's thoughts, feelings, and actions that represent instances of this individual counselee's problem and that might contribute to creating a more high-fidelity map of the territory.

What Steps Are Involved in Setting Objectives?

Perfection of means and confusion of goals seem—in my opinion—to characterize our age.—*A. Einstein*

Throughout the book, we have shown clearly that we believe the client is master, that client goals are the driving force of the process, and that helping the client achieve his or her objectives is why the counselor is in the counseling relationship. A crucial part of the relationship is working with the client to identify his or her objectives.

Arriving at a counseling objective with a client is the result of a process that involves listening carefully and encouraging clients to explore potential goal areas. It involves pinpointing the specific changes the client desires and identifying the context in which the change is desired. Steps in the process and the skills needed for each step are described next. We hope these steps are beginning to seem familiar.

INVITING THE CLIENT TO SHARE CONCERNS

As the counselor, you need to learn what has brought this client to you, the current status of the problematic situation, and what the client hopes to achieve in counseling. One way to begin is to let the client know that this information will be important to the success of the process. Appropriate counselor use of attending, following, and pinpointing skills will also be important to the process.

RECOGNIZING POTENTIAL GOAL AREAS

As you attend to and follow the counselee's discussion of his or her concerns, you must listen closely and recognize and mentally list counselee utterances and nonverbal messages that are potential goal indicators. Listen particularly for expressions of pain, dissatisfaction, frustration, discomfort, self-deprecation, unhappiness, and similar states. These can be presented as "I'm lonely," "I'll never get . . . ," "I just felt a big knot in my stomach," "I can't take another day like . . . ," "I'm no good at . . . ," "It made me so mad."

Listen also for expressions of hopes, wishes, aspirations, desires, ambitions, needs, improvements, and change. These may appear in statements beginning with "I just wish . . . ," "I'd like . . . ," "I hope that . . . ," "If only I could . . . ," "Maybe it would be better if . . . ," or "Wouldn't it be neat if . . . "

AGREEING ON A GOAL

Expressions of distress and hope such as those just given indicate areas in which the client is seeking change. Once a client has "told his or her story," the counselor can use the goal indicators that have emerged as a menu of possible counseling goals, discussing them with the client and helping the client decide which area to work on first.

One of the best counselors we know frequently asks her clients, "What do you need right now?" This habit of checking in with the client helps keep her on track with her counselees. Don't assume; ask.

SETTING CRITERIA FOR FUNCTIONAL COUNSELING OBJECTIVES

A useful objective statement conveys the same image to everyone who hears it. Disappointment in counseling, as in other interpersonal relationships, stems from confusion or disagreement about what is to be done or accomplished, when or where it is to happen, and how well or how much will be accomplished.

Objective statements must address each of these three dimensions if disappointment in counseling is to be avoided and expectations of success are to be realized. Successful counseling is an outgrowth of mutual counselor–counselee agreement about three issues: (1) what is to be achieved, (2) when or where is it to be achieved, and (3) how well or how much is to be achieved.

Moving from Goal to Objective

Let's take the complaint, "I freeze up during exams," as an example of how to move from goal to objective. After discussion, the complaint becomes the basis for a *goal statement*: "I don't want to freeze up during exams. I want to do my best."

The counselor was aware of several fuzzies in the complaint and the goal statement. Some pinpointing of "freezing up" and "doing well" led to a clearer understanding of the client's problem and what the client hoped to achieve, as reflected in the following statements:

- Reduce my feelings of anxiety, particularly the shakiness in my knees, sweaty palms, shallow breathing, and butterflies in my stomach.

- Stop saying things to myself such as "I feel awful. I'm going to blow this thing. I can't remember anything I've studied."
- Start saying things to myself such as "I have read the material carefully. I've studied my notes. The excitement I feel can energize my performance. I'm going to go from item to item and do the ones I'm sure of first."
- Complete the Test Anxiety Workshop offered next month.

These statements are a refinement of the broad objective given earlier, but all the pieces are not yet in place. We need to examine three important elements of the statements to determine how they can be improved.

1. We *assume* that the behavioral events or tasks named in the first two statements are indeed part of what the counselee means when he or she says, "I freeze up during exams," but we have no verification of this. We *assume* that the tasks in the last two statements are directly related to the problem area, but we are not sure. Ethical practice requires that the relevance of proposed counseling objectives be confirmed by the counselee.

2. Each goal statement must be specific enough that the counselee will easily be able to determine reliably whether the goal has been accomplished. The preceding statements lack that specificity. Being able to recognize accomplishment is crucial to client self-esteem.

3. None of the first three example statements above says anything about when or where these events will occur, or how well or how much they will occur. Commitment to a specific context and level of performance prompts us to *action*. In *Annie Hall*, Woody Allen indicates he's been in counseling for 14 years, with no sign of progress. Few of us would be interested in "help" that took *that* long in coming!

As you help a client move from goal to objective, you must ensure that the objective is what the client wants, that he or she can assess progress toward it, and that the stated performance level requires the client to take prompt action in a clear direction. The following are examples of objective statements that do include information about all three criteria:

Example 1
    Complaint: "I freeze up during exams."
    Goal: "I want to be able to do my best during exams."
    Objective: To . . .
        What: Reduce feelings of anxiety, particularly the shakiness in my knees, sweaty palms, shallow breathing, and butterflies in my stomach
        When: During my next midterm exams
        How well/much: To the level I felt during my weekly quizzes

Example 2
    Complaint: "I just got some terrible news."
    Goal: "I want to talk to someone about it."

Objective: To . . .
    What: Talk with the counselor about this letter
    When/where: Here and now
    How well/much: For up to an hour

Practice

For each of the following objective statements, write the appropriate part under the appropriate heading. The first one is done as an example.
    Example: Talk with the counselor about this letter right now for an hour.

1. Smile and speak first to at least one different person on my floor each week.
2. Stop smoking during the next month.
3. Say "Thank you. I appreciate . . ." to Pat each time I am aware of a way she has helped me this week.
4. Practice the self-hypnosis routine for 15–20 minutes each evening this week.
5. Keep a log of every bit of food I eat during the next seven days.

What	*When/Where*	*How Well/Much*
Talk with counselor about letter	Now	For an hour
1.		
2.		
3.		
4.		
5.		

Now, compare your analysis with the key.

KEY TO PRACTICE		
What	*When/Where*	*How Well/Much*
1. Smile and speak to a different person	On my floor	Each day for the next week
2. Stop smoking	Everywhere, always	For one month
3. Say "thank you" to Pat	Each time I'm aware of . . .	This week
4. Practice self-hypnosis routine	Evenings	15–20 minutes each night this week
5. Keep a log of food eaten	Everywhere, anywhere	Every bit . . for next seven days

If your list looks similar to ours, we're on the right track.

Power of Functional Counseling Objectives

Objective statements that are functional contribute to ethical discharge of the counselor's responsibility to the client in the following ways:

1. They ensure that counselor and counselee are on the same track. (In the only study of its kind that we have found, Thompson and Zimmerman [1969] found a "marked discrepancy" between what clients said they wanted from counseling and what their counselors thought they wanted!)

2. Functional objective statements enable both counselor and counselee to continually assess progress in counseling.

3. They prompt the counselor to introduce new activities when it becomes apparent the current plan is not meeting the agreed-on objective.

4. They give the counselee a clear yardstick of achievement and an unequivocal definition of personal success.

5. Functional objective statements allow large goals to be expressed as a series of manageable objectives. Success in each smaller step builds motivation in the client to do the next and to persist to the ultimate goal.

Counselors represent only one of many groups who claim an ability to help people improve their lives. Understandably, claims of this sort are often met with skepticism. In his farewell address as president of the American Psychological Association (1970), Donald Campbell stated that the primary challenge facing psychology was *demonstrating* that counseling makes a difference. With the current competition for resources, it's even more important today. Being clear about counseling objectives is the best way to ensure that counselee expectations of success are realized and disappointment is avoided.

Will the Outcome Be Satisfactory?

An objective can meet the three criteria (what is to be done, when, and how well or how often) without being a good counseling objective. A good objective, from the *counselee's* point of view, is one that is achievable, "costs" the counselee the least, and will be satisfying to the *counselee* to achieve.

We sometimes still set goals that aren't achievable, and our clients do so as well—goals like these: "I want to end the relationship but I don't want to hurt him," or "I want us to quit fighting so much." The only muscles we control are our own. We need to rethink goal statements like these and set ourselves tasks that are within our power to achieve. What *can* we achieve?

A person usually has a number of possible ways to pursue an objective. All change requires some extra investment of time, attention, psychic energy, and other personal resources. As the counselor/servant, I owe it to my counselees to find the most affordable, most efficient means of making the changes they seek. As a counselor, my familiarity with the treatment literature affects my ability to serve my clients efficiently.

There is no lack of people, including counselors, who are willing to set goals for others. As Mark Twain said, "Nothing needs reforming so much as other people's habits." But it's very hard for any of us to do something that brings us no satisfaction whatsoever, that makes no personal difference to us. Clients are no exception. Client goals must involve change that the client experiences as consequential. Goals that don't make an important difference to the counselee are not likely to cause anything but frustration. The worth of any prospective goal must be validated in the perception of the counselee.

Further Practice

Now you are aware that functional counseling objectives have three essential components. It is not easy to make good objective statements; your first attempts may seem awkward. One way to develop your skills is to practice. Listed below are five statements representing goals/complaints. Write at least one objective statement for each that contains the three essential components we have been considering.

1. "I'm lonely."

   What _____

   When/Where _____

   How Well/Much _____

2. "I'd like to communicate with her better."

   What _____

   When/Where _____

   How Well/Much _____

3. "Our life together is just a round of fights and cold silences."

   What _____

   When/Where _____

   How Well/Much _____

4. "I'm not getting anything done in any of my classes this semester."

   What _____

   When/Where _____

   How Well/Much _____

5. "I've got to get a job."

What _____

When/Where _____

How Well/Much _____

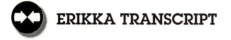 **ERIKKA TRANSCRIPT**

Counselor Readiness

As our demonstration counselor develops his empathic understanding of Erikka and her concerns, additional self-instructions are important. That's right. The self-talk that began at Step 1 and continued at Step 2 again serves to help the counselor stay focused and on track.

> I need to listen for the "hurt," "pain," and "discomfort" in Erikka's life.
>
> I need to help Erikka get beyond "the story" of her problem to the actual thinking, feeling, and acting elements of her distress. I want to respond to her in ways that encourage a more specific, accurate, and complete view of the territory of her experience.
>
> We need to collaborate on developing a clear picture of what the desired outcomes look like in terms of specific thoughts, feelings, and actions. I want to pay attention to those behaviors that are working for Erikka while helping her to define what we need to add or replace.
>
> I want to keep myself from mixing up my personal values and experiences in this search for a desired outcome. I'm still *following* Erikka and using her experience to guide our development of goals and objectives.

The Interview

This section of the session moves toward achieving a mutually agreeable counseling objective, the task in Step 3. Notice the various ways the counselor pinpoints the action, thought, and feeling elements of Erikka's concerns.

CO25:   What are some things we would be shooting for to make things right again? These might include the way you think about yourself, feelings, or something you do that would be desired outcomes.

CL25: I see my outcome as not wanting to bring things up to my head level and get these headaches, and to do that, I see myself as getting back on schedule and attending to the things I know. I derive pleasure from productivity, so I am off the track right now. I derailed myself somewhere during the last two weeks and have ended up causing major havoc with my body.

CO26: What do you mean when you say you are "off the track" and you've "derailed" yourself?

CL26: I've let school go to a certain extent. My pay job has ended up being rushed. I send my work back to Los Angeles and I ended up letting that go a whole week and then rushing to get it mailed in. Things like that, that are very immediate, have just taken place this past week.

CO27: Things that have to do with school responsibilities, pay job responsibilities . . . Do you have a job you *don't* get paid for?

CL27: Um-hmm. My practicum.

CO28: How's that going?

CL28: That's excellent. Really, it's something I was just thinking about today driving back from there. I'm out at Flowing Wells at Project Inscape. That has just clicked. I'm doing so much with that. I'm doing that and my Nautilus. It's like that's all I've been doing for the past two weeks. I don't know. I'm not getting anything else done. Those are two great areas right now in my life, but I'm letting things slide.

CO29: OK. So it sounds like life isn't a total disaster. Your practicum at Inscape and the program at Nautilus are going just fine. [CL: Yeah. It's just great. It's fine.] And somehow it's very easy for you to follow through on those two parts of your responsibilities.

CL29: And there's very . . . At Nautilus there's not an external responsibility to someone else. It's to me. Inscape's pretty personal, too. I have responsibilities to the people there, but it's still pretty free. Not for when I show up there, but I don't feel that's a real heavy responsibility on me; that comes very comfortably.

CO30: So what we're looking for in these other two areas of your life is you feel like you need to get on track and follow through on some things. [CL: Um-hmm.] And then you said you didn't want this stuff, whatever it is, to be coming up (*gestures with hands moving up from stomach to head*) [CL: Um-hmm.] What would be happening instead of that?

CL30: It would be like catching it before it grew. Like knowing there are reading assignments to do, not waiting till there are *five* reading assignments due, but getting it when there's one. I see things as just stacking up. (*gestures with hands*) And they stack up so far that they get up to here (*points to head*). [CO: Um-hmm!] Before, they never stacked up that far. If they ever stacked up, up to two, not five or six (*chuckles*). Just visually, picturing it for myself, I see that as having happened. When there's just one or two things to attend to, it stays right down here (*makes waist-level gestures*). So if there's a little tension about it, it will get me here (*gestures to stomach*). But now, there are so many other things that have stacked up (*gestures to head*). And that's just striking me now, that's it's a kind of stacking throughout my body (*gestures*). It's come up to here (*gestures to top of head*) now, whereas it never got there before.

CO31: Good. . . . Is there anything else that we're looking for in terms of a . . . It sounds like we're looking for an end to your headaches.

CL31: Yeah. (*chuckles*) Oh, yeah!

CO32: I'm pretty clever [CL: Um-hmm! (*chuckles*)] to have figured *that* out. And something else physically, feelingwise, that we're looking toward changing?

CL32: Umm, the first one that just came to my mind was relief. And I don't know, I don't know where that came from, except, I dislike the thought that anything is controlling me or impeding my progress. And it would be a *relief* not to have the headaches or the continuing knowledge that things are stacking up. And not having that would be a relief; I guess that's where relief comes from.

CO33: Some sense that life isn't overwhelming, [CL: Um-hmm.] that you've got a handle on things. Sounds like control in your life is real important.

CL33: Yeah. Very important.

CO34: And what would you like to be saying to yourself? Like maybe something different from "I'm lazy; I'm really disappointed in myself."

CL34: That I'm taking care of business, and that business comes before my pleasure. I feel like I've been sticking pleasure way up there as Number One. And having business, I've been letting that . . . So I think I'd like to be saying to myself, "Business is coming before pleasure. I'm taking care of that. Now you can go and have fun."

CO35: OK. OK. So, again we're talking about some organizational ability that you've demonstrated real well in the past [CL: Yeah, yeah.] and kind of kicking that in gear again so that . . . so that you can take care of things and still enjoy your practicum, Nautilus . . . [CL: Um-hmm.] Umm, this is sort of the Negotiate Counseling Objective point in the process that we were talking about.

The counselor has been pinpointing, verifying, pinpointing, verifying, and so on. Open to the possibility that there's more to be put on the table, the counselor always says, "And what else . . ."

Assuming for now that the menu of possible objectives is complete, the counselor addresses "How will we know we've arrived?" by posing the following question to Erikka. This is another opportunity to validate mutual client/counselor understanding of the client's counseling objectives.

CO35: (continues) What's going to be a way that we can observe or measure that you have in fact accomplished these things?

CL35: Ummm . . . I would say a way I could really click into would be a day-to-day reference of whether or not I'm getting the headaches, but also, kind of returning to my check-off list. I don't know whether that became ineffective for me two weeks ago for some reason. I think it must have or I would still be holding on to it. Maybe returning to that and laying out priorities. I do that right now; I have one in my book right now, and all it has on it is Nautilus, and Call Tim, . . . for us to go out tonight (chuckles). It's like I have nothing else, when I know I have a tremendous amount of school stuff to do. That's all that's on my list of things to do now. It's silly. So I need to re-look at re-scheduling, a recommitment to those organizational check-off things.

CO36: OK. So if you had one thing we would be shooting for it would be for you in fact to have a check-off list and be using it? [CL: Um-hmm. Um-hmm.] Another thing we're looking at is monitoring the headaches and looking at what, frequency of zero as kind of the target? [CL: Um-hmm.] Anything else?

CL36: Um, I don't know that it can be monitored, but checking in on my feelings about what's going on. The production that I see taking place is the check-off correlating with the decrease in headaches. If it's not, then I've been going on the wrong path. [CO: OK.] So maybe cluing in to the correlation between the two, and how I am feeling about that. With my productivity, is it lessening, is it bringing things back down? (hands move from head down to waist)

CO37: OK! So it sounds like what you're saying is that you're operating under an assumption [CL: Yeah! Right!] and one thing that you want to do is see whether you can validate that assumption, or whether we have to go in a different direction. [CL: Yeah. Right.] Speaking of that assumption, I guess one thing I want to do is ask you, have you seen a doctor?

CL37: No! (chuckles)

CO38: OK. Is that anything that you'd consider doing?

CL38: No. (chuckles) I don't do that very often.

CO39: So that's not an option you turn to when you have any physical discomfort.

CL39: No. Not at all.

CO40: All right. And it sounds as though that usually works out for you [CL: Yeah.] when you take care of it yourself. [CL: Um-hmm, um-hmm.] Is there anything else that we're looking for in terms of a desired outcome?

CL40: Um . . .

CO41: So we're looking at getting back on the checklist. [CL: Um-hmm.] OK. Making sure that you're using that. . . . There was something else that you said and I've lost it. Do you remember . . .?

CL41: Well, checking in to the decrease in headaches, and the feeling of am I getting a relief or a sense of productivity from getting back on the checklist. [CO: OK., OK.] Yeah. I think that pretty much covers it.

CO42: Do you have some sense when all of this started?

CL42: Two weeks ago.

CO43: Two weeks ago.

CL43: Two weeks ago . . . Monday? . . . Two weeks ago.

CO44: OK. [CL: Yeah.] How is it that you remember that? You seem to have it pretty clearly in mind.

CL44: Um, I don't know why. I just know it was all last week during classes, and early on the week before I started noticing I was getting headaches. And I just know that that was around two weeks ago. [CO: Um-hmm.] Um, I don't know why. I just know I wouldn't say three weeks and I wouldn't say just a week ago. It's around two weeks.

What follows is a clear demonstration of counselor creativity in pinpointing. The counselor, sensitive to Erikka's verbal and nonverbal language, uses her metaphor of things "stacking up" as the basis for a kind of "psychodramatic" pinpointing of Erikka's present awareness of her situation. Notice how helping

Erikka get in touch with the data results in a much more accurate map of the problematic territory in her life at present.

CO45: OK. I'd like to do something with you. Could you stand up? [CL: Yeah.] (*they both stand*) I want to look more at this . . . You've used the term *stack up* a lot. [CL: Um-hmm.] I'd like to look at what it is we're stacking up here in your life. [CL: OK.] It might have some relationship to this checklist that you're going to be beginning. [CL: Yep. Yep.] These things that are stacking up will probably be on this list? [CL: Yep. Yep. Yep.] What's one thing that's stacking up right now?

CL45: Reading. A lot of necessary class textbook reading.

CO46: OK. (*looks around, finds a sheaf of papers, and hands to CL*) Will you hold this? [CL: Um-hmm.] (*holds papers in both hands in front of her*) OK. Reading. What's another thing that's stacking up?

CL46: Um . . . Doing a second assignment that's due for a class a week from Wednesday.

CO47: A second assignment?

CL47: Yes. It's the second part of a three-part assignment that's due. [CO: OK] I need to be taking a closer look at a case study that I'm doing with one of the kids at Inscape, and I haven't been doing that.

CO48: OK, OK. What does that involve?

CL48: It's just taking a look at implementing logical consequences for a behavior of one of the kids out at Inscape. I chose that. Everyone can choose her own.

CO49: I chose the first symbol. (*touches papers CL is holding*) What would be something to symbolize *that* stacking up, more paper? Or . . .

CL49: No. Something like that eraser (*points to chalkboard eraser*) because it's not really that heavy, but it's something that needs to be there.

CO50: It's something significant.

CL50: Yeah. (*CO adds eraser to the "stack" CL is holding*)

CO51: What else is stacking up?

CL51: (*looks up into space; deep exhale*) Ohhh, God. (*wry chuckle*) Oh! I have a test this coming Monday and I'm going home to L.A. on Friday and don't know how I'm going to get all the studying done for it.

CO52: OK.

CL52: That's a big one.

CO53: That's a big one, huh?

CL53: (aside to fellow class member) You got a headache, too?

CO54: What would be a good symbol for this big one that's coming up?

CL54: That bag. (points to backpack)

CO55: (puts backpack on top of stack CL is holding) That *is* a big one. [CL: Um-hmm.] What else is stacking up?

CL55: (deep sigh) The confrontation I'm going to have with my boyfriend when I go home.

CO56: The confrontation you're going to have with your boyfriend? OK. Is that something that's been brewing for a while?

CL56: (starts chuckling) About two weeks. (ducks head, holds hand to face, keeps chuckling; audience murmurs and exclaims)

CO57: About two weeks . . . What would be a good symbol for the conflicts with . . . ?

CL57: Joel

CO58: Joel? (turns to class) Would you help us out, Joel?

JOEL: (approaching CL) Where do you want me? (Joel is an attractive male fellow student about 3 inches taller and 60 pounds heavier than the client)

CL58: Over here, in front of me.

CO59: As you have a sense of . . . as you anticipate this conflict brewing with your boyfriend, what would be a good way to symbolize that stacking up, too?

CL59: Unnh, (to Joel) stand on the chair. (he does) Put your hands (points to her shoulders; Joel puts hands on her shoulders, leaning forward a bit) That's IT! (chuckles)

CO60: OK. OK. (CL sighs) And what else is stacking up?

CL60: Money. Hoping I get my scholarship money through soon.

CO61: Money. OK.

CL61: That's a big one.

CO62: That's a big one.

CL62: Not as big as this one.

CO63: How big is the money issue?

CL63: I'd put it as, like, the trash can.

CO64: (CO fetches trash can) Where would you like this?

CL64: (chuckles) I'll just put [the rest] of this on top. There we go. (CL is now holding trash can with papers, books, and backpack on top, and Joel's hands pressing on her shoulders) That's it.

CO65: There you go. Organizing things, hunh? OK. What else is stacking up?

CL65:   Letters to write to friends.

CO66:   Letters to write. What's a good symbol for them?

CL66:   (*looking around*) Just those stray papers. It's not . . . That's fine.

CO67:   What else?

CL67:   (*pauses, head down, sighs*) That's about it. (*in a soft voice*)

Notice how the counselor keeps asking, "What else?" and doesn't move on until Erikka says the picture is complete.

Counselor self-talk now goes something like this: "Erikka's map of the situation has been changing in the last few minutes. I want to use the indicators we discussed earlier to see how she's doing. I want to see which piece she wants to address first."

CO68:   That's about it? OK. How're you feeling?

CL68:   (*head comes up; chuckles*) I want to go to Nautilus and work out! . . . I'm feeling really bogged down.

CO69:   Bogged down?

CL69:   Very much so.

CO70:   And where do you notice that in your body right now?

CL70:   A lot of stress right across here, (*gestures to forehead*) and my stomach's starting to get a little worse. More than it was . . .

CO71:   OK. Stomach's a little "grindy"?

CL71:   Um-hmm. Nervous, it's a nervous stomach.

CO72:   OK. And the tension's where, right here? (*CO places hands around CL forehead*) [CL: Um-hmm, Um-hmm.] And the pressure's what, like that? (*CO moves hands to frontal part of CL head*)

CL72:   More on the side, on the side. [CO: (*moving hands*) Like that?] Yeah. yeah. Right, that's right, right there. That's it.

CO73:   And (*walks around to stand just behind CL on left side, and says, in "voice" of CL*) as I'm sort of paying attention to all this pressure in my head and I've got all these things stacked up, and my stomach's getting "grindy," what am I saying to myself?

CL73:   I'm saying, "God, you need to take care of things. You need to get things sorted out," and, uh . . .

CO74:   (*continues for CL*) This isn't like you. [CL: No.] How'd you get yourself in this fix? [CL: Right!] Does that fit?

CL74:   Right. You screwed up. (*head down*)

CO75:   OK. You screwed up. (*CL, head down, nods*) OK. (*walks from behind CL to face CL*) Is there anything that you've no-

---

ticed since we've stacked things up? Anything that's become any clearer that's related to the issue you came up here for?

CL75: I think I've substantiated my hypothesis that there are all these things I need to attend to that I've let stack up; that there's no need for me to see a doctor about my headaches. I definitely know that all these things need to be attended to. In a way, I followed up on my assumption, [CO: Um-hmm.] and that my boyfriend issue is a lot larger and looming in front of me than I thought it was. [CO: OK.] Very much more.

CO76: Sort of seems like it may be a priority in terms of . . .

CL76: In a way, it was something that I thought, "Oh, well, I'll take care of it when I get home." And now I'm realizing that home is only in three days. And it's a lot more. It's bigger than I thought it was. A lot bigger.

CO77: OK.

CL77: And weighing me down a lot more.

CO78: Weighing you down a lot more? And, is there any connection between your headache and that, too?

CL78: Yeah. I think so. I don't think I've equated it with something in the last couple of weeks, something I needed to do, like do an assignment, or do this. But, so I don't see it as part of the stack-ing up . . . I *didn't*, but now I'm seeing it as kind of encasing all the other things I need to do.

CO79: OK.

CL79: It's like, it's seeping through everything else. It's like, when I study for the 623 test, I've got to address this issue. (*indicates Joel/boyfriend with head*) And when I read up for behav-ioral counseling I still have to address it. It's like it always keeps jumping back in the picture. [CO: OK.] These things, (*nods toward stack*) you do them and the door closes on them. This (*nods toward boyfriend*) . . . it just keeps being there.

CO80: OK. Shall we go ahead and come up with a plan to deal with this?

CL80: (*chuckles*) I think so.

CO81: (*taking wastebasket, backpack, and other items from her hands and sending Joel back to audience*) We'll give you a bit of a rest. (*CL and CO are once again seated facing each other*)

We'll end the transcript segment here, with the counselee's agreement that it's time to make a plan (Step 4) to achieve her objective as previously defined.

Debriefing

OBSERVER: Does the counselor always use a psychodramatic technique to pinpoint the components of the problem situation? What if he wasn't trained in the use of action methods?

COUNSELOR: I don't think of the methods as a "psychodramatic technique." It is one of many ways that I observe what Erikka is going through. Counselors use a variety of methods to accomplish each of the tasks in the counseling process. Each counselor brings a unique combination of experience, theoretical perspective, and skills to each counseling session. If the counselor is attending to the client's world, he or she will respond with the tools that fit the task, rather than requiring the client to respond in ways which fit the tools. "I am a(n) _____ (psychodramatist, cognitive behaviorist, Adlerian)" is an easy way to set yourself and your client up for a process driven by an agenda from the counselor's world instead of the client's.

OBSERVER: The identification of the boyfriend issue was a type of "Ah, ha!" experience for Erikka. Isn't that the goal of counseling, to bring the unconscious to the surface? How did the counselor know that this issue was a part of Erikka's distress?

COUNSELOR: The counselor depends totally on the client to define the goal of counseling. While it may be satisfying for the counselor to participate in an "Ah, ha!" experience, the counselor's attempt to make that happen will distract him or her from a client-centered counseling process. The counselor had no idea about Erikka's boyfriend or any other "missing piece." By following Erikka's map and pinpointing the thoughts, feelings, and actions of Erikka's "out-of-control experience," the counselor facilitated Erikka's identification of her relationship conflict as one aspect of her distress.

OBSERVER: Most counseling sessions don't take place with an audience of readily available counseling students to represent boyfriends and other issues. What would the counselor have done if the session had taken place in his office?

COUNSELOR: If I chose to use an action technique, I might have used an empty chair or another object to represent the boyfriend. I could have asked Erikka to represent her experience in two dimensions, using pad and paper, or a marker and drawing board. A visualization activity might accomplish the same purpose.

 ## SUGGESTIONS FOR INTEGRATING ACTIVITIES

1. Write a specific counseling objective that might develop from each of the following goal statements. Remember, a good objective (a) names what will be done, (b) tells when or where it will happen, and (c) specifies how well or how much.

a. "I want to end this relationship."
b. "I want to be a better father."
c. "I want to be less anxious while taking the final exam."
d. "I want to get this term paper written on time."
e. "I want to decide on a major."
f. "I want to figure out whether or not to get a divorce."
g. "I want to feel better about myself."
h. "I don't want to just sit there quietly while she plans my life for me."

2. Think back to a moment in your life that was an example of special *achievement*, or think of a time when you *overcame a barrier*. Think of a time when you experienced a moment of success, perhaps in getting through a hard time in your life. Pinpoint and report the feelings, thoughts, and actions that you were aware of at the moment of success. If you can't recall them exactly, imagine what you most likely felt, thought, or did.

At the *moment* of success I was
Feeling   Thinking   Doing

And in the moment just before this, I was
Feeling   Thinking   Doing

And in the moment just before this, I was
Feeling   Thinking   Doing

And in the moment just before this, I was
Feeling   Thinking   Doing

And in the moment just before this, I was
Feeling   Thinking   Doing

And in the moment just before this, I was
Feeling   Thinking   Doing

And in the moment just before this, I was
Feeling   Thinking   Doing

Now, complete this sentence: "I am successful in accomplishing personal goals when . . ."

   3.   Try one of the following for more practice in pinpointing actions, thoughts, and feelings.

a.   Identify a situation in your life that is producing or has produced frustration for you, is likely to recur, and for which you wish less discomfort.

   •   In an example of the situation, pinpoint as clearly as possible the moment in which you were first aware of a feeling of frustration.
   •   As clearly as possible, identify the actions, thoughts, and feelings that preceded this moment, the actions, thoughts and feelings that preceded those, the ones that preceded those, and so on, until you get to the beginning.
   •   Examine the chain of actions, thoughts, and feelings that precede the feeling of frustration. Does the feeling appear to be a logical result of this chain of actions, thoughts, and feelings? How might the chain be changed to make frustration less likely?

b.   Identify something in your life that you have intended to do and have not yet accomplished.

   •   Think of a moment when you were about to do this task and pinpoint the words you may have said to yourself that stopped your movement toward achievement.
   •   Chart the chain of actions, thoughts, and feelings that terminate in the thoughts noted above.
   •   How might the chain be changed so that the event at last occurs?

   4.   Now try the pinpointing process in simulated counseling. Audiotape or videotape this exercise, if possible, so you can observe your own work. Find a classmate willing to exchange services with you as a counselee for this exercise. Set up an initial counseling interview. Record it. Use attending and following skills to encourage your "client" to tell his or her story. As the client's situation emerges, find an appropriate place to try the following:

a.   Select one of the distressing feelings your counselee has mentioned. It probably makes sense to select the one that seems most important, of most concern, to the counselee. Think of this as the "target feeling."
b.   Ask the counselee to recall his or her most recent or most intense instance of *experiencing* the target feeling. Help the counselee locate a single example that he or she will be able to recall in some detail.
c.   Locate the example as specifically as possible in time and space. What day? Time? Location?
d.   Locate the beginning of the example event. One way is simply to ask the counselee, "How did it start? And when was that? Where were you sitting, standing? Who else was there?"

e. Verify the beginning by making sure the target feeling has not yet begun: "Were you aware of any distress at that moment?" If you get a "Yes," go back in time to the point when you get a "No."

f. Walk through the event from the beginning, as though it were a movie, frame by frame. Your objective is to finish the walk-through in such detail that you will both be aware of the counselee's actions, thoughts, and feelings *in each frame* of the "movie."

    In practice, it usually doesn't work well to get actions, thoughts, and feelings one frame at a time. The better way is to get the actions or thoughts from beginning to end, and then to go back and fill in the missing pieces as well as you can.

g. Use following responses to clarify and to verify the details as you go along.

h. Note where in the sequence of actions or thoughts the counselee first reports awareness of the target feeling. This is *important*. Verify that *this* feeling is the target feeling, the feeling that the client may want to change. Pay particular attention to the moments in the event just prior to the counselee's awareness of the target feeling. Somehow, it is logical, in the person's private logic, to experience this distress. The "reason" for the distress is usually contained in a thought, a piece of self-talk. It's not unusual for the counselee to be unaware of this thought. When this is the case, work together with the counselee to discover a statement that makes the distress "logical" and that fits for that individual. This private logic often seems to involve a "should" in some form.

Pinpointing the actions, thoughts, and feelings that immediately precede the onset of the target feeling should reveal the elements of personal experience that make the feeling "logical." Reviewing this sequence and verifying its accuracy with the counselee frequently results in a kind of insight about how the feeling occurs.

i. Locate the moment when the counselee loses awareness of the target feeling or when the target feeling is superseded by another feeling. Get a frame-by-frame picture of the sequence of actions, thoughts, and feelings that immediately precede the end of the distress. If the distress doesn't seem to end ("I'm *always* anxious"), find the moment when the intensity of the feeling seems to drop. Information about how the distress ends is often valuable when considering ways to reduce the distress.

j. Your counselee may not be able to recall an incident clearly enough to get a very complete picture of how the target feeling starts and ends. One recourse is to send the counselee out with the assignment of making a mental videotape of the target feeling episode the next time one occurs.

    Another recourse is to "script" a typical episode based on general recollections. Even though the client's recollections are general, the script can contain specific actions, thoughts, and feelings that seem credible as personal behaviors to your client.

k. Use the information gained to verify that *this* episode, and others like it, are of real concern to the counselee at this time.

If it isn't, what is? Use the information to arrive at a counseling objective: What, specifically, would the client like to change? Use the information to arrive at a way of gauging the progress of counseling: What, specifically, will be observed that represents the desired change?

⏱ CONSULTATION TIME

Scenario 1

COUNSELOR: So, you are feeling resentful that the teacher called child protective services?

CLIENT: Yeah, it's none of her business how I discipline my kid!

COUNSELOR: You're telling yourself that . . .

CLIENT: Don't you think that a few swats on the backside are the best way to handle a bad attitude when nothing else has worked?

What are the counselor's options?

- "I want to focus on your beliefs about disciplining your children, not mine."
- "Can you give me an example of Henry's bad attitude? When was the last time he had a bad attitude?"
- "So, a few swats on the backside is your last resort. When you say nothing else has worked, what things are you trying in response to Henry's bad attitude?"
- "You want to know whether I agree that spanking Henry is effective discipline when your other options have failed? How can my opinion be helpful to you?"
- How would you respond?

Scenario 2

COUNSELOR: You want to be less anxious . . . ?

CLIENT: Yes, I just know that I would feel better about myself if I were relaxed when I was talking with my supervisor at work.

COUNSELOR: And what is one way that you would notice that you're more relaxed?

CLIENT: I would just know it. I can tell the difference between feeling tense and relaxed.

What are the counselor's options?

- "It would help me to understand more about how you will know that you're successful in being relaxed when talking with your supervisor."

- "You believe that it will be obvious to you when you're less anxious with your supervisor?"
- "If we were going to measure your level of relaxation right now on a scale from 1 to 10, 1 being very relaxed and 10 being anxious, what rating would you give yourself?"
- "Are there any differences in the way your body feels when you're relaxed compared with when you feel anxious?"
- How would you respond?

REFERENCES

Ellerbroek, W. C. (Spring 1978). Language, thought and disease. *CoEvolution Quarterly*, pp. 30–38.

Mager, R. F. (1972). *Goal analysis.* Belmont, CA: Fearon Pittman.

Thompson, A., & Zimmerman, R. (1969). Goals of counseling: Whose? When? *Journal of Counseling Psychology, 16,* 121–125.

SUGGESTED READING

Egan, C. (1994). *The skilled helper* (5th ed.). Pacific Grove, CA: Brooks/Cole.

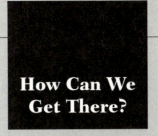

How Can We Get There?

An Overview of Steps 4 and 5

At this point where a mutually agreeable "there" has been determined, an outcome that both counselee and counselor are committed to pursuing, it is time to address directly the central task of Step 4, *Identify Plan for Achieving Objective*. Although a very effective planning process is described in Chapter 9, often little planning needs to be done. Once counselees have examined the issues, developed more accurate maps, and described a specific outcome as their next agenda item, they often know exactly what they need to do next—and do it.

It's not accidental that the first two-thirds of this book addresses process and techniques related to "Where are we going?" For most of us, most of the time, when we have a clear answer to this question, we know what to do. It often works the same way with counselees.

So, Step 4 can go very quickly. Even when it does, we still think you should pay attention to Step 5, *Support the Plan*. Note especially the checkout procedure described there. Checkout is an effective way (clients seem to enjoy it) for counselor and client to confirm that the client *is* committed, prepared, and aimed in the right direction with the necessary tools to get the job done.

Almost always, clients report back that things didn't go exactly as planned. Sometimes the unplanned surprises are inconsequential and sometimes they're serendipitous. Sometimes, however, unplanned events disrupt the client's attempt to follow the plan, blocking client progress. When objectives remain unmet in spite of client effort, and they're still important objectives, the performance analysis model described in Chapter 10 can help diagnose the interrupted plan and lead to more effective planning.

CHAPTER 9

Step 4:
Identify Plan for
Achieving Objective

*If that little green man from Mars arrived and asked us to
explain our techniques for effecting human change, and if
we then told him, would he not scratch his head (or its
equivalent) in disbelief and ask us why we have arrived at
such complicated, abstruse and farfetched theories, rather
than first of all investigating how human change comes
about naturally, spontaneously, and on an everyday basis?*
—Paul Watzlawick

Plan, Map, and Territory

Each of us makes plans to achieve objectives every day.

- "I'm going to leave the house before 8:00 A.M. to make some calls at the
  office before my first meeting."
- "I want to take my lunch today to help toward my goal of saving money
  for a new bike."
- "I'm going to send my girlfriend flowers; that will put some spark in our
  romance."

We know what we want to do and set out, with the best of intentions, to act
in ways that will get it done. Generally, at the end of the day, we can look
back and experience considerable satisfaction: There was time to make
those phone calls; the homemade turkey and swiss sandwich cost a third

of cafeteria lunch and tasted better; my beloved couldn't believe how beautiful the roses looked.

And there are those occasional times when, no matter how hard we try, we reflect back on a day when we didn't put the plan together very well.

- "I should have remembered that this was my day to take Nicole to the baby-sitter. I barely made the meeting on time . . . and still haven't returned those calls."
- "My adviser wanted to meet over lunch at the cafeteria. I had no choice but to spend four bucks on the enchilada special."
- "I just remembered: I was going to send flowers to Irma and I forgot."

What is the difference between the days when we do what we say we're going to do and those when we come up short of our expectations? Let's go back to our map and territory metaphor to understand this difference between successful and unsuccessful plans. Remember that our personal territory of experience comprises our thoughts, feelings, and actions. The words we use to describe this experience create a map of that territory. Our ability to negotiate successfully the territory of our day-to-day experience is greatly facilitated by an accurate map, and is impeded by an inaccurate or incomplete map.

If my map hasn't incorporated my duties as a father who shares the responsibility for getting his daughter to the baby-sitter, then my experience will not leave me with enough minutes in the morning to achieve my phone-calling objective. If I tell myself that I should leave my sack lunch behind and buy the enchilada special, the territory looks quite different from the way it did when I was focused only on saving money for my bike. And if my plans to buy flowers for my girlfriend are not based on up-to-date, true feelings, my forgetfulness may be more representative of the past than the present.

In each step of the counseling process, we've emphasized the use of such counselor skills as attending, following, and pinpointing in helping the counselee create a more representative map of those thoughts, feelings, and actions that make up the *real* problem to be addressed in counseling. At its best, this more representative map provides the client and the counselor with a behavioral description of the client's discomfort and identifies past and present events and circumstances associated with the discomfort.

The counselor task in Step 4, Identify Plan for Achieving Objective, is to help the counselee to map the future. The plan provides the behavioral directions leading from the counselee's present problem situation to the desired outcome. These directions include the sequence of goal-achieving actions, the thoughts that can most effectively support the performance of these actions, and the skills to monitor and respond to feelings as the plan unfolds.

What can the counselee *do* to "be more assertive with my mother-in-law," "become more organized in my studying," "reestablish my friendship with Paul," or "control my temper when my wife and I disagree"? An effective plan is a sequence of actions likely to achieve the desired outcome. We think the emphasis on *action/outcome* linkage is especially appropriate for counselors. We need to be reminded that *outcomes* aren't likely to change if *actions* don't change, and conversely, that different actions are likely to result in different outcomes. To us, an unmet counseling objective suggests that a new plan may be needed to achieve the desired result.

The new plan must address the questions prompted by the counselee's desire to experience new and more satisfying territory as identified by his or her objective: "When and where is my first opportunity to be more assertive with my mother-in-law?" "What can I do this evening to begin a more organized study process?" "What is the first thing I want to say when Paul answers the telephone?"

Step 4, Identify Plan for Achieving Objective, is the step in the counseling process that shifts counselor and counselee focus from "Where are we going?" to "How do we get there?" Although we speak of a shift in focus from identifying a desired outcome to means of achieving it, we hope it is obvious that any "means" under consideration must be linked to the currently sought "end." During the planning process, counselors should validate their assumption that the client's identified goal remains the same. Priorities can and do change.

We alluded earlier to a predilection of many helpers toward advancing their own favorite answers to other people's questions. Sue and Zane (1987) suggest that a major reason for counselor ineffectiveness is that counselor-nominated remedies too often don't make sense in the client's world. The "Empty Hogans" story at the beginning of Chapter 4 is an example of how the best of intentions by culturally sensitive helpers can misfire.

"Doing for others" is not a good planning maxim, especially when the "others" will be doing the plan. We believe the best planning occurs when the person who will be doing the plan is involved. If you create a plan for someone else and assume that person has the resources, motivation, and confidence required to realize it, you can easily be mistaken. Further, if you identify a plan for someone else and assume that what works in *your* world will work in that individual's world, be prepared for disappointment.

In counseling, creating a plan to meet the counselee's objective is most successful when it is done as a mutual activity involving both the counselor, who knows how to plan, and the client, who is the world's foremost source of information on his or her own resources, motivation, sense of self-efficacy, and ways things work in his or her world.

In point of fact, most of our clients seem not to need much help with "How can we get there" once an objective is clear. Time spent clarifying an objective, pinpointing, as Dave has been doing with Erikka in the transcript, is time saved in the long run. Clients, like us, are capable human beings, using their skills and resources effectively most of the time when their objectives are clear.

Pinpointing as Planning Tool

It is not enough to be busy. The question is . . . what are we busy about?—*Thoreau*

Just as there are problems and *real* problems, there are plans and *real* plans for achieving successful results. We believe that a *real* plan, like a well-written recipe, provides unambiguous information as a basis for effective action toward a predictable result. In the planning process, the counselor's use of pinpointing assists the client in generating the step-by-step sequence of actions necessary to achieve the desired objective.

The same pinpointing subskills that serve clients in understanding their concerns and identifying objectives are the most efficient tools for developing real client-centered plans. We consider each of these four subskills here.

1. Discriminate fuzzies (generalizations *about* behavior) from specifics (reports describing behavior). Example:

CL: I guess this Sunday's baby shower will be the next chance I have to be assertive with my mother-in-law.

CO: What is one way you can *act* more assertively on Sunday?

CL: I want to stick up for myself when she starts to take over the baby shower.

CO: You want to "stick up" for yourself by doing . . . ?

CL: By telling her that I would feel more comfortable if she just relaxed and let me handle things.

2. Attend to three domains of awareness: actions, thoughts, and feelings. Example:

CL: My wife and I are going to talk about our budget tomorrow. I just hope that I don't lose it!

CO: You don't want to "lose it." What do you want to do instead of "lose it"?

CL: I want to stay calm.

CO: So, you want to feel calm. What is one thing that you can say to yourself to be calm?

CL: Well, we've been talking about being better listeners with each other. I need to remind myself to be quiet and listen to her viewpoint!

CO: And if you're thinking about being a listener and feeling calm, what will you be doing as the budget discussion progresses?

CL: I guess that I'll be able to keep my voice down and stay seated at the table until we finish the budget.

3. Focus on actual experience in a single event rather than on generalized impressions (personal myth, map) of many events. Example:

CL: If Paul and I can be friends again, my life will be so much more fulfilling.

CO: Do you want to let Paul know how you're feeling?

CL: I think he knows. I just hope he feels the same way.

CO: When will you have the next opportunity to talk with Paul?

CL: I'm not sure. I guess I'll call him when I get my courage up.

CO: Would it be helpful to talk about what you want to say when you call Paul?

CL: Yes. I guess I'm not sure what to say to him.

4. Discover the temporal sequence of elements in the critical incident. Example:

CL: Yes, I feel better now that I'm clear that a more organized study routine will help me to feel less scattered.

CO: What would you be doing in a "more organized" study routine?

CL: Oh, you know, sitting down at a regular time and hitting the books.

CO: How would you determine that regular time?

CL: I guess that it would depend on my class schedule.

CO: So, you would have to look at your class schedule *before* you could set up a regular study time?

CL: That's right, and I guess I need to know about my work schedule and when my girlfriend and I are going to see each other.

CO: So, there are lots of considerations to think about before you schedule study time. [CL: Uh-huh.] How do you *feel* when you're thinking about class schedules and time with your girlfriend and study time?

CL: Well, I guess, that's when I feel scattered and overwhelmed.

CO: So, let's see, what else could you say to yourself as you're beginning to feel overwhelmed?

CL: I guess—"Just pay attention to classes and study time first. I'll enjoy time with Loranne more if I have my homework done."

The Erikka transcript at the end of this chapter demonstrates the counselor's use of pinpointing to collaborate with Erikka in developing a plan. Notice how many of Dave's responses are similar to those in Steps 1, 2, and 3 of the counseling process, but now oriented—with his client—toward the future. How is Erikka going to achieve her objectives—fewer headaches, calmer stomach, and so on? The counselor's pinpointing responses are intended to help Erikka map her path to this objective.

CO80: OK. Shall we go ahead and come up with a plan to deal with this?

CL80: (*chuckles*) I think so.

CO81: (*taking wastebasket, backpack, and other items from her hands and sending Joel back to audience*) We'll give you a bit of a rest. (*CL and CO are once again seated facing each other*) Where do you think we should start?

CL81:   Empty the trash can . . . I don't know. Start with the most immediate need. For me, that's taking care of things. Time sequencing . . . Take care of behavioral counseling, because I need to address that before I go back to L.A. Otherwise, all of a sudden it will be Monday and I'll have the tape due, and I'll need to do that. But even saying that, I can't seem to do that without addressing the issue with my boyfriend, but that's just become so rote I even hate discussing it, so that's probably also why it didn't come up earlier. It's something I keep saying, "I'll just take care of it. It's no problem."

CO82:   OK. It sounds like it's something that you've addressed before and it hasn't worked out real well.

CL82:   It keeps going up and down, up and down. . . . It's to the point now where I'm disgusted with myself that it keeps becoming a problem, so I don't talk about it.

CO83:   So on the one hand, it seems like that kind of encases everything, and "I can do all that stuff. I can make a checklist. I can change my priorities around and I can cut back some Nautilus time right now, and pay more attention to my school, but, I don't know. I still have . . . what's his name? [CL: Robert.] I still have Robert around, kind of peering over the whole situation." Is that the way it feels?

In one sense, the counselor is *following* the counselee in creating the plan, but following in a very active way, helping Erikka to continually validate or question the probability that the steps in her plan will lead her to where she wants to go.

Client Resources

The counselor is also attending to Erikka's experience to help identify the places in her cognitive map that are going to assist or impede her goal attainment. As Erikka and her counselor walk through the plan, pinpointing the thoughts and feelings associated with the actions Erikka has been prescribing for her future, it becomes apparent that her map needs further refinement to match the territory of her experience with her boyfriend and the interaction of this relationship with her other responsibilities.

Motivation and Sense of Self-Efficacy

The counselee's motivation is a critical variable in the planning process. The counselor and counselee must be convinced that the action prescribed by the plan is likely to lead to counselee satisfaction. The counselee must also believe that he or she has the ability to perform the plan well enough to achieve the desired results.

As the counselor and Erikka are building a plan, the counselor continues to help Erikka assess her motivation. CO82—"It sounds like it's something that you've addressed before and it hasn't worked out real well"—is a motivation check. Does Erikka want to give it one more try? CO85 and CO92 check out Erikka's hesitation and what she really *wants* to do. The counselor is attempting to confirm that Erikka's motivation is real. If this very necessary condition for goal achievement is not present, counselor and client must not only reevaluate the plan but the objective as well.

One of our favorite ways for counselors to help their clients determine whether there is enough motivation and self-efficacy to drive a plan to its successful outcome is through action methods such as role-play. In the session with Erikka, the counselor sets up an opportunity for her to practice one element of her plan: telling Robert to leave. Although this role-play is just an approximate representation of real life, it offers Erikka the opportunity to notice how her thoughts and feelings do or do not support her sense that the plan will lead to her satisfaction.

Existing Client Skills

For several reasons, we have a bias in favor of plans that involve behavior already existing in the client's repertoire. For one, experience has taught us that generally our clients are capable people who have a history of effective living. Using existing skills or tuning up old skills reminds clients of past and present capabilities and boosts their morale. Further, clients have more confidence in their efficacy with familiar skills than with something unfamiliar. Plans that heavily involve the client's existing behavioral repertoire are also more likely to be culturally appropriate in the anticipated context where they will be applied. Finally, using existing skills tends to be more efficient. Why spend client resources building a new set of stress-reduction skills if the client has some that worked in the past and just need to be dusted off or fine-tuned?

Counselors get clues about existing pertinent client resources throughout the counseling process. As clients tell their "story," get in the habit of noting the skills, resources, and achievements they report in passing (Erikka's list making is an example). It's not often that clients will need to learn everything from scratch. Keeping a mental inventory of what's already in place may be useful in the planning stage.

Consider clients who are complaining of poor grades or of a faltering relationship. These folks might consider themselves ineffective, but there are undoubtedly some skills and information in their present repertoire that will be useful in improving their situations. Listen for these, recognize them, and value them. The more existing client skills and resources you can identify and acknowledge, the more likely it is that the client will carry out the after-session plan with confidence. We tend to repeat those things that have been successful for us in the past when we know enough and are calm enough to do so.

It may be useful to ask clients, "What have you tried in the past?" or "How have you dealt with similar situations in the past?" and listen for the parts that worked.

Action techniques like role-playing and behavior rehearsal can reveal useful client behavioral skills as well (see the Erikka transcript for examples).

A plan is a hypothesis yet to be verified. We take care to identify a plan we believe has a high probability of success when used in the environment for which it was designed, but the best-laid plans are still uncertain. Talk with your counselee about trying the plan as an experiment (which is what it is, really). Setting it up as an experimental trial can help the counselee focus on doing the tasks and observing the results, gathering information about the process and outcomes of the plan. Trying out a plan as an experiment sets the counselee up as an experimenter and data gatherer. With this perspective, the results of the new ways of being are less likely to be critical to the self-esteem of the counselee and more likely to be feedback about the effectiveness of the plan.

Viewing the outcomes of a plan simply as feedback helps reduce any counselee tendencies to make success/failure judgments about themselves and their capabilities, and it puts the focus on "What have we learned that can help us improve the plan?" Adopting an experimental mind-set about plans helps diffuse the pressure to succeed that some counselees may be feeling; instead, it sets up an expectation that whatever results will be useful information about the plan.

A Process for Creating Plans

A *plan* is a sequence of actions that produces a specific result. Much of our daily routine consists of action sequences that are so practiced we do them without thinking. Getting dressed, tying shoes, starting the car, driving to school are all sets of actions that have a fairly predictable specific result. No two of us do these things exactly the same way. Our plans fit us and our unique environments.

When we are faced with the need or wish to achieve something outside our routine, we ask ourselves, "What should I do?" At the risk of seeming redundant, we'll reiterate our belief that being clear about intention, goal, and objective is crucial to subsequent planning and achievement. Being clear about one's objectives is a central part of personal empowerment. Empowerment is confirmed as objectives are realized. The planning process links objectives to the sequence of actions most likely to achieve them. The four-phase planning process described next is one way to discover what needs to be done to achieve a valued outcome.

Phase 1: Identifying the Objective

It's almost impossible to plan effectively without an identified purpose, result, or objective in mind. So, the first stage in creating a plan is to develop clarity about what the plan is meant to achieve, accomplish, or produce as a result. An objective that is clear about *what* is to be accomplished, *when* or *where*, and *how well* or *how much* is an excellent place to start. (See Chapter 8 for identifying objectives.)

Phase 2: Thinking Backward
from the Objective to the Beginning

To discover *how* an outcome can be achieved, think backward in time. Start by assuming the objective has just been accomplished, then ask yourself, "What *action* had to occur just before the objective was accomplished?" Write the answer to this question in a statement that begins with a *verb*. Verbs are action words; results come from actions.

Then ask, "What action had to occur just before that?" Add this to your list with another statement that starts with a verb. And keep on asking, "And what had to occur just before that? And just before that? . . . " until you get to what seems to be the starting place. (If you're not clear about this process, there is an example coming up soon.)

By starting at the objective and thinking backward, you can identify a series of actions (the *plan*) that result in the specific objective to be achieved. You will have a list of actions that, if performed in the sequence in which you named them, should lead to the desired result. (Note that action statements also help identify people, information, and other components important to the proposed plan.)

But, have you missed something? Left something out? Before you actually try the plan, complete the next phase.

Phase 3: Simulating Operation of the Plan

Using the list of actions developed in Phase 1 and Phase 2, start at the beginning and mentally walk through the actions from the beginning, one by one. Add any actions that seem to be needed to create a logical sequence of actions that appear to lead to the desired outcome. If each action seems to lead to the next, and so on to the final desired result, the plan may be complete.

In doing the simulated walk-through, you may find places where more than one sequence of actions is possible, or where sequence doesn't appear to matter. This happens in the real world. (It probably doesn't make any real difference whether the cream or sugar goes in the coffee first; what matters is that they both get there.) Whatever works for you is fine.

Phase 4: Identifying the Conditions
Necessary for Success

The success of this plan assumes that four critical conditions have been met:

1. The *objective* must be known to all participants.
2. The necessary *resources* must be available as required.
3. The counselee's *motivation* must indicate that the planned activities will be more satisfying than the alternative.

4. The counselee's *sense of self-efficacy* must indicate a belief in his or her ability to perform and to achieve success.

Keeping track of these four conditions as a plan evolves is good strategy. As counselees consider action, their incentives, objectives, and commitment can change. It is entirely reasonable, we believe, for clients in the process of considering change to have second thoughts. We have known clients whose priorities changed but who kept quiet in order "not to upset my counselor"—not a good choice.

It's usually more efficient problem solving to borrow a plan rather than invent your own. Later, we'll provide some ideas about where we've found existing plans. If you do locate an existing plan that looks promising, you may have saved yourself the time and trouble of doing Phase 2; you can begin checking it out with Phases 3 and 4 to see how well it fits your situation. Fine-tuning a borrowed plan may be a real time-saver.

The best place to look for a plan to help a counselee reach a current objective is in the counselee's own past. Most human beings cope very well with most parts of their lives. This means we all have a repertoire of effective plans. The most efficient problem solving may be helping someone find a plan he or she already has and applying it to the current situation.

One advantage of using a plan people already know is that they have experienced success with it in the past; past success is a major source of confidence that they can deal with the present effectively. A second advantage of using an already familiar system is that its validity in the world of the counselee is known; there is no transplant shock to deal with.

Action Plan Format

The Action Plan format (Forms 9.1 and 9.2) is a tool for integrating your awareness and skills in identifying and describing a plan for achieving a counselee objective. We've presented one completed example and left a blank form for you to apply in the first Integrating Activity at the end of this chapter.

The Counselor Toolbox

The planning process is one tool available to counselors collaborating with counselees in their objectives. We think this process is a particularly useful tool because it emphasizes the identification of a sequence of actions that lead to achievement of the objective. In other words, this planning process is outcome-oriented and action-specific in the sense that real plans must be if they are going to increase the likelihood that the counselee will achieve successful results.

The planning process does not have the bells and whistles of many other tools available to counselors. It is a basic and relatively methodical process unattached to

ACTION PLAN: COUNSELING OBJECTIVE

OBJECTIVE

What? *To tell Paul that I want to renew our friendship.*

When/Where? *Before next weekend. Anywhere—as long as we are face to face.*

How well/much? *To express my thoughts and feelings directly, without acting angry or defensive.*

Final step: *Listening to Paul's response to my request to be friends again.*

Preceding step: *Looking at Paul eye-to-eye and stating that I want to be friends.*

Preceding step: *Listening to Paul's thoughts and feelings about our break-up.*

Preceding step: *Asking Paul to talk about his feelings about our break-up.*

Preceding step: *Telling Paul the things I never told him about the stress in my life when we broke up.*

Preceding step: *Meeting Paul at a place he chooses.*

Preceding step: *Asking Paul to meet me to clear up the "unfinished business" between us.*

(continued)

any particular counseling theory. It is not a strategy or technique that tends to inspire lay observers to want to become counselors—unlike psychodrama, Adlerian Family Counseling demonstrations, or the session in which my "Gestalt therapist" encouraged me to do "empty chair work" on my issues with my father.

Preceding step: *Telling Paul that I want to get together to talk.*

Preceding step: *Calling Paul today.*

Start by: *Telling myself that I have the courage to be honest with Paul.*

PREREQUISITE CONDITIONS/ASSUMPTIONS

1. Objective: *I know I want to tell Paul that a friendship with him is important to me. He will know that after I talk with him.*

2. Resources: *I have practiced my talk in the role-play with my counselor. I feel ready to say what I need to say.*

3. Motivation: *Even if Paul doesn't want to see me again, just getting this off my chest will help me feel better.*

4. Self-Efficacy: *I have Paul's phone number and I know we're both available next weekend.*

In our experience, effective counselors are helpful to counselees because they attend to the elements of the Counseling Process Model, regardless of the specific strategies and techniques they apply.

At the same time, Step 4, Identify Plan for Achieving Objective, is the step in the Counseling Process Model that does encourage me, the counselor, to "borrow"

ACTION PLAN: COUNSELING OBJECTIVE

OBJECTIVE

What?

When/Where?

How well/much?

Final step:

Preceding step:

Preceding step:

Preceding step:

Preceding step:

Preceding step:

Preceding step:

(continued)

plan-making tools. I would look for those that have demonstrated efficacy with counselors and objectives similar to the desired outcome I'm addressing in this session.

Where do I borrow these tools? First, your colleagues can provide a generous collection of information and the support to apply strategies and techniques skill-

Preceding step:

Preceding step:

Start by:

PREREQUISITE CONDITIONS/ASSUMPTIONS

1. Objective:

2. Resources:

3. Motivation:

4. Self-Efficacy:

fully. We hope that the Integrating Activities presented in this book help you to experience the benefits of peer supervision and encouraging feedback.

Second, the professional literature is a potentially rich resource for practitioners, particularly those relatively new to practice or those encountering problem areas beyond their previous training and experience.

The last 40 years have brought an increasing volume of published counseling case literature, research, and reviews. Counselors need to be familiar with the literature related to their areas of practice for several practical reasons. The literature provides general models as guides to understanding problematic situations such as fears, stress, abuse, and low self-esteem. Case literature tells the step-by-step story of a clinician and a client engaged in working to achieve a specific counseling objective. Research reviews collect and examine research evidence regarding the efficacy of various approaches to an issue (such as enuresis) or examine the efficacy of a selected strategy (such as a systematic desensitization) for an array of problems.

Finally, recipe books are useful when you need specific information about steps in a process likely to lead to a specific desirable result. We feel most confident about recipes that have stood the test of time; Grandma's cornbread recipe worked for everyone who followed it like Grandma did. A good recipe is one that we can do with our resources (equipment, skills) and that appears very likely to deliver something we find attractive. Familiarize yourself with behavior change models; read Bandura (1977) on response facilitation and Meichenbaum (1977) on self-talk; and learn about applications of these principles to specific behaviors described in textbooks and in case literature. Some current examples of useful recipe books for counselors are listed at the end of this chapter.

 ERIKKA TRANSCRIPT

The counselor's emphasis now moves to articulating a plan, a sequence of actions, that has a high probability of achieving the agreed-on objectives (fewer headaches, calmer stomach, and others).

Counselor Readiness

> It seems that Erikka is now pretty clear about just what things she needs to take care of in her life.
>
> Erikka says she's ready to come up with a plan to deal with the boyfriend issue. I wonder how much help she needs in getting ready to actually do whatever it is that must be done.
>
> Erikka seemed to find the action technique helpful in clarifying the issues; perhaps more action would help clarify what needs to happen to deal with the boyfriend.
>
> More action might also provide some clues about whether she already knows what she needs to do and whether she can do it.
>
> First, let's pinpoint what *dealing with* means; it's hard to think about how to get there until we're clear about where we're going.

The Interview

CO80: OK. Shall we go ahead and come up with a plan to deal with this?

CL80: (chuckles) I think so.

CO81: (taking wastebasket, backpack, and other items from her hands and sending Joel back to audience) We'll give you a bit of a rest. (CL and CO are once again seated facing each other) Where do you think we should start?

CL81: Empty the trash can . . . I don't know. Start with the most immediate need. For me, that's taking care of things. Time sequencing . . . Take care of behavioral counseling, because I need to address that before I go back to L.A. Otherwise, all of a sudden it will be Monday and I'll have the tape due, and I'll need to do that. But even saying that, I can't seem to do that without addressing the issue with my boyfriend, but that's just become so rote I even hate discussing it, so that's probably also why it didn't come up earlier. It's something I keep saying, "I'll just take care of it. It's no problem."

CO82: OK. It sounds like it's something that you've addressed before and it hasn't worked out real well.

CL82: It keeps going up and down, up and down. . . . It's to the point now where I'm disgusted with myself that it keeps becoming a problem, so I don't talk about it.

CO83: So on the one hand, it seems like that kind of encases everything, and "I can do all that stuff. I can make a checklist. I can change my priorities around and I can cut back some Nautilus time right now, and pay more attention to my school, but, I don't know. I still have . . . what's his name? [CL: Robert.] I still have Robert around, kind of peering over the whole situation." Is that the way it feels?

CL83: That's *exactly* the way it feels.

CO84: "But, geez, I've already tried to do this, and I just think it's going to be the same old thing."

CL84: Yeah . . . Probably . . .

CO85: You just hesitated. Is there . . .

CL85: Because it just, it just really tees me off that it's still something that I'm trying to . . . Oh, here's another weekend when we're going to be talking about *this* again, and, uh . . . I don't know. I don't like to give it any air time. I don't think it warrants that. There're too many other things.

CO86: Is that the way you're feeling right now? You talk about "the issue," but, it's like, "Oh, I don't want to get into it right now because . . ."

CL86: Yeah. And it's not just right here. That's been pretty much the feeling the last couple of weeks. It's just, "Gosh. Forget about it. Let me just go ahead and get some other things done."

CO87: Uhm-hmm!

CL87: (*laughs*) But I'm not *doing* anything, so . . .

CO88: Would you stand up again? (*they stand; CO hands her the wastebasket, books, papers, calls Joel up from audience; and recreates the position CL was in before they sat down at CO80*) Why don't you go ahead and let Robert know what you want to do with him.

CL88: (*snickers, laughs*) Shall I physically tell him? [CO: Yeah. Do whatever you want.] (*CL looks up at "Robert"*) Would you please leave? (*Robert doesn't move*) You just don't fit in right now. Could you please leave? (*no movement from Robert; CL laughs*) Leave! (*pauses, then backs away from Robert about four steps, carrying wastebasket and other items*).

CO89: Where are you going?

CL89: I'm coming back to Tucson.

CO90: Coming back to Tucson, from . . .

CL90: Los Angeles. That's where Robert is.

CO91: Did you take all this [other stuff] with you?

CL91: Um-hmm.

CO92: Is that the way you want to go to L.A., to see Robert?

CL92: That's not the way I *want* to, but that's what's going to happen.

CO93: That's what's going to happen. OK. I'm going to L.A., and do . . . something with Robert?

CL93: Say, "That's it. Kaput. Can't handle it. Too much going on here to try and maintain this."

CO94: And then you're going to take all this, and take it back to Tucson. (*pause*)

CL94: Because I'll have this done by next Wednesday. I mean I know I'll do this, once that's taken care of. [CO: OK.] I know I'll do it on Sunday.

Debriefing

OBSERVER: What was the counselor thinking that Erikka should do with the boyfriend issue? How can the counselor advise her if he hasn't met the boyfriend?

COUNSELOR: I wasn't thinking about the boyfriend. My client is Erikka. This plan is designed within Erikka's world of experience. My lack of experience with her boyfriend is not salient to the accomplishment of her objective.

OBSERVER: If Erikka indicated that her previous talks with her boyfriend hadn't worked, why did the counselor suggest that she bring him up again?

COUNSELOR: I heard Erikka say that he kept coming up in her life. Bringing her boyfriend back into the scene was representing what is her reality. By observing how Erikka responded to his "coming up in her life," both my client and I have the opportunity to experience the parts of the interaction that "feel" as if they have or haven't worked and what thoughts, feelings, and actions actually seem successful to Erikka. In other words, we can learn more about how *not* to throw out the baby with the bathwater when it comes to developing a plan.

 ## SUGGESTIONS FOR INTEGRATING ACTIVITIES

1. In your own life, identify some task or goal long deferred—like organizing the basement or learning to dance. Using the Action Plan format, create an objective statement. Then, use the four-phase process in this chapter to create a plan for action that would seem to lead to achieving your objective. Finish the assignment by (a) identifying conditions essential to the success of the plan, and then (b) identifying the conditions that account for the objective currently being unmet. Are the lists for (a) and (b) the same? The next step is up to you.

2. This can be a one-time or a continuing activity that is intended to help you expand your knowledge of plans or strategies that already exist in the professional counseling literature. Your goals in this activity are (a) to acquire knowledge of existing intervention strategies pertinent to a particular counseling problem area, (b) to become familiar with the professional literature as a resource, and (c) to start assembling a "toolbox" of counseling strategies.

This activity works best when a small group of two to three students selects a counseling problem area as a focus. You could choose from relationship issues, stress management, self-esteem, substance abuse, anger management, family violence, career choice, eating disorders, or others. The *team product* consists of the following:

a. Three strategy abstracts from each team member, each from a different source, typed on Form 9.3. Team members supply each other with copies of abstracts, each person thus expanding his or her strategy library. When there are several teams, all can exchange abstracts.

(*text continues on page 161*)

FORM 9.3 Strategy abstract form (blank)

Abstract author: _____

Intervention Strategies for [problem area] _____

1. Name of intervention technique: _____

   _____

2. Usable with whom?

3. Under what conditions?

4. With what expectations? .

5. Description of intervention technique:

(continued)

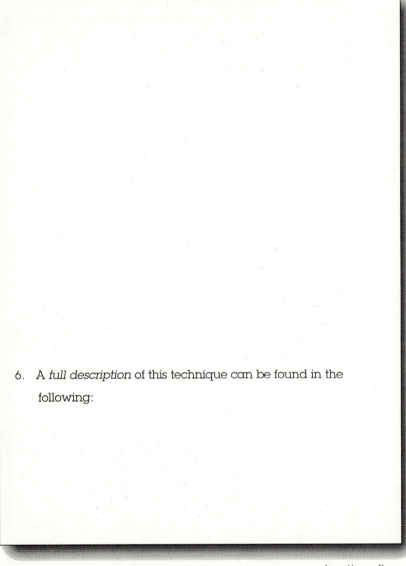

6. A *full description* of this technique can be found in the

   following:

(continued)

FORM 9.3 *(continued)*

7. A report of *results* achieved with this technique can be found in

FORM 9.4 Sample strategy abstract (filled in)

Abstract author: ___David R. Harvey___

Intervention Strategies for ___Developing Social Skills___

1. Name of intervention technique: ___Imagined (Covert)___
   Modeling

2. Usable with whom? *Adults, teenagers, and older children
   who want to learn to communicate assertively, modify phobic
   respones, e.g., test anxiety, or develop other skills that increase
   their capability to interact effectively.*

3. Under what conditions? *(1) The client is actively involved in
   learning to apply the strategy; (2) the client demonstrates
   an ability to use imagery; (3) imagined modeling is
   combined with actual practice.*

4. With what expectations? *Many clients demonstate gains in
   coping responses and skill development within a few weeks.*

5. Description of intervention technique:
   a. *Describe the procedure and discuss the rationale for
      using imagined modeling with the clients.*

   b. *Encourage the client to think of a model who is
      demographically similar to, and respected by, the client.*

(continued)

    c. Ask the client to describe the model in detail so that the model's characteristics can be used in creating the image in Steps 5 and 6.

    d. Present a two-minute stimulus scene and encourage the client to visualize the scene as it is presented.

        (1) Describe the context in which the target response is appropriate.

        (2) Ask the client to imagine someone modeling the target response within the context.

        (3) Describe a favorable outcome following the model's response within the scene.

    e. Present five to seven scenes within a one-hour session. Implement the procedure in three to five sessions within a one- to two-week period of time.

6. A full description of this technique can be found in the following:

Watson, D. L., & Tharp, P. G. (1993). Self-directed behavior: Self-modification for personal adjustment (6th ed., pp. 169–175). Pacific Grove, CA: Brooks/Cole.

Cautela & Kearney. (1996). The covert modeling handbook. In P. C. Kendall (Ed.), Advances in cognitive-behavioral

(continued)

research and therapy *(vol. 3, pp. 103–129). New York: Academic Press.*

Kazdin, A. E. (1984). Covert modeling. In P. C. Kendall (Ed.), Advances in cognitive-behavioral research and therapy *(vol. 3, pp. 103–129). New York: Academic Press.*

7. A report of *results* achieved with this technique can be found in the references listed above.

b. A single-page cover sheet for the collection of abstracts. The cover sheet should be headed by the name of the problem area. The sheet should contain paragraphs addressing the following ideas:

    (1) "We defined this problem area as including . . ."

    (2) "We sought information about ways to deal with this problem . . ." (How and where did you search? Sources? Results?)

    (3) "As a result of our search, we learned . . ." (Nature of information available, status of techniques in this area, evidence of negative or positive results, what is needed, and so on.)

    3. When there are several teams, a team performance can be included. The performance consists of an in-class demonstration of a segment of counseling that begins with the counselor (or co-counselors) working with a counselee to select an intervention and ends with the counselee departing to try it out.

🕐 CONSULTATION TIME

Scenario 1

COUNSELOR: And, you've seen a counselor before?

CLIENT: Yes, two years ago, but I wanted to see a woman this time.

COUNSELOR: You saw a male counselor two years ago and now you've chosen to see a woman. How do you think that seeing a woman will be helpful to you?

CLIENT: I won't have to deal with you coming on to me sexually . . .

What are the counselor's options?

- "Your previous counselor "came on" to you sexually? (*Client nods*) Can you tell me more about that experience?"What are the counselor's options?
- "That is a very serious breach of professional ethics, if what you say is true. Can you tell me the counselor's name and what he did?"
- "One of your primary concerns in seeing me for counseling is to feel safe from any sexual advances? In what other ways do you want counseling to be helpful?"
- "And if you don't have to worry about your counselor making sexual advances . . . ?"
- In what other ways might you respond?

Scenario 2

The counselor has been seeing a client referred by the Employee Assistance Program at the client's workplace. The counselor receives a call from the client's work supervisor.

COUNSELOR:	Yes, how may I help you?
CLIENT'S SUPERVISOR:	I just wanted to ask your opinion. I know that you've been working with Fred on his ability to manage stress. Can you tell me how he might handle a change in position right now?
COUNSELOR:	Does Fred know that you were going to call me?
CLIENT'S SUPERVISOR:	No, I didn't want him to get anxious about it.

What are the counselors options?

- "I'm sorry, but that information is confidential and my client would have to sign a release before I could respond to your questions."
- "If you have a copy of the Employee Assistance Program guidelines handy we could go over the section of confidentiality and what I can and can't disclose about the clients referred by your company."
- "Fred may feel that it would be appropriate for me to discuss this subject with you. I'm wondering whether you could ask him to sign a release of information giving me his permission to respond to your questions."
- "If you're concerned about his anxiety over our discussion, I'm wondering how much you trust his ability to manage the stress of a position change."
- Other counselor responses?

REFERENCES

Bandura, A. (1977). *Social learning theory*. Englewood Cliffs, NJ: Prentice Hall.

Meichenbaum, D. H. (1977). *Cognitive behavior modification: An integrative approach*. New York: Plenum.

Sue, S., & Zane, N. (1987). The role of culture and cultural techniques in psychotherapy. *American Psychologist, 42*, 37–45.

SUGGESTED READING

Belkin, G. S. (1975). *Practical counseling in the schools*. Dubuque, IA: William C. Brown.

Blatner, A. (1988). *Acting-in: Practical applications of psychodramatic methods* (2nd ed.). New York: Springer.

Cautela, J. R. (1977). Covert conditioning: Assumptions and procedures. *Journal of Mental Imagery, 1*, 53–65.

Cormier, W., & Cormier, L. (1991). *Interviewing strategies for helpers* (3rd ed.). Pacific Grove, CA: Brooks/Cole.

Ellis, A., & Grieger, R. (1977). *Handbook of rational-emotive therapy*. New York: Springer.

Goldfried, M., & Davison, G. (1976). *Clinical behavior therapy*. New York: Holt, Rinehart & Winston.

Haley, J. (1987). *Problem-solving therapy* (2nd ed.). San Francisco: Jossey-Bass.

Ivey, A., Ivey, M. B., & Simek-Downing, L. (1987). *Counseling and psychotherapy: Integrating skills, therapy, and practice* (2nd ed.). Englewood Cliffs, NJ: Prentice Hall.

Jacobson, E. (1938). *Progressive relaxation*. Chicago: University of Chicago Press.

Kanfer, F., & Goldstein, A. (1980). *Helping people change* (2nd ed.). New York: Pergamon Press.

Kanfer, F., & Schefft, B. (1988). *Guiding the process of therapeutic change*. Champaign, IL: Research Press.

Kazdin, A. G. (1978). Covert modeling: The therapeutic application of imaginal rehearsal. In J. L. Singer & K. S. Pope (Eds.), *The power of human imagination: Newer methods of psychotherapy*. New York: Plenum.

Lange, A., & Jakubowski, P. (1976). *Responsible assertive behavior*. Champaign, IL: Research Press.

Mahoney, M. J. (1970). Toward an experimental analysis of coverant control. *Behavior Therapy, 1*, 510–521.

Meichenbaum, D., & Turk, D. C. (1987). *Facilitating treatment adherence: A practitioner's guidebook*. New York: Plenum.

Passons, W. R. (1975). *Gestalt approaches in counseling*. New York: Holt, Rinehart & Winston.

Rogers, C. R. (1951). *Client-centered therapy*. New York: Houghton Mifflin.

Shelton, J., & Levy, R. (1981). *Behavioral assignments and treatment compliance*. Champaign, IL: Research Press.

Smith, J. C. (1985). *Relaxation dynamics: Nine world approaches to self-relaxation*. Champaign, IL: Research Press.

Watson, D., & Tharp, R. (1993). *Self-directed behavior: Self-modification for personal adjustment* (6th ed.). Pacific Grove, CA: Brooks/Cole.

Wolpe, J. R. (1958). *Psychotherapy by reciprocal inhibition*. Stanford, CA: Stanford University Press.

CHAPTER 10

Step 5:
Support the Plan

Don't walk in front of me,
I may not follow.
Don't walk behind me,
I may not lead.
Walk beside me . . .   —Albert Camus

A plan is just a plan, a map for a journey considered but not begun. In counseling, plans may be discussed, formulated, and revised, and still the client's life outside the counseling hour may remain unchanged. As counselors, we have worked with counselees to develop plans to achieve important objectives. Sometimes clients leave with their plans, perform them as planned, and achieve important goals in their lives. Sometimes clients leave with their plans, and return to say, "I didn't try it" or "I tried it and it didn't work." Sometimes clients leave counseling having exercised their right to reject the plan and maintain the status quo in their lives, at least for now.

As counselors, we are committed ethically to supporting clients' rights to make informed choices about the ends and means of change in their lives. This chapter describes a process called Checkout: Informed Choice that we believe supports the client's right to make an informed choice about a planned process of change. For clients committed to change, the second section, Priming Client Readiness for Action, provides hints for facilitating the client's readiness and ability to perform the needed tasks. Finally, for those times when the client returns and reports unexpected results, Performance Problem Analysis suggests a diagnostic procedure that should help pinpoint the impediment.

Counselors have an ethical responsibility to help counselees make good choices. Clients have every right to decide whether to pursue a proposed plan. We believe people make the best choices when they have the most information possible about available options and expected outcomes. Checkout is a way of verifying that counselees understand clearly what the plan entails and what they can reasonably expect if it is followed.

Checkout: Informed Choice

Checkout is a procedure to increase the probability that counselees can indeed make an informed choice about pursuing the proposed changes in their lives. Checkout seems to fit best at the point when you and your counselee have drafted a plan for achieving the desired and agreed-on counseling objective. The checkout procedures briefly recapitulate the counseling process to the present moment. Checkout is presented in this section as a series of unfinished statements posed by the counselor, to be completed by the client. We are most assured we have been working in our clients' world when they can supply the words that describe where they are going, how they expect to get there, and how they will know they've arrived.

Checkout might start something like this:

COUNSELOR: Let's take a few minutes to go over the ground we've covered so far. So what you've been concerned about in your life is . . .

The counselee is encouraged to restate the problematic situation. It's all right for the counselor to prompt the client's response but he or she should use the client's own words.

An important part of this restatement is articulating the distressing feeling that accompanies the situation, the feeling the counselee wants to change. Helping clients stay in touch with the distressing feelings that brought them to counseling sometimes seems to strengthen their resolve to persist, to make changes.

COUNSELOR: And what you would like to change is . . . (from what? to what?)

This is the goal/objective that has been negotiated; this is what the counselee hopes to accomplish through counseling.

COUNSELOR: And what you can do to change it is . . .

This is the plan, the sequence of actions through which the counselee intends and expects to achieve the objective.

COUNSELOR: And when you have accomplished these tasks you will

be feeling . . .
and saying to yourself . . .
and doing . . .

that will tell you that you have met your goal.

This step is important for two reasons. Asking clients to identify the thoughts, feelings, and actions they expect after completing the plan (1) affirms the presumed link between the plan and the reason they sought counseling (the counseling objective) and (2) affirms that they know what indicators signal their achievement of change.

It's important to affirm that clients can recognize their achievements. With some clients we might even build in some sort of minicelebration at this point. It could be no more than asking clients to say to themselves: "Good for me! Instead of staying stuck in (the old situation), I decided to do something about it, and I did!"

COUNSELOR: And so, on a scale of 1 to 10, with 10 being absolutely certain, how confident are you that when you leave here you actually can/will do the plan?

Clients usually have no trouble coming up with some sort of estimate. We're looking for at least a 7. If we get a lower estimate, we might say something like the following:

COUNSELOR: It sounds as though you think something might keep this plan from happening. I wonder how the plan could be changed so you'd be at a 7 or 8? . . . I wonder if doing the plan seems like more effort than the change would be worth to you?

This probe provides an opportunity to address something that was missed or misunderstood earlier. Sometimes as counselors we get enthusiastic about certain kinds of interventions and "sell" them to an agreeable client, who may have reservations he or she can express by saying "5 or 6."

When we get a lower estimate, it may be because the planned first step is too ambitious. When this happens, we're inclined to scale down the first homework task to increase the chances of success for the client. We may also need to visit an earlier stage, taking another look at Step 2, Understanding the Client's Concerns. For an example of how helpful this probe can be in the counseling process, look at the Erikka transcript beginning at CO116 (at the end of Chapter 11).

What is important, of course, is not that checkout happens just like our example, but that it happens. Checkout usually takes no more than 8 to 10 minutes and has the effect of focusing attention on the client's distress of the present situation, the actions to be taken to change it, the desired results, and the expectation that the client can and will take action. Checkout verifies that counselor and counselee are on the same track, that they are focused on work that's important to the counselee, and that the counselee clearly understands what's involved.

Priming Client Readiness for Action

Strong client expectations of success are important precursors of achievement. Expectations for success that are founded on experience are more durable than others; they last after the client has left the counselor's office. We offer the following hints for priming the client's readiness and ability to perform homework assignments.

Encourage the counselee to identify cues for performing the plan. It helps to have a reminder that now is the time to do it. Here are some examples:

- "As soon as I get in the car to go to work, I'm going to tell myself . . ."
- "I'm going to put my homework card on my calendar so that I'll see it when I'm asked to schedule my time."
- "Whenever my husband says, 'We have to do something about a budget,' I'll know it's time to practice my calming skills."

Have the client role-play the task. Actually practicing the assigned task gives the counselee a successful attempt before he or she leaves the office. Don't assume that a discussion about "using my sense of humor when I make a request of a co-worker" will magically become a request-making skill at the counselee's job site tomorrow.

COUNSELOR: Dean, would you like to set up a role-play situation so that you can try out some ways to use humor when you ask Debbie to put your tools away?

DEAN: What do you mean?

COUNSELOR: Well, let's pretend you're at the shop tomorrow. We can even make my office seem more like the shop. Let's see, where shall we put your toolbox and where shall we put Debbie's? . . . Now, if I were Debbie, where would I be when you wanted to ask me about replacing your tools? . . . How would I be acting? . . . What would be the look on my face? . . . OK. Let's run through a rehearsal of how you want to make your request.

The rehearsal of behavioral assignments can also be done cognitively through imagery and self-instruction techniques. Once counselees have been through an in-office cognitive rehearsal of their plan, they have another tool they can apply at any time to rehearse the plan.

Encourage the counselee to make an explicit public commitment to perform homework tasks.

COUNSELOR: So, what is your plan for these next two weeks before we meet again?

MIMI: I'm going to try some of the things we talked about and see how it goes.

COUNSELOR:	Which particular things did you want to commit yourself to doing before our next session?
MIMI:	Well, I liked the plan we came up with about ignoring my son's critical comments about his aunt.
COUNSELOR:	So, for the next two weeks you will . . .
MIMI:	I will ignore all my son's comments about his aunt's appearance.

(*Note*: Some clients prefer to write out their commitment and to have it available as a reminder.)

Prepare counselees for possible negative effects of performing the tasks that are expected to lead to change. Change often has a down side, at least in the short term. If your counselee has always avoided conflict by not speaking up, an assertive response may draw some fire he or she has never before experienced. When Mom decides to ignore her son's comments about "Aunt Fatty," he may persist by expounding on more of his aunt's personal characteristics. This situation illustrates the maxim that "it always gets worse before it gets better."

If counselees are invited to anticipate possible adverse responses to their experiments, they can build in strategies to reduce these effects and prevent their own discouragement. The following exchange is one example:

COUNSELOR:	How do you expect your husband to react when you say you want to wait until after the kids are in bed before you talk about money problems?
MARIA:	I don't know. I've never said anything like this before—except in here. I don't care how he reacts. We have to stop fighting in front of the kids.
COUNSELOR:	You're not sure how he'll react, but this is too important to back away from.
MARIA:	Yes, I just hope we don't have a fight over *when* we're going to talk about our finances.
COUNSELOR:	Are there any circumstances—a certain look on your husband's face, something he might say when you bring up the subject— that might lead you to say to yourself, "Maybe this isn't such a good idea right now"?
MARIA:	I'm not sure.
COUNSELOR:	Should we identify some worst-case scenarios and fine-tune your plan so that you can be encouraged by your own efforts, regardless of how your husband responds?
MARIA:	Yes. I think that I'd better be prepared.

Change is not easy, no matter how well-designed the counselee objective and plan may be. The checkout process is a way to verify that the counselor and counselee are focused on matters significant to the counselee. Checkout bolsters client self-efficacy estimates by helping the client articulate the discomfort of the current situation and reinforce his or her own ability to alleviate the problematic situation.

Performance Problem Analysis

Every counselor has had the experience of working with a counselee to arrive at a course of action and seeing the counselee off to carry out the plan. A week later, the counselee comes in as scheduled:

COUNSELOR: Hi, Charlie. How are you doing? How did it go last week?

CHARLIE: Not so good. I didn't really get a chance to do what we talked about.

COUNSELOR: (*thinking*, "That's *not what I expected to hear*.") Sorry to hear you're not doing so well. Tell me what happened.

The counselor begins to suspect that there's a problem; the performance expected of Charlie has apparently not happened. A performance problem exists when an important difference is noted between what is *expected* (you thought your client would come back to this session and tell you how well it went) and what actually *occurs* (the client did nothing new). We notice that a bad feeling is usually part of the sequence: Expectation → Opportunity for action → Observed default → Disappointment (frustration, anger, guilt, blaming).

Recognizing Performance Problems

Many of the problems people seek help with can be viewed as *performance* problems, situations in which an expected or desired action did not occur. Here are some examples of performance problems.

* Mom expected the garbage to have been taken to the alley and she sees that it is still sitting in the kitchen sink.
* Sarah is waiting on the corner of 2nd and Cherry for Ralph to pick her up. It's 2:30 and she heard him say he would be there at 2:00.
* I promised to call the dentist and schedule a check-up before school started; it will soon be November and I still haven't called.
* My client didn't show for his appointment this week. When he called he said he would be here.
* My client said he hadn't done the homework we planned last week.

Clients often need help in understanding and responding to situations when they experience disappointment, frustration, anger, and eventually depression and guilt

---

because their expectations or someone else's were unmet. In the first example, Mom knows there is a problem because she did not expect to see the garbage still sitting in the sink. She *expected* the garbage to be gone; she *observed* that it was still here. The potential for a problem exists when an individual notices a difference between what *is* and what is *expected*. This deficit is a problem if the observer thinks it is, and feels like it is (disappointment, frustration, anger, guilt). In the example with Sarah, for Ralph to be 3 minutes late is probably not a problem (unless it's raining); for Ralph to be 30 minutes late almost certainly is a problem.

A problem exists for an individual when he or she experiences a *difference that matters* between what *is*, and what is *expected*. Our definition implies that expectations play a key role in defining performance problems. One of the ways we keep ourselves and others from meeting our expectations is by expressing them in vague, nonspecific terms. For example, did your parents ever tell you to "act more grown up"? Were you sure what that meant? Were they? Expectations expressed in general terms like "acting more grown up" seem to mean different things to different people in different situations. One of our colleagues characterizes such goals as being in a race with a receding finishing line. No matter what happens, you never seem to meet expectations, to succeed.

Diagnosing performance problems and finding and fixing what's keeping us stymied depends on clarity about what is expected and how we know it is not occurring. When the performance is *clearly described*, and it is *expected*, and it is not *occurring*, then we know there is a *problem*.

Diagnosing and Remedying the Problem

Asking the following four diagnostic questions, in the order given, can pinpoint factors contributing to performance problems. (We owe a debt to Robert Mager, 1970, for the concept; any errors in application to counseling are ours.)

QUESTION 1:   IS EVERYONE INVOLVED AWARE OF THE EXPECTED PERFORMANCE?

One of the major reasons we have performance problems when two or more people are involved is that some of the participants did not get the message or did not get the complete message.

- "I didn't know you wanted me to carry out the garbage." (Performance)
- "I didn't know you wanted me to carry out the garbage before dinner." (Performance + Time)
- "I didn't know you wanted me to carry the garbage out to the alley before dinner." (Performance + Time + Place)

The checkout process we described earlier builds in an attempt to confirm that the client understands clearly what is to be done, and when, and where. If others are involved, they need to know precisely what's expected of them, and when, and where.

When clients return with the expected tasks undone, you need to verify once again that you and they shared common expectations about what they were to do. Words spoken in the counselor's office may assume different meanings when clients carry them out into their world. Check it out. A statement of purpose that reduces ambiguity includes the clearly described *expected performance* and *when* and *where* it is to occur.

QUESTION 2: ARE THE RESOURCES REQUIRED FOR THE PERFORMANCE AVAILABLE TO THE PARTICIPANTS?

Every performance requires resources. If the participants know what is expected and it still is not happening, the next area to check is whether the *resources* required for the task are available to the participants. Things don't get done when there is a lack of time, energy, tools, essential knowledge, skills, money, power, competencies, and the like.

It is easy to overlook resources essential to achieving the desired result. We sometimes get ourselves in trouble by agreeing to accomplish something without taking stock of our available resources. We act as though time and energy are infinite, and we volunteer for one more committee or one more task. We can be puzzled by lack of performance because we *assume* capabilities exist when they may be absent, or rusty from misuse, or not really available because they have never been mastered at all. It may not occur to us that not all adults can read and write English; not all women can sew, or cook, or take minutes; not all men like sports or are good in business; not everyone can walk up to a stranger and ask a question; not everyone has mobility; not everyone can initiate a conversation; not everyone can speak on his or her own behalf; not everyone will tell you if he or she is in pain; not everyone can do many things you and I take for granted.

Role-playing (simulation) is one way to verify the availability of information, skills, or other tools needed for plan performance. It's also a way to determine what information and skills may be required by the performance. Dave uses simulation with Erikka when he asks her to face Joel, who is posing as Robert, and tell him what she needs to tell Robert. Simulating the task in the counselor's office is an inexpensive way to verify that words and skills are available to the performer.

QUESTION 3: IS THE PERFORMANCE REWARDING TO THE PERFORMERS?

When all participants know what is expected and all participants have the resources needed to do what is expected, and still the performance does not happen, the reason may be that the participants see the performance as unrewarding. Three situations can exist in which it is better *not* to achieve the expected result.

• Not achieving the expected result may be more immediately rewarding than achieving it. For example, John gets lots of attention for not yet having taken out the garbage. Once he carries the garbage out, the attention ends.

- Achieving the expected result may bring more pain than pleasure. For example, going to the dentist will bring more pain than I have now. Or John's buddies may tease him if he goes against peer norms and is a "good boy." So, avoiding the performance means avoiding the pain.

- Achieving the desired result is no more rewarding than not achieving it—and it costs more. For example, we think of a teacher who expended incredible amounts of effort in getting all his students to come in from the hall and be at their desks when the bell rang "so we can get started on time." But what the students had learned was that nothing important happened for the first 5 minutes anyway; being tardy or being on time had no real or important consequences for them.

To this point, we believe the expected performance is most likely to occur if everyone involved knows exactly what is expected, has the resources necessary to do it, and believes that doing it will be personally rewarding. And, we have seen occasions when all these seemed to be in place, and still the expected performance did not occur. That's why we have the next question.

QUESTION 4: DOES THE PERFORMER BELIEVE HE OR SHE IS CAPABLE OF ACHIEVING THE TASK?

When all conditions for successful performance seem to have been met, and even when it is clear that performance would be in their own best interests, some individuals do not perform. Such people have been described variously as discouraged (Dreikurs, 1953; Nikelly, 1971), having a low sense of self-efficacy (Bandura, 1977), exhibiting learned helplessness (Seligman, 1975), or having a negative self-concept.

What seems to be missing is a belief in one's own ability to act successfully. Jerome Frank (1973) observes that all people who seek counseling are demoralized to some extent. Thus, attention to morale-building or esteem-building experiences is always sensible and may be the most crucial factor in successful counseling more often than we think.

Two major elements in esteem-building are respect and achievement. A client's self-respect is nourished by a counselor who shows respect. Messages of respect for the client's value and integrity as a unique human being are sent by a counselor whose intention and skills demonstrate empathic understanding.

Personal achievements contribute to self-esteem only when they are recognized as real accomplishments. Many people have been taught that only perfect achievement counts; less than perfect means failure. Our society reinforces this with rampant Number One-ism; only the best counts. If our self-esteem depends solely on those occasions when we are perfect or best, we are in deep trouble. In the real world, we can only do the best we can do at this time and place; with experience, support, and more resources, we may become capable of doing better.

Recently we read, "There is no failure in nature." We understand this to mean that failure—or success—is a judgment we make about something relative to a set of expectations. The expectations, and the judgment, are ideas, human opinions that exist apart from accomplishments. Accomplishment can be viewed as an esteem-building achievement if expectations are set at human rather than godlike levels. For many in today's world, simple survival is a major accomplishment. Just being able to get oneself through the day is reason enough for a sense of achievement and a healthy self-esteem.

Performance objectives are most likely to be reached when the participants

- Are aware of the objective
- Have the necessary resources to achieve it
- Believe the objective will be satisfying
- View themselves as capable of achieving it

When performance problems do occur, you can discover the reasons by considering each of the four elements in the order given. The performance analysis process is shown in Table 10.1. For each problem status, the table gives the diagnostic question, identifies common sources of interference, and suggests the task needed to remediate the situation.

 **ERIKKA TRANSCRIPT**

Counselor Readiness

Erikka seems clear about what she needs to do and what she can expect as she does it.

Erikka's incentive to resolve the issue with Robert seems to vary. I'll need to pay attention to that.

Erikka seems confident that she can do what the plan requires. I'd like to help her have some experience of what it feels like to do the plan.

I'm concerned about how much time is available in the session. I want to leave enough time to evaluate before we end.

The Interview

CO95:   OK. Can we try this one more time? [CL: OK.] (*CO sets up the situation again, but without wastebasket and other items, just with Robert looming overhead, hands on CL's shoulders*) What are you going to do with Robert?

CL95:   (*sighs, looking up at Robert*)

The session continues, with CL delivering her message to Robert. The videotape operator missed this portion while changing cassettes. Sorry. The transcript resumes just as the role-play has ended.

TABLE 10.1 ■ PERFORMANCE ANALYSIS PROCESS

	Problem Status	Diagnostic Question	Common Sources of Interference	Remedy
The tasks in the plan weren't done; counselee didn't do as counselor expected . . .	Expected performance did not occur.	Were counselee and counselor expectations the same?	Counselor *assumes* mutual understanding.	Inform all parties. Validate their understanding.
All parties know what is expected, but . . .	Performance did not occur, or did not occur to expected standard.	Does counselee have all resources required to do plan?	Resources not available; resources not at level required for success.	Validate availability of resources at level required by task. Equip counselee for success.
All parties know what is expected, have required resources to do the plan, but . . .	Performance did not occur.	What does plan actually bring: loss of positives, gain of negatives, or no important consequences?	Incentives for counselee are not all identified, or are mistakenly identified.	Validate significance of outcomes for counselee.
All parties know what is expected, have the resources to do it, and value the anticipated outcome, but . . .	Performance did not occur.	Counselee may not see self as capable of "success" or achievement.	Discouragement; self-concept as incapable, as loser.	Build self-esteem through awareness of resources, achievements, caring.

One can infer from the material immediately following that CL has walked through a sequence of actions (a tentative plan) toward "doing with Robert," then coming back to Tucson and addressing the Tucson issues.

CL100: I think I could have gotten more and more out with him. I wasn't aware of anything else. It was just him. And when I come back here, I want to address these things (*points to wastebasket and other items*) singularly. Independently from one another, and not just the whole thing. Just to pick up the letters, or just the assignment.

CO101: How's your headache?

CL101: It's not really that, not really that pressing now. It's pretty non-existent now.

CO102: Really! How about your stomach?

CL102: It's OK. [CO: OK, meaning . . .] It's fine. There's nothing really going on.

CO101–102 are Step 6: Evaluate tasks, assessing current status of CL counseling objectives. Planning, doing, and evaluating are not necessarily linear in the counseling process.

CO103: Um-hmmm! . . . Do you have any idea what happened?

CL103: (big exhale, pause) Um . . . I think I took things more inde-pendently rather than grouping them all up. I didn't feel I was inadequate in any situation. I felt a lot more strength and adequacy and power in dealing with just this issue, rather than 10 of them at once. That's the most predominant thought right now. Looking at the issues in a more realistic manner.

CO104: Do you think that's something you might do this weekend?

CL104: Um . . . Yeah. I think that's something that I'd *like* to do. I don't know. These [local] things still have to be done. It's a matter of leaving some things behind, in a way, or putting a pause on them and going off and doing the other things I need to do.

The last several CO comments verify CL map of the preceding experience, and CL's intent to follow the map after the session. Notice tentativeness in CL response to CO104 ("I think that's something that I'd *like* to do"). Will our counselor pick up on this tentativeness?

Debriefing

OBSERVER: What if the client says "No" when you ask her to try some-thing—like a role-play? Wouldn't it be better just to direct the client to do an activity that you believe can help her?

COUNSELOR: If the client says "No," she is letting me know that (1) she feels she has a choice in the matter, (2) she has a right to say no, and (3) the master-servant relationship is working the way it needs to if counseling is to be successful.

My responses to "No" can include (1) facilitation of my client's disclosure of the thoughts and feelings, facial expressions, and posture that are part of "No"; (2) a request for a suggestion from my client about what she wants to do next; or (3) the option of another consultation suggestion that can help us get to where we have agreed to go. If I take away the question that introduces the activity, I take away my client's right to be in the driver's seat of the counseling process.

OBSERVER: Couldn't there be explanations other than Erikka's for why her headache and stomach distress went away, such as catharsis, endorphins released through her assertive actions, increased self-esteem? Wouldn't she benefit from the counselor's interpretation of what happened in the session?

COUNSELOR: I am focusing my awareness and skills as a counselor on how Erikka's own map of her experience—her "talk" about headaches, Robert, and things piling up—can better represent the territory of that experience—her thoughts, feelings, and actions. She is in the best position to validate the success of that endeavor. My analysis or alternative interpretation is not only less valid, but downright distracting to our collaborative efforts to develop Erikka's map-making skills.

 ## SUGGESTIONS FOR INTEGRATING ACTIVITIES

1. We recognize performance problems in our own lives by feelings of anger, guilt, frustration, or blame when something we tell ourselves we are expecting does not happen. The next time you find yourself experiencing these feelings, use the four diagnostic questions and write your analysis of the situation in your journal. Does knowing *how* the problem was created make a difference in how you think about it?

2. Here's another assignment in self-study. During the next week, notice how you anticipate, prepare for, and rehearse the tasks in your life. Some of us prepare for success; some of us prepare for failure. Are your rehearsals more of the "Do this . . ." or of the "Don't do this . . ." variety? Do you rehearse before or after the fact: "I want to say this . . ." versus "I should have said this . . ." What do you observe about how you get ready for an important task? What really helps? How?

 **CONSULTATION TIME**

Scenario 1

COUNSELOR: Our time is up for today.

CLIENT: This has been a good session. I still feel shaky about next week, but I think I can handle it.

COUNSELOR: Yes. You have some options now.

CLIENT: I know. But maybe I'll get in trouble, get in over my head. Can I have your home number in case I need to call you before next week?

What are the counselor's options?

- "I'm sorry. I don't see clients out of the office. You can handle it."
- "If it's an emergency that can't wait until our next session, here's the number for Help on Call, the crisis phone line."
- "Sure. My number is xxx-xxxx. Please call before 9:00 P.M. if at all possible."
- "Do you still have the information sheet I gave you before our very first session? It has a paragraph about what to do if you need to contact me outside your scheduled session."
- How might you respond?

Scenario 2

The counselee has arrived 25 minutes late for the scheduled one-hour counseling appointment.

COUNSELOR: Hello, Marie.

CLIENT: I can't believe the traffic today. I thought I'd never get here!

What options does the counselor have?

- "I suggest that we reschedule our session so that we can have the full hour to address your concerns."
- "I have the next 35 minutes available as we scheduled; then I have another appointment. How do you want to use the time?"
- "It seems that this part of your day hasn't worked out as planned . . . What are you feeling right now?"
- "Before we begin the session, it might make sense to review our initial counseling agreement and what we discussed about scheduled appointments."
- How might you respond?

Scenario 3

COUNSELOR: You're saying that you can't get your ex-partner's accusations out of your mind, and the only way to get his attention is to threaten him with a gun?

CLIENT: The son-of-a- _____ will *have* to take me seriously if he's looking down the barrel."

What are the counselor's options?

- "Have you ever threatened someone with a gun before?"
- "You must be feeling very desperate to consider going to such extremes to influence your ex-partner . . ."
- "Are you willing to discuss other options for addressing your feelings about your ex-partner?"
- "I want to clarify my responsibility in this situation. If you leave my office today with the intention of threatening your ex-partner with a gun, it is my professional duty to warn him about his risk of harm from you. I may have to call the police to assist with this warning. What is your response to what I've just said?"
- What else might you do as the counselor?

REFERENCES

Bandura, A. (1977). Self-efficacy: Toward a unifying theory of behavioral change. *Psychological Review, 84,* 191–215.

Dreikurs, R. (1953). *Fundamentals of Adlerian psychology.* Chicago: Alfred Adler Institute.

Frank, J. (1973). *Persuasion and healing.* Baltimore: Johns Hopkins University Press.

Mager, R. F. (1970). *Analyzing performance problems or you really oughta wanta.* Belmont, CA: Fearon Pitman.

Nikelly, A. B. (1971). *Techniques for behavior change.* Springfield, IL: Charles C Thomas.

Seligman, M. E. P. (1975). *Helplessness: On depression, development, and death.* San Francisco: Jossey-Bass.

SUGGESTED READING

Kanfer, F. H., & Schefft, B. K. (1988). *Guiding the process of therapeutic change.* Champaign, IL: Research Press.

Shelton, J. L., & Levy, R. L. (1981). *Behavioral assignments and treatment compliance: A handbook of clinical strategies.* Champaign, IL: Research Press.

How Will We Know We've Arrived?

An Overview of Step 6

Our role as counselors demands that the first person to know that a counseling objective has been met must be the counselee. We're committed to this position for several reasons. For one, it's the clients' lives in which change is being sought, so any change will be observable first by them. Second, although the desired change will occur in their lives, some folks have developed blind spots to their own achievements, with a consequent loss of an important source of self-esteem. The last part of the model addresses these issues.

Step 6, *Evaluate Counseling*, is designed to identify those events that will signal progress toward the established objective, and ultimately, clients' arrival at their goal. By charging counselees with the responsibility of monitoring the results of their efforts, the stage is set for them to be aware of what they have achieved and for them to accept their own role in improving their life status. This is the point when counselees experience themselves as people capable of positively changing their own lives.

We hear a lot about self-esteem these days. None of us has more than we seem to need. One esteem-building factor is a sense of agency, bolstered by the experience of successful effort in our own behalf. Step 6 has as a primary focus helping counselees experience themselves as agents in their own behalf, successfully creating for themselves a more satisfactory life.

CHAPTER 11

Step 6:
Evaluate Counseling

Everything that happens, happens as it should, and if you observe carefully, you will find this to be so.
—Marcus Aurelius

Process and Outcome Criteria

If you're flying to Cleveland, you don't wait until you have disembarked to see if you're on the right plane. We've learned to pay attention to the *process*: having the right ticket in our pocket, getting to the right gate at the right time, and listening for the flight attendant to say, "Welcome to Flight 446 for Cleveland." If all these indicators are in place, our chances of finding ourselves in Cleveland at the end of the flight seem good.

For counselors, it's getting the client to the right place that matters. We want to remind you that the six-step Counseling Process Model, like any other behavior (see Chapter 2), is a hypothesis: "*If* the counselor performs each task in the model effectively, *then* the client will be most likely to achieve the desired result." Information about client outcome will be needed to gauge client progress and achievement of counseling objectives.

Although evaluation is labeled the final counselor task in this model, the counselor has been busy gathering data and making assessments throughout the process. Counselors who want to arrive at their clients' expected destinations learn to monitor each step in the Counseling Process Model. *Process evaluation* for the counselor means continually monitoring progress in achieving each of the six tasks in the Counseling Process Model.

Process Evaluation Criteria: Staying on Track

Our thinking about process evaluation is grounded in assumptions we presented in Chapter 3. Given these assumptions, the successful counselor is one who efficiently and effectively performs the tasks identified in the Counseling Process Model, tasks that are intended to result in a satisfactory final destination for the client. Let's consider how the counselor can monitor progress for each of the six process tasks along the way to the expected outcomes.

Although the progression in actual practice is not often this linear, think of each step in the counseling process as dependent on completion of the preceding step. Put another way, the purpose of each step is to reach the next one. Thus, one way of evaluating the ongoing process is by determining for each step whether achievement is sufficient to move on to the next level, and so on, to the end of the process. Let's see how the counselor might stay on track by using the three familiar guiding questions to attend to process evaluation during a session. Unless otherwise noted, what we describe is how the counselor is thinking during the session, not as dialogue with the client (although it could be).

Step 1: Initiate Counseling Relationship

Where are we going? We're going to Step 2, Understand Concerns. I need to hear why this person came to counseling, what's problematic in her life, and what she hopes to achieve through counseling.

How can we get there? I'll invite the person to tell me why she came. I'll use attending and following skills to elicit client talk about her concerns. I may need to teach this person about counseling, process, roles, and limits.

How will we know we've arrived? The best indicator will be for the client to begin talking about what brought her to counseling.

Step 2: Understand Client Concerns Empathically

Where are we going? We are trying to understand as accurately as possible what the client experiences as problematic and what she desires to change in her life.

How can we get there? Attending and following responses will be our first choice; other means, such as simulation or observation, may be useful.

How will we know we've arrived? We'll know when the counselor's description of the client situation is interchangeable with the client's, when the client is ready to consider possible objectives for change.

Step 3: Negotiate Counseling Objectives

Where are we going? We expect to achieve mutual agreement on what is to be accomplished through counseling, when or where it will happen, and how well or how much it will happen.

How can we get there? We must agree on the first problem or goal area to address; we'll pinpoint the changes we are seeking.

How will we know we've arrived? We will have arrived when we agree on a specific objective as our target.

Step 4:   Identify Plan for Achieving Objective

Where are we going? We need to discover and agree on a plan the client believes will achieve her goal.

How can we get there? We will inventory client resources and draw on counselor resources to develop a plan of action within the client's capabilities.

How will we know we've arrived? The client will report confidence in her ability to perform the required tasks.

Step 5:   Support the Plan

Where are we going? The aim is for the client to perform tasks as described in the plan, with appropriate modifications if needed.

How can we get there? We will move toward the goal because the client finds her current status intolerable, has participated in development of the plan, has evidence that the identified tasks are within her capability, values what the plan can achieve, and believes she is capable of performance.

How will we know we've arrived? The client will report performance of the plan as described, with appropriate modifications if needed.

Step 6:   Evaluate Counseling

Where are we going? We are seeking evidence that the process has achieved the client's desired outcomes.

How can we get there? We will gather evidence as defined in Step 3 about the status of the client's desired outcome.

How will we know we've arrived? The evidence will support achievement of the desired outcome, as described in Step 3, when we are successful.

It should be clear that evaluation is an ongoing process throughout counseling. The counselor is always paying attention to relationship building and to evaluating, by asking the guiding questions. A critical requirement for counselors committed to serving the best interests of the client is that counselor and client are talking about, focused on, and working toward achieving the same result, some specific aspect of client experience.

Because words can take on so many shades of meaning, counselors take special care to verify the accuracy and completeness of their understanding. We referred above to two tools frequently used by Erikka's counselor for verifying consensual meaning: *following responses* and *pinpointing*. These tools are also valuable in helping the counselor keep the process on track.

FOLLOWING RESPONSES

The task of understanding the client's concerns (Step 2) is crucial to success in subsequent steps in the process. Successful understanding requires attending to the client's verbal and nonverbal communications and verifying counselor understanding of the problematic concerns. Counselor use of *following responses* provides opportunities for client feedback to affirm or modify counselor understanding, thus increasing the fidelity of the counselor's image of what's going on in the client's life.

In the Erikka transcripts, you have probably noticed the relatively high frequency of counselor following responses throughout the entire session. Each use of a following response yields an opportunity for ongoing assessment of the accuracy of the counselor's understanding. Erikka's behaviors that let the counselor know his following responses were on track included head nods, saying "Yeah, yeah" or "Unh-hnh," and her continuing on-topic responses. The counselor has probably been responding to less overt clues as well, such as her facial expressions and tone of voice.

PINPOINTING

Another frequently used device for ensuring shared meaning is *pinpointing*. Pinpointing, as it yields clear, descriptive language, contributes to verifying that counselor and client are on the same track and leaves less room for persistent misunderstanding. Erikka's counselor frequently requested specific examples of her self-talk, feelings, and actions to validate that the two of them were focused on the same concerns.

Counselors need to constantly verify that the tasks in the counseling process are focused on the client's problematic experience in the client's world. *Following responses* and *pinpointing* are two tools that evoke client feedback regarding the accuracy of counselor understanding. It's hard to imagine a successful counseling outcome if the process has been flawed by counselor misunderstanding of the client's world.

The Erikka transcript exemplifies the kind of pervasive attention we believe counselors need to give to keep on track with their clients. This aspect of assessment, in map-territory terms, impels Dave to continually verify how well the map he is using (and constantly revising) fits the territory of the client's immediate concerns. The counselor's territory includes the client in the present moment of counseling as well as the client's problems outside counseling.

Counselors, in addition to drawing inferences from client behavior about how the process is going, can ask directly. The checkout procedure described in Chapter 10 exemplifies a means of directly assessing progress for each counselor task in the process.

Perhaps somewhat naively, we believe that counselors who remain committed to their role in determining *Where are we going? How can we get there?* and *How will we know we've arrived?* have best ensured their chances of staying on track with their clients.

Outcome Criteria: The Bottom Line

HOW AM I DOING?

We all want to know how we're doing. It is especially important for professional counselors because we advertise our ability to help people in distress. Counselees have the right to expect that we advertise truthfully, that we can, indeed, deliver what we advertise. The American Counseling Association's ethical standards require that members gather data on their effectiveness and be guided by the findings (American Counseling Association, 1995).

As counselors, we want to consider counselor performance from two perspectives: How am I doing with this client? What does my experience with this client teach me that can make me more effective with future clients? Implications of the first question are considered here. The second question regarding implications of current experience for work with future clients is considered in Chapter 12.

HOW DO I KNOW I AM EFFECTIVE?

As professional counselors, we determine our effectiveness ultimately by the extent to which our clients reach the objectives we agreed on. If the client's objective is unmet, we haven't been effective with that person. It's as simple as that. We like this definition of counselor effectiveness because if we were counselees, it would seem fair to us.

HOW CAN WE DETERMINE WHETHER COUNSELING WAS SUCCESSFUL?

We need to look to the counselee to answer this question. Specifically, we need to look at the performances or events named in the agreed-on objective to determine whether counseling has been successful. Counseling succeeds to the extent that the negotiated objective is met in the client's life.

Although looking at the client's life to assess results seems obvious, it's often hard to achieve. It usually assumes the client as a source of data. The modal number of counseling sessions counselors have with clients is one (Sue & Zane, 1987). For a number of clients, counselors get just one shot. Erikka is fairly representative in that way. Counselors who do seek follow-up data may find it very difficult to obtain.

In her life outside the counseling session, Erikka identified headaches, tasks left undone, and her dislike of herself, expressed in dissatisfaction with the way she was dealing with some things in her life, as areas she wanted to change. As counseling goals, she identified fewer headaches, "taking care of business," and being at a 10 on a 10-point scale of liking herself. Beginning at around CO139 in the transcript, Dave and Erikka work out how she can monitor her progress in these areas. The monitoring procedures they identify will serve as yardsticks against which the effectiveness of the proposed plans can be measured.

The counselor makes a point of setting up a way of learning from the client how the plan has worked out a week or two down the road. We think it's really important for counselors and clients to check in after a plan has been initiated. Sometimes all that's required is to schedule a phone call to give the client a chance to talk about how it went and to share in celebrating the effort. (*How did it go? . . . Sounds like you handled it well. Call me if you think we need to get together again.*)

Counselor Error

Counselors don't practice very long before discovering that not every client makes progress. In Chapter 3, one of the assumptions we stated was that lack of client

---

progress was the counselor's responsibility. One reason we prefer *counselor error* as an explanation for lack of client progress is that we can do something about it. Counselor error almost always indicates a need on the counselor's part for more information, for better understanding, for revalidating some critical assumption, and/or for more attention to understanding the client in the client's world. These simple words refer to a most difficult counselor task.

Sarason (1985) describes the challenge of clinical understanding like this:

> Understanding does not come full blown but rather is a result of grappling with three major obstacles: underestimating the scope and complexity of the process, failure to use one's own life experiences creatively, and resistance to the idea that the process is a never-ending one. (p. 191)

In the Erikka transcript, counselor Dave gives ample evidence that he is aware of each of these three primary hurdles to understanding. The major share of counselor time and effort was given to creating a comprehensive, high-fidelity map of Erikka's problematic territory. It was only through this careful, painstaking process that the central issues emerged. Complexity was added by Erikka's having attempted several times previously without success to get Robert out of her life. It's not unusual for clients to come to counseling for help with some persistent, recalcitrant issue.

The importance of the counselor's continually pursuing understanding was exemplified by the issue of Robert. It became necessary to clarify just what messages Erikka had sent to Robert, and in what ways, and with what effects on her views of herself as well as on her views of Robert.

Had Dave assumed at any time prior to that point that he understood Erikka's problem well, the result would surely have been different. Had he cut the process short, the client's issue with Robert could well have remained problematic. At best, the client might have returned to the counselor for a second session, giving him another chance to become effective. Clients do sometimes return in situations where they feel vulnerable and counselors are warm and well intentioned.

Because it's costly for clients to strive without progress, diminishing their sometimes meager stores of hope, we cannot overemphasize the role of counselor understanding in the counseling process. The process of understanding does not of itself guarantee desired outcomes, but it certainly seems a necessary precursor to planning for and achieving desired change.

Client priorities change—and counselors may not notice. One potential source of counselor error is the possibility that during the process of counseling, a client will change his or her mind about the counseling objective. That clients' perceptions of themselves and their own situations may change during counseling seems quite reasonable. Nevertheless, counselors sometimes assume that once an objective is set, it's set for the duration of counseling. Counselors need to be alert to the possibility that client perceptions and priorities are continually subject to change. Yesterday's answer to "Where are we going?" may not be the best answer today.

Nourish counselee expectations that you are interested in details about the effects of your work together. If plans are set up as experiments designed to check out assumptions (hypotheses) about how things will go, then getting data about the results of the experiments may come more easily.

We've never gotten in trouble by being too interested in the results. We *have* gotten in trouble by *assuming* we knew how things were going. Make it a habit to get feedback about staying on track and the effectiveness of plans for change. Check it out!

Mark Twain observed, "In the absence of fact, a firmly held belief will suffice." It's easy for us as counselors to *believe* we are helpful to our clients. Many of us assume relative to our clients that no news is good news. We say, "Things must be going well. He hasn't called for another appointment so there must not be a problem." It's as though we've paraphrased Twain: "In the absence of data, wishful thinking becomes fact."

For ethical professional counselors, "no news" and "wishful thinking" are *not* the evidence of counselor efficacy that must support the offer of professional services and continued practice. Make evaluation of your work a priority.

Counselors as well as clients need feedback about the consequences of their work. With Erikka, Dave's work throughout can be viewed as a hypothesis about how counselors help people change their lives outside the counseling session. Dave finds numerous occasions to monitor change in Erikka during the session, such as asking "How's your head feeling now?" His assumption that this process will have the desired postsession effects for Erikka will remain unsubstantiated unless and until Dave makes provision for gathering follow-up information about Erikka's later experience.

It is in their interest and the interest of their future clients for counselors to gather information about the effects of their work. An important factor in counselor efficacy is the counselor's expectation that he or she can help clients. Counselors who gather information from clients about the effects of their work together are in the strongest position to develop a well-founded confidence in their abilities as counselors. Wouldn't you prefer to be served by a counselor whose clients had told him or her of the positive changes counseling had effected in their lives?

ERIKKA TRANSCRIPT

Counselor Readiness

> I need to be as clear as possible about how Erikka experiences her distress.
>
> Erikka reports headaches and a "grindy" stomach as elements of her distress and as her purpose in seeking this session; we need to monitor these indicators as we work to see if we're on track.

We're hearing about things "stacking up"; we'll need to keep track of those things, and of their relationship to headaches, stomach.

The Interview

CO104: Do you think that's something you might do this weekend?

CL104: Um . . . Yeah. I think that's something that I'd *like* to do. I don't know. These [local] things still have to be done. It's a matter of leaving some things behind, in a way, or putting a pause on them and going off and doing the other things I need to do.

CO105: Robert's continued presence here is somewhat intentional. Is there anything you want to do with him for the remainder of this session?

CL105: Umm . . . I think his continued presence is going to be around for a *long* time. I don't know. I'd like to put him out of my sight for a while. That's what I'd like to do. That sounds so terrible.

CO106: Unh-hnn. . . . Go ahead and try that. Put him out of your sight.

CL106: (*starts pushing Robert toward the other side of the room, with Robert resisting but going; as she begins to ease the pressure, Robert starts coming back; she pushes harder; impasse*)

CO107: Is that sort of the way it feels? Is it an effort to put him out of your sight?

CL107: (*emphatic nod*) Big one.

CO108: A big one.

CL108: Huge. Yeah. Yeah. And it's this hard. It's harder, harder.

CO109: So is that realistic? Are you going to be able to put him out of your sight?

CL109: Maybe this far, just this far. Not even that far. (*drags Robert back toward "home" a few steps*) Maybe this far. Right there.

CO110: Would you stay there for a second, Robert? (*to CL*) Let's go sit down. Have we come up with anything that has to do with a plan that might help you work toward some of those things you wanted: fewer, possibly zero headaches; checklists; checking out your assumptions about the relationship between the headaches and the organization in your life?

CL110: I think the plan, I don't know if it can be termed a plan, but a recognition that I've had is that I let a lot of things stack up in the last couple of weeks, and I think it's all been in this kind of mode of "I can't even deal with those until I deal with Robert," but Robert has been something I've just kept . . . It's just going to be the same old thing. So in a way, I've let these things sit, and I just did what I felt good about. [CO: Um-hmm.] That just represents my recognition of what I've been doing and how these headaches have come about. I've let all this unfinished stuff surround me.

CO111: And what are a couple of things you might want to experiment with?

CL111: Definitely taking a look at where I can let some things rest for a while and attend to the main thing that's keeping me from doing all the other things I'm very capable of handling, and checking off on my list, [CO: Um-hmm.] which is dealing with Robert. And it's coming up real soon. It's not like it's a month from now. It's very immediate. So I know I'll be able to get to those things real soon afterward.

CO112: OK. So, are we talking about making that checklist and establishing some priorities before you go see Robert?

CL112: Um-hmm. I already feel I'm more interested about putting my energy into doing these things now because I can't keep thinking there's nothing to attend to with Robert. I know there is. And just with that knowledge now, I feel like there may be even a few things I can get to before I go there [CO: Um-hmm!] because I know I would be doing them afterward anyway. Now would be easier. Prioritizing them.

CO113: And that's something you know how to do, you've done in the past . . .

CL113: Yeah. Yeah.

CO114: And as far as Robert goes . . . (CL points to Robert and chuckles wryly) What . . .

CL114: He's just *looming* there, and I know, I just know what's going to happen.

CO115: How's your head feeling right now? [CL: Fine.] Stomach? [CL: Fine.] What are you saying about yourself, just to reflect on what we've been doing up here?

CL115: That I usually take care of things wonderfully, and I'm not taking care of them now. I'm doing a half-assed job of doing it. And on a scale of liking myself, I'm about at a 3 on a scale of 10.

CO116: What's it going to take for you to like yourself? What is it you want to rate yourself out of 10?

CL116: 10.

CO117: What's it going to take for you to get to a 10?

CL117:   Ummh, take care of things in the way I've been accustomed to, just dealing with them, and getting them done, and not having them lying around, . . . and facing this issue with Robert, and just getting it out of the way and moving on, instead of having it there, and in my life all the time.

CO118:   OK. Are you ready to do that, to face that issue?

CL118:   Oh, yes! I have to. I have to.

CO119:   Why don't you go tell him that? I'll wait here for you.

CL119:   What, that I'm ready to face the issue? (*CO nods. CL walks over to where Robert has been standing and faces him*) I'm leaving everything else behind right now and I'm just talking to you. And, umm, we're just going to figure this out and I'm going to tell you just how it is with me, living in Tucson, and you, living here. It's just not going to continue. I don't feel real good about what's happening. My independence is something you haven't been able to get hold of. You haven't been able to understand it for so long. It's only going to get more bitter. It just keeps getting worse and worse. And I don't feel good about what's happening between us, at all. So . . . Maybe one day we can be friends, but I know right now we can't be friends. (*CO walks over to stand beside CL as she finishes speaking*)

CO120:   I decided to join you. I'm going to ask you to reverse roles, just for a second. (*CL stands with head down, hands clasped in front of her, tears welling up in her eyes, for several seconds*) What's going on right now?

CL120:   (*hands to face, covering eyes, crying, speaking through her tears*) I just know, I just know how upset he's going to be.

CO121:   Unh-hnn. . . . I guess if we reversed roles that's one thing he'd probably feel, how upset he's going to be. . . . (*CL in tears*) Is that what keeps this thing going on and on and on is your knowing how upset he's going to be? (*pause; CL's tears are lessening*) Why don't you go ahead and say that to him.

CL121:   (*speaking through sniffles*) I just know how hurt and disappointed you are, but I'm sorry, I can't keep this going. (*pause*) [CO: Because if I keep this going . . .] Because if I keep this going I'm just not taking care of myself and what I want to do. . . . I'm being dishonest with both of us. . . . It's not fair. It's not fair to you and it's not fair to me. And I'm sorry. . . .

CO122:   What's going on right now?

CL122:   It's just kind of sad.

CO123:   Kind of sad. Unh-hnn.

CL123: Disappointed in myself that I couldn't live up to what he wanted. . . .

CO124: And one thing I'm saying about that to myself is . . .

CL124: I didn't come through for him. I let him down.

CO125: Say that to him.

CL125: I couldn't be what you wanted me to be, and I just, I can't be that. It's not *me*. And I just let you down. . . .

CO126: It's tough to be me in a relationship with you.

CL126: *Yeah.* It's not even me. I don't even know me. I have to pretend to be something with you. . . . [CO: And what that pretending does to me is . . .] It makes me feel dishonest, and it makes me feel rotten that you don't really love *me*, because you don't love the part of me that goes out there and is independent, and goes after what I want, and moves away from you . . . and . . . talks to other males. I mean, it's ridiculous!

CO127: (*placing a hand on each of CL's shoulders and pressing down*) And it feels like this.

CL127: (*softly*) Yeah. (*CO has Robert, facing CL, put his hands on her shoulders*)

CO128: And there's something about it that's tough to give up.

CL128: Yeah. . . . 'Cause there's still that feeling that I'm being cared for in a way that's real strong and real watchful . . . secure . . . Keeps me in line . . . (*several big sighs*)

CO129: What are you feeling?

CL129: *This* is how he feels, and . . . breaking away from it . . . I don't know, he's been around so long. [CO: You're kind of used to this.] Um-hmm. (*sighs. CL reaches up and moves Robert's hands down from her shoulders, and Robert moves them back; and then once again*)

CO130: What am I going to do about all that stuff that I like, being cared for, being involved in a relationship I'm used to?

CL130: I don't know. I go back like I have.

CO131: Um-hmm. . . . It's easy.

CL131: Yeah. (*sighs*)

CO132: How's my head feeling right now?

CL132: Sore.

CO133: Sore. Right here? (*places hands on CL's temples*)

CL133: Um-hmm.

CO134: Stomach?

CL134:   Not really anything. (*CL's voice is softer now*)

CO135:   (*to Robert*) Let me step in right here (*facing CL*) What do you want to *do* with this at this point?

CL135:   I don't know. There's not really very much I can do, except to decide what I'm going to do. [CO: Decide what you're going to do.] And then do it. . . . That doesn't have much validity right now, because it's something I did last spring, and it's something I did the year before that.

CO136:   Did you decide what you were going to do? (*CL nods*) Did you *do* it? [CL: Un-hnn.] And then what happened?

CL136:   (*ruefully*) I went home for the summer [CO: Un-hnn.] and everything was there. And it was, yes, like we're going to be different. [CO: Un-hnn.] And I came back with all this vim and vigor. And it's no different.

CO137:   So is it kind of hard to trust yourself, trust that you can decide what to do and do it?

CL137:   (*nods agreement*) And this is the only area of my life that's like that because . . .

CO138:   One of those areas where it doesn't seem like me?

CL138:   Yeah . . . yeah (*nods agreement*)

CO139:   (*asks "Robert" to sit back down; CO and CL take seats again*) How can you make this weekend seem like it's *you*? The you that you want to be, the you that you want to rate a 10.

CL139:   Ummm. . . . Honest keeps coming through, and I feel like when the breakup has happened before it hasn't really been an honest one. The reasons haven't been honest. The reasons have been temporary ones. And that's just coming through now, it's been temporary.

CO140:   So you might have some reasons or some things to say that might be different [CL: Um-hmm.] this time, [CL: Um-hmm.] a little more true to you. [CL: Um-hmm. Yeah. Yeah.] Well, we're talking about making lists and checking things out. Do you want to make a list of those reasons?

CL140:   (*softly*) Yeah, yeah. That would be a good idea.

CO141:   Could you do that before you go to L.A. this weekend?

CL141:   Yeah. Yeah. I'd want to. (*10-second pause*)

CO142:   One thing I have a sense of is that we've been working pretty hard here for a while, and you've been working hard, and we've managed to get through all six steps of the process. (*CL chuckles*) I guess I need to check in and see what else we have to do.

CL142: Not much, really. Since I'm a master at list making, I know I'll be able to do that fine. So I don't need any extra skills or practice at making lists. I know what to take care of as far as that's concerned.

CO143: OK. How are you going to work this out in terms of keeping track of headaches and also figuring out what kind of correlation there might be between your taking care of some of this structure we've been talking about and your headaches? Do you have a plan for that?

CL143: Once again, I just see some sort of chart or a list, maybe putting down the parts of the day. My mornings seem to be clumped, my afternoons are clumped, and my evenings—not hourly so much as just a morning time, an afternoon time. Ummm, maybe documenting it that way. Did I have a headache in the morning, and what did I do that morning. Really, looking at my parts of the day, and what I've done, and then if I have a headache.

CO144: Have you done that before with anything? Just to get some feeling for whether you think you can do that.

CL144: Oh yeah, I feel I can do that fine.

They agree on a time to get together for a follow-up session.

Debriefing

OBSERVER: I was disappointed when Erikka wouldn't completely put Robert out of her sight. Why didn't the counselor put more pressure on her to move him out of her life if that's what she really wanted?

COUNSELOR: While I heard Erikka *talk* about wanting to put Robert out of sight, I was also paying attention to her experience— the thoughts and feelings indicating that at this time and place, she is not ready to make a complete break with him. In other words, her *map*—"Get Robert out of my life"—was not fitting the *territory*—crying, feeling cared for and secure, not trusting herself. If I'm responding to my own agenda about what Erikka *should* do, I'm not able to respond to her experience and readiness to change.

OBSERVER: How does the counselor know whether this was a successful session? It seems that there are still some unresolved issues.

COUNSELOR: I heard Erikka say some things that matched up with her goals and objectives. She reported relief from headaches and stomach distress. She feels capable of accomplishing a plan to monitor her headaches and their relationship to daily events. She reports that she has a better idea of what to communicate to Robert and how to do it when she sees him.

OBSERVER: How does the counselor know that Erikka will do what she says she is going to do?

COUNSELOR: I don't. Erikka will have to let me know whether this counseling session made a difference in her life.

SUGGESTIONS FOR INTEGRATING ACTIVITIES

As a culminating exercise, we suggest that you and a fellow student agree to serve as each other's "client" in a counseling relationship that takes you through all six steps of the Counseling Process Model. Most of our students find that this exercise works best with two or sometimes three sessions a week apart.

We ask each counselor to tape-record each session and to use these tapes in an extensive self-analysis of the counseling process. A rather lengthy form has evolved as the Case Report for this exercise. (See Forms 11.1 through 11.6 on pages 197–208.) Although it may initially appear overwhelming, trust us. Our students consistently evaluate this experience as very helpful and tell us it was well worth the effort that goes into doing it.

When we assign this culminating exercise, we also include a scheduled review session with each pair of client-counselor students once they have completed the assignment. At the review session with the instructor, each counselor has about 20 minutes to present the case. (We like having the student-client available during the review as an additional source of data.)

CONSULTATION TIME

Scenario 1

Client does not show up for appointment. The counselor calls the client.

COUNSELOR: Hello, Emelia. I'm calling because you missed your appointment yesterday.

CLIENT: I just didn't want to go. Things don't seem to be getting any better and I feel like I'm wasting my time.

(text continues on page 209)

FORM 11.1 Case report form

CASE REPORT

Step 1. *(Initiate Counseling* has been accomplished when the exercise begins.)

Step 2. *Problem/predicament/complaint (in counselee's own words)* (Attach verbatim transcript containing sequence of five of the best counselee-counselor exchanges in which counselor does the following.)

   A. As first described:

   B. Changed to (if changed):

   C. Pinpointed example of counselee problem: (attach Form 11.2, Pinpointing Actions, Thoughts, and Feelings)

Step 3. *Goal (in counselee's own words)*

   A. General goal:

   B. Negotiated objective

      (1) *What* is to be done?

      (2) *When/where* will it happen?

      (3) *How much/how well* will it happen?

(continued)

(4) *Evidence* of progress/success will be . . .

C. Counselee assets, strengths, resources:

D. How does counselee culture influence view of problem? Goal?

Step 4. *Plan* (how the objective is to be achieved)
   A. Initial plan (attach Form 11.3, Action Plan)

   B. Revised plan (*if* revised, show changes):

Step 5. *Performance* (counselee performance of tasks in plan)
   A. What did you do to increase probability of counselee performance of tasks in agreed-on plan?

   B. Level of counselee confidence in/commitment to plan (0–10):

   C. To what extent did counselee do the planned tasks?

    D. Did unexpected changes occur in counselee performance? How did you respond?

    E. How does counselee culture affect planning? Performance?

Step 6. *Results*

    A–B. (attach Form 11.4, Evaluation of Results)

    C. Unexpected Results:

FORM 11.2 Pinpointing actions, thoughts, and feelings

ACTIONS, THOUGHTS, AND FEELINGS

1. Focus on the part of your interview in which you are eliciting the counselee's report of the actions, thoughts, and feelings associated with the "target feeling" in *one single example* of the problem situation.

2. Using the audiotape as a source, list below the counselee's actions, thoughts, and feelings reported in the order in which the counselee *originally experienced them*. Check action, thought, or feeling for each event reported. Circle the "target feeling," one or more of the problematic feelings that prompted the counselee to seek help.

   A. When, where, and with whom did the episode occur?

   _____

   _____

   _____

   B. In counselee's words from the the transcript:

                                                    Action Thought Feeling

   (1) _____

        _____   ___   ___   ___

   (2) _____

        _____   ___   ___   ___

   (3) _____

        _____   ___   ___   ___

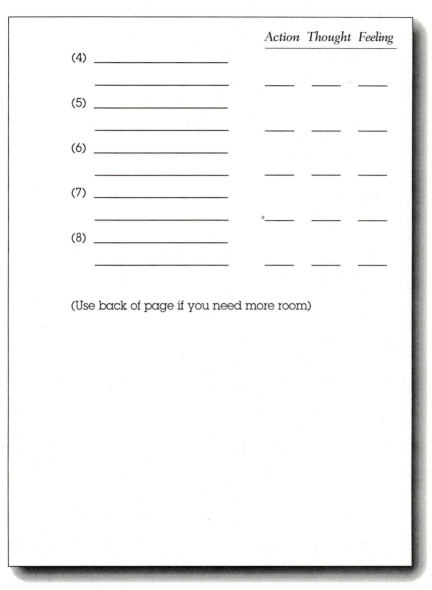

Action Thought Feeling

(4) _____

_____   ____ ____ ____

(5) _____

_____   ____ ____ ____

(6) _____

_____   ____ ____ ____

(7) _____

_____   ____ ____ ____

(8) _____

_____   ____ ____ ____

(Use back of page if you need more room)

FORM 11.3　Action plan form

ACTION PLAN:　COUNSELING OBJECTIVE

OBJECTIVE

What?

When/Where?

How well/much?

Final step:

Preceding step:

Preceding step:

Preceding step:

Preceding step:

Preceding step:

Preceding step:

Preceding step:

Preceding step:

Start by:

PREREQUISITE CONDITIONS/ASSUMPTIONS

1. *Objective:*

2. *Resources:*

3. *Motivation:*

4. *Self-Efficacy:*

FORM 11.4 Evaluation of results

EVALUATION OF RESULTS

1. Compare results *expected* with results *obtained*.
   A. Objective is . . .
   B. Current status is . . .

2. Is objective met?
   A. Yes—CELEBRATE!
   B. No (go to Step 3)

3. Is progress satisfactory?
   A. Yes, continue plan (go to Step 4) because _____

   _____

   B. No (go to Step 3C), because _____

   _____

   C. Did counselee perform the plan (Step 5)?
      (1) Yes . . . review/revise plan (go to Step 4)

      Yes, but _____

      (2) No . . . (go to 5A)

         Objective valid?   Resources available?

         Valid incentive?   Self-efficacy for plan?

      No, because _____

      _____

4. Set new objective?
   No. Terminate counseling? _____
   Yes: _____

FORM 11.5   Counselor performance self-evaluation

COUNSELOR PERFORMANCE SELF-EVALUATION

Step 2.   Following responses (transcript).

- Did counselor acknowledge counselee messages? Stated or implied feeling?

- Did counselor stay at counselee level of detail?

- Did counselor show evidence of empathic understanding?

Step 2C.   Pinpointing. Write the inferable "prescription" of actions, thoughts, and feelings that culminate in the target feeling:

Step 3B.   Negotiated objective.

- *What* the counselee is to achieve is:

- Evidence of progress/success will be:

Step 4A.   Action Plan.

- Is each step clearly described; *action* indicated?
  Yes   No

(continued)

- Are the steps in logical order, functionally related?

  Yes   No

- Will doing the Plan lead to the desired objective?

  Yes   No

- Are important assumptions identified?

  Yes   No

Step 5A. Preparing counselee for successful Plan performance. (*How* was each element assured?)

- Did counselee know the objective?
- Were sufficient resources available to counselee?
- Did counselee have sufficient incentive?
- Did counselee have self-efficacy for performing the Plan?

Step 6. Evidence of successful counseling is/will be:

FORM 11.6 Case report critique

CASE REPORT CRITIQUE

1. How do you explain the results attained with this counselee?

2. How did similarities/differences in counselor and counselee cultural heritage affect the process?

3. What did you learn that you might use another time?

   A. About yourself as a helper?

   B. About *understanding* someone?

   C. About what *helping* means?

4. Your comments about the experience:

(continued)

A. What worked?

B. What didn't work as expected?

C. What can I do to improve my skills?

D. What would I like to know?

Please rewind your tape cassette so that when it is dropped into the tape player it will start at the place your first transcript begins. Thanks; it really helps!

What are the counselor's options?

- "You sound like you're very discouraged and don't see how counseling will be able to help. Can you tell me about what's been happening since last week's session?"
- "I'm concerned about not being able to work with you to help you make the changes you want to make. With your permission, I'd like to discuss our work together with my supervisor and call you back afterward."
- "I don't see how you can make progress if you don't show up for your appointment. Why don't we reschedule and talk about this in the next session?"
- "I want to learn more about how I can be helpful to you. What do you mean when you say that things don't seem to be getting any better?"
- How would you respond?

Scenario 2

COUNSELOR: And how did you do with your weight-loss plan this week?

CLIENT: The same as last week, the week before, and the week before that . . . Lousy. I didn't follow my diet, never made it to the gym, and forgot to practice that "self-talk" stuff until this morning as I was getting ready to come to our session.

COUNSELOR: There's not much evidence of progress toward your objective to lose 25 pounds.

CLIENT: Actually, I've gained seven pounds since I started seeing you a month ago.

What are the counselor's options?

- "Is losing weight really that important to you? How motivated are you to reach your goal?"
- "I'm concerned about our lack of progress. Can we step back and evaluate my counseling services over the past month to determine what I'm doing that is and isn't being helpful to you?"
- "I'm wondering if we should discuss a referral to another counselor who might be more effective in helping you to lose weight?"
- "I'd like to take some time to discuss our lack of progress with the other counselors in the agency and get some suggestions on how to proceed. I want to do some reading as well to be sure that I'm aware of other approaches that have been effective. How do you feel about this plan?"
- What other responses might you have?

REFERENCES

American Counseling Association. (1995). *Code of ethics and standards of practice*. Alexandria, VA: Author.

Sarason, S. B. (1985). *Caring and compassion in clinical practice*. San Francisco: Jossey-Bass.

Sue, S., & Zane, N. (1987). The role of culture and cultural techniques in psychotherapy. *American Psychologist, 42,* 37–45.

PART

3

Professional
Development

CHAPTER 12

Promoting Professional Growth

In practical situations what you need to know is what you need to know. You need to know what to do. And that is all. —Wendell Johnson

We started in Chapter 1 by telling you our view of the process of becoming a counselor—as the melding of person, knowledge, and skills. Now, after going through each step in the Counseling Process Model, it's time to address matters related to your using your counseling experience to improve your counseling effectiveness.

Most of what we know about how counselors gain effectiveness has been learned with students in practicum and internship supervision seminars. The issues we address in this chapter are those that have seemed most important to our students and graduates. The first part continues the focus on evaluation, which we began in Chapter 11. The emphasis here is on what we can learn from our experience with one client that may help us do a better job with the next. We close with a look at some issues lying in wait when you begin actual work as a professional counselor.

What Accounts for Counseling Success?

To use the map/territory metaphor once more, we see counselors as building maps that reflect their perceptions and beliefs of the counseling territory. Counselors use these maps to guide their thoughts and actions during the process of counseling clients. Through classes, reading, discussion, and experiences with clients, counselor maps are extended, elaborated, and amended. Some maps, or parts of maps, seem to go for extended periods without question or revision, apparently losing their metaphoric "as if " quality. At their worst, some counseling maps appear to become Procrustean frameworks in which every client is embedded.

We are very interested in how our counseling students build and revise their maps of the counseling territory. How our students view their experiences and how their experiences become incorporated in their map of counseling bear directly on what their next client can expect, how that person will fare in counseling. Predictably, we are advocates of regular supervision of one's work as a counselor.

Following a successful counseling experience, a question we like to ask counselors in supervision is, "How do you account for your success with this client?" The importance of this question is obvious if one accepts Kelley's (1958) view that behavior is hypothesis. Counselor behavior in counseling is analogous to a series of "If . . . , then . . ." statements, generalizable for counselors as "If I do or say _____ then counseling will be successful." If indeed counselor hypotheses are in the service of counseling success, the beliefs the counselor holds about what leads to success are crucial. We, too, advance beliefs about what leads to success in counseling. We hope you recognize the ideas in this book as hypotheses to be examined, refined, and replaced as your experience leads to more effective ones.

Comments from Successful Counselors

Often, we ask counselors how they understand and explain their success. In this section, we provide some of their answers and discuss them. Their responses suggest the maps they are constructing of their counseling territory as they understand it.

"The client was easy to work with." When asked to clarify "easy to work with," counselors say that these clients behaved as though they knew what counseling was for—to focus on their own life and take responsibility for finding ways to be more successful and less uncomfortable. In short, easy-to-work-with clients acknowledged that they had a problem or need, and they wanted to do something about it.

"The client was 'motivated' to work." When asked to define *motivated*, these counselors described motivated clients as those who not only talked about their important issues but also disclosed very personal experiences related to their concerns. Motivated clients were willing to express difficult, sometimes painful, feelings in counseling sessions. Their willingness to risk self-disclosure of thoughts and feelings and past actions to their counselor indicated their motivation to work.

"The counselee did the plan," or *"The client came up with a better plan and did that."* Counselors report that successful clients left their sessions intending to take action in pursuit of the desired outcome. They knew what to do and how to do it. They came back to the next session reporting that they had followed through on the plan, making any adjustments necessary to accomplish the objective. These clients reported increased confidence and ability to devise and follow through on plans over time.

"The client really wanted . . ." Counselors observed that clients who *really* wanted to address particular concerns and accomplish their objectives acted in ways that appeared congruent with their expressed intentions. In other words, these clients were not saying one thing in the session and doing another during or after that session. Counselors reported that successful clients' actions validated their expressed intentions.

Please note that all these counselor comments credit or attribute the reason for successful counseling outcomes to the client. Counseling success in the counselors' views resulted from clarity of client intent, client capabilities, the intensity of client commitment, and client perceived self-efficacy.

We see counselors' tendencies to explain counseling results in terms of client attributes as a good news/bad news situation. We'll consider the good news first. Counselors do recognize the reality that clients' lives change through client effort. We each move our own muscles; no one can move them for us.

Further, our counselors seem to have a good grasp of four essential elements of successful behavior change (described earlier in Step 5, Support the Plan). Thus, counselors' linking client focus, client motivation, and so on, to desirable new client behavior appears quite reasonable. It fits what counselors have observed when clients achieve desired change.

Questions for Successful Counselors

We believe, however, that counselor beliefs or attributions implying that the present successful status is due to the client reflect only part of the story. Attributions that focus on the client may serve to deflect attention from the *counselor's* participation in this interactive relationship. We believe it is important for counselors to be able to articulate their participation in the process of successful client change. We ask our successful student counselors more questions:

OUR QUESTION:	Had the client made the desired change *before* working with you?
STUDENT RESPONSE:	Obviously not.
OUR QUESTION:	Then, how was this client so easy for you to work with if he or she had not been successful earlier?
STUDENT RESPONSE:	It's important for the client to believe that working with a counselor will make a difference. Counselors need to convey a commitment to *serve* the client with individual attention to his or her concerns and goals, personal needs, and resources. It is not only important for the client to have a clear objective to feel successful; the counselor needs to be involved in an outcome-referenced process to support his or her own belief that counseling is making a difference in the client's life.

OUR QUESTION: *In the case of the "motivated" client,* how did it happen that this client was motivated to work?

STUDENT RESPONSE: Clients come to counseling expecting help on issues of consequence *to them*. Counselors who attend to these issues and help clients to identify desired outcomes that are positive and meaningful to them will have motivated clients. Counselor attending, following, and pinpointing skills nourish clients' experience of being understood and expectations of successful change.

This process sustains the counselor's motivation as well. The counselor's total commitment to understanding why the client is there and what he or she hopes to accomplish encourages the attention and self-talk that the counselor needs to fulfill the role and responsibilities of an effective helper.

Focusing on client needs and desired outcomes prevents the counselor from being sidetracked by labeling, stereotyping, and value conflicts that sap counselor motivation and contribute to burnout.

OUR QUESTION: How did the client come up with a better plan *and* do it?

STUDENT RESPONSE: Clients are encouraged to see themselves as an impressive reservoir of experience, strategies, and skills. How can clients mobilize their strengths and compensate for limitations to achieve their objectives? When the counselor functions as consultant and catalyst to planning rather than as a prescriber of plans, clients become the architects of their plans. They have ownership and need no one's permission to adapt their plans as needed.

Every counselor needs to feel that he or she has the resources available to navigate the counseling process successfully. Counseling works best when the counselor has the energy, information, skills, and self-confidence to follow the Counseling Process Model. Professional training, literature, and supervision are invaluable resources for professional growth, especially when the counselor's experience doesn't appear to match up with a particular client's needs ("Uh-Oh! . . . My client has just told me he is HIV positive and I've never worked with . . . I'd better look for some help.").

OUR QUESTION: How did your client come to believe that he or she was capable of reaching his or her objective?

STUDENT RESPONSE: We consistently convey the respect and support to the client that says, "You can do it. . . ." This respect is

---

communicated through a process that puts the client in the driver's seat: "This is your life and you are capable of identifying your uppermost concerns, understanding what changes are needed to successfully address these concerns, and mobilizing the resources and plan to accomplish these changes in your world."

Clients' belief in their own ability to accomplish tasks and objectives is nurtured by their counselor's efforts to attend to and pinpoint strengths and accomplishments as well as concerns and limitations.

And there's nothing like a strong sense of counselor self-efficacy to increase counselor effectiveness. Counselors need to practice appropriate self-talk and to become skillful and candid reviewers of their own performance. We advocate self-monitoring procedures that give as much or more attention to skills and accomplishments as to skill deficits and perceived shortcomings. Peer and supervisory relationships that support counselor self-efficacy make more sense to us than those that undermine counselor confidence.

Counselors who think about *how* they happen to have clients who are easy to work with, motivated, and able to come up with new responses to problematic situations are counselors who are likely to be open to change and growth. They grow by acknowledging their own influence in the counseling relationship, building their repertoire of relationship skills, and being ready to examine *their* contribution to situations where counseling bogs down and confusion sets in.

So, how do you increase the probability that your clients will be focused, motivated, and so on? We think the best way to find yourself working with successful clients is to use the client-centered approach we have described in this book. This approach assumes that the most productive counseling relationship is one in which the client is convinced that the counselor's primary concern is for the client's best interests, and both participants share a common purpose, a purpose the client believes is important. The relationship results in a means of achieving the client's purpose, using resources available to the client in a way that is credible in the client's world.

Distractions for Counselors

Consider the following terms: *defensive, unmotivated, unfocused, resistant.* Be honest. Who comes to mind as you say these words: counselor or client?

We earlier commented that counselor attributional tendencies were a good news/bad news situation. The bad news as we see it also has to do with counselor tendencies to look only to the client.

As counselors, we also tend to attribute *lack* of counseling progress to clients. These are representative of comments we've heard from counselors who were unhappy with the way counseling was going:

"He's in denial; resistant; unmotivated."

"She's a borderline; what can you expect?"
"She's a controller; passive-aggressive."
"He's playing games."

We believe there are strong cultural mechanisms that systematically bias our perception and understanding of the world and of our participation in it. We offer here two observations in support of the existence of counselor perceptual bias. First, in our experience, most counselors report that the terms that opened this section evoked "client." In counseling, we're accustomed to hearing terms such as these applied to clients, not counselors. Second, the counselor culture is replete with rhetoric enabling us to blame clients when the counseling process isn't meeting our expectations. Counselors have an elaborate vocabulary that refers to clients who disappoint them.

It is difficult to be an accurate participant/observer. We are struck with the importance and the continuing challenge of discriminating between inference and observation: inside world and outside world. We believe that counselors who view their work as hypothesis, subject to validation in the lives of their clients, will become increasingly effective and efficient helpers. We hope and believe that ideas described earlier in this book can be helpful to counselors attempting to monitor and learn from their own performance.

Counseling in the Real World:
Ideals, Environment, and Integrity

There are always issues you will encounter when, having learned the counseling basics, you begin actual work in a job where you are called *counselor*. We have presented in this book what we believe is an effective approach to professional counseling, along with the assumptions on which it rests and the conditions under which it can be ethically practiced. We believe that only as we are scrupulous in honoring the assumptions and conditions that undergird our view of professional counseling do our clients have a reasonable chance of actually receiving the help we advertise. In other words, what we present in this book represents our ideals as professional counselors.

Our self-esteem as counselors rests in large part on the extent to which we see ourselves living up to our ideals. Practicing in the world as it is today provides counselors with many encounters that challenge their ideals of service. We hear statements like these:

"We're expected to bill 40 units of service each week. The paperwork keeps me here an extra 2 hours each night."
"By the time these clients have negotiated the system and get to me, they're so used to being told what to do they won't open up."
"I get one 50-minute session with each client. That's all."

"Can anyone suggest an intervention I can use with the brothers and sisters? They've been court-referred for 10 sessions."

Counselors who make such statements sound frustrated, discouraged, even angry. They became counselors to help people improve their lives, and they find themselves with clients and in settings where their best efforts seem to achieve little. Like the counselor who made the last comment, they often seem to think that somehow, if only they had the elusive right intervention, they could achieve success.

One of us took a job as a school counselor right out of graduate school. During that first year, two situations consistently recurred, each adding to the counselor's confusion. Part of the counselor's job involved reviewing the midterm "failure" notices and calling those students with multiple F's to the counselor's office. When the student appeared at the counselor's door and said, "I got this notice to come down this period," the counselor would respond with something like this, "Hi. Come in and sit down. . . . How are things going? Anything you'd like to talk about?" The student would generally respond, "Things are going OK." And then, silence. The counselor would think, "Now what do I say? Thanks for coming in?"

The other recurring event involved those students who, given the choice of a 2-day suspension or visiting the counselor, had opted for the counselor. These encounters went pretty much like the others.

COUNSELOR: Hi. How are things going?

STUDENT: Mr. Hanlon said I could come here instead of taking a suspension.

COUNSELOR: OK. Anything you'd like to talk about?

STUDENT: No. Things are OK now. Do I have to come back here again?

It took a while for this counselor to discover that he was playing "Let's Pretend," operating from a set of expectations, a counseling map, that didn't fit the real-world territory where the students were living. The counselor was acting as if these situations were beginning counseling relationships. They were not. The students' appearances were mandated by other people. This was the "counselor's office"; the "counselor" was there; students were called in or referred for "counseling"—none of this meant that *students'* expectations included participation in *counseling*.

Calling It Counseling Doesn't Make It Counseling

What is called counseling (or therapy) is an increasingly popular and diverse menu of activities and conditions. Courts, employers, parents, and social institutions include "counseling" as an option (intervention) for problematic people and people with problems. As limited resources are stretched further, administrators set service delivery rules (eligible diagnoses, duration, deadlines, service locations, and so on) without much evident sense of how their decisions profoundly affect possible counseling outcomes. It's still all called counseling (or therapy), and people called counselors (or therapists) are part of "service delivery teams." We see much of what's happening today as more pervasive examples of "Let's Pretend"—namely, "Let's pretend that people we call counselors, doing what we call counseling, under the conditions we set, can actually develop counseling relationships through which clients can experience success."

Our point is that it's easy to see how counselors today can become frustrated and confused. The school counselor in our example was frustrated and ineffective because he didn't notice that assumptions and conditions fundamental to initiating a professional counseling relationship were not present in the real world of the student and the counselor. We believe that unless and until these essential conditions are met, there can be no effective counseling relationship.

Both of the previous examples called for mandated participation. So-called clients found themselves required by others to appear for "counseling" (or "therapy"). Because of a number of social, political, and economic factors, mandated counseling appears on the increase. In our view, involuntary counseling is incongruous both with the philosophical and ethical heritage of counseling and with the theoretical and empirical foundations from which current practice derives. In short, we view counseling as something done *with* people rather than *to* people or *for* people.

Whether mandated by courts, parents, agency, or partner, a person's appearance at a counselor's office brings with it, at best, the *possibility* of a counseling relationship. In our school counselor example, mandatory appearance at the school counselor's office represented a potential opportunity for a student to choose to become involved in counseling. To get to the point where the student was capable of real informed choice about participation, the school counselor must recognize that *potential* for a counseling relationship exists in the first moments of contact. Acknowledging the student's immediate realities seems a crucial first step.

COUNSELOR: You're probably wondering why I called you in today.

STUDENT: Yeah. What's this all about?

COUNSELOR: Part of my job here at Ashland High School is to offer help to students who might need it. I was going through the midterm failure notices and . . . (and so on)

We'd like the student and all our potential clients to experience counselor empathy in the process of establishing common understanding about what each is bringing to this contact, what counseling might offer, and under what conditions. When we've done our best to establish the potential benefits and costs of counseling participation for this individual, the choice of whether to continue is his or hers.

In the school counselor example, the school administration would have supported the counselor's offering these mandated participants informed choice about entering a counseling relationship. Some situations don't support this option with mandated participants. For example, when the court says "30 days, $1,000, or 10 weeks of counseling," those who choose counseling are expected to appear for 10 sessions.

When we do provide services under forced-choice conditions, we prefer not to think or act as if it's counseling. We don't want the participants, officers of the court, or any others involved to think so either. We want to name these sessions more accurately, to keep us on the same page with the participants. Instead of language that refers to "counseling services" provided by "counselors," we prefer "leader" or "monitor" or "caseworker" to refer to the person in charge (keeps records; files reports), and we think in terms of "participants" or "members" who attend "program sessions" or "group meetings" or "discussions."

We think it is important that we do all we can to preserve counseling as a professional relationship. We would wish prospective counselees to know they are the masters; it is they who decide whether to participate, and in what ways, and toward what ends.

Counseling is a process that can help those who choose to use it to become stronger and more capable. At best, counselors can help people find the means to come closer to realizing a greater measure of personal satisfaction in their world. At its heart, professional counseling assumes and respects the capability, integrity, and right of self-determination of individuals in a democratic society. Otherwise, it's not counseling.

What about the Mental Health Language and Culture?

For beginning counselors, agency and hospital settings can be like a foreign country where the counselor may experience a kind of "culture shock." Counselors encounter human service workers and administrators with different ways of thinking, different language, and different values and expectations. Many counselors spend part or all of their professional lives working within a system (the mental health culture) that has patterns of speech and thought that appear to reflect assumptions and beliefs different from some of those presented here. The language and customs of some mental health "cultures" may be very different from the language and customs of the counselor following this book's counseling process. For example, some mental health systems use the *Diagnostic and Statistical Manual of Mental Disorders* (DSM-IV) (American Psychiatric Association, 1994) as the framework for assessment, treatment planning, and payment for services rendered. These organizations will use a very different language from that of a system that encourages the pinpointing of specific thoughts, feelings, and actions to identify problems and develop consensus about counseling goals and strategies.

How can a counselor respond when he or she encounters persons or systems with perhaps fundamentally different views of counseling? Counselors respond in different ways. Some flee, seeking out more familiar territory. Some counselors "go native." They become immersed in the new culture, learning the talk and the walk of their new community, giving up the heritage they brought from home so they can blend with the new. Some counselors attempt to convert the new system, changing what they don't like. It's probably apparent that none of these coping methods is satisfactory.

Choosing an environment in which to work and adapting to differences in the workplace is a difficult process. We believe that what's needed first is a clear understanding of ourselves—our beliefs, our values, our own identity as counselors and how we relate to other people. Next, we must begin to build an understanding of the beliefs, language, rules, and behaviors of the workplace. Being clear about one's own counselor identity (assumptions, language, beliefs, behaviors) best equips one for encounters with different modes of expression. Our own clear map of the counseling territory helps us locate and understand how new ideas relate to the familiar, how to translate new events in terms familiar to us, and finally, how to integrate a new culture in ways that preserve our integrity, our identity as counselors, and our ideals.

The culture shock some counselors experience when they encounter individuals and institutions with different understandings and expectations signals an opportunity for learning and growth. We recommend an attitude of openness to learning. The process we describe as collegial confrontation in Chapter 7 is a powerful mechanism for examining apparent differences, resolving misunderstanding, establishing common ground, and helping counselors maintain their ideals in the workplace.

In the preface to this book, we stated that our mission is to help you think like a counselor and act like a counselor. We are eagerly curious about the meld of person, knowledge, and skills you're achieving as you work to become a counselor. Anything you could tell us about your interaction with these materials would be sincerely appreciated. Your willingness to communicate your experience will greatly assist our ability to account for our successes and limitations in supporting counselor training and professional development.

REFERENCES

American Psychiatric Association. (1994). *Diagnostic and statistical manual of mental disorders* (4th ed.). Washington, DC: Author.

Kelley, G. A. (1958). Man's construction of his alternatives. In G. Lindzey (Ed.), *The assessment of human motives*. New York: Rinehart.

APPENDIX A
Code of Ethics
American Counseling Association

Preamble

The American Counseling Association is an educational, scientific and professional organization whose members are dedicated to the enhancement of human development throughout the life span. Association members recognize diversity in our society and embrace a cross-cultural approach in support of the worth, dignity, potential, and uniqueness of each individual.

The specification of a code of ethics enables the association to clarify to current and future members, and to those served by members, the nature of the ethical responsibilities held in common by its members. As the code of ethics of the association, this document establishes principles that define the ethical behavior of association members. All members of the American Counseling Association are required to adhere to the Code of Ethics and the Standards of Practice. The Code of Ethics will serve as the basis for processing ethical complaints initiated against members of the association.

As Revised by Governing Council, April 1995 Effective July 1, 1995. Reprinted from *ACA Code of Ethics and Standards of Practice*, pp. 1–19. Copyright © 1995 ACA. Reprinted with permission. No further reproduction authorized without written permission of the American Counseling Association.

Section A:
The Counseling Relationship

A.1. Client Welfare

    a. Primary Responsibility. The primary responsibility of counselors is to respect the dignity and to promote the welfare of clients.

    b. Positive Growth and Development. Counselors encourage client growth and development in ways that foster the clients' interest and welfare; counselors avoid fostering dependent counseling relationships.

    c. Counseling Plans. Counselors and their clients work jointly in devising integrated, individual counseling plans that offer reasonable promise of success and are consistent with abilities and circumstances of clients. Counselors and clients regularly review counseling plans to ensure their continued viability and effectiveness, respecting clients' freedom of choice. (See A.3.b.)

    d. Family Involvement. Counselors recognize that families are usually important in clients' lives and strive to enlist family understanding and involvement as a positive resource, when appropriate.

    e. Career and Employment Needs. Counselors work with their clients in considering employment in jobs and circumstances that are consistent with the clients' overall abilities, vocational limitations, physical restrictions, general temperament, interest and aptitude patterns, social skills, education, general qualifications, and other relevant characteristics and needs. Counselors neither place nor participate in placing clients in positions that will result in damaging the interest and the welfare of clients, employers, or the public.

A.2. Respecting Diversity

    a. Nondiscrimination. Counselors do not condone or engage in discrimination based on age, color, culture disability, ethnic group, gender, race, religion, sexual orientation, marital status, or socioeconomic status. (See C.5.a., C.5.b., and D.1.i.)

    b. Respecting Differences. Counselors will actively attempt to understand the diverse cultural backgrounds of the clients with whom they work. This includes, but is not limited to, learning how the counselor's own cultural/ethnic/racial identity impacts her/his values and beliefs about the counseling process. (See E.8. and F.2.i.)

A.3. Client Rights

    a. Disclosure to Clients. When counseling is initiated, and throughout the counseling process as necessary, counselors inform clients of the purposes, goals, techniques, procedures, limitations, potential risks and benefits of services to be performed, and other pertinent information. Counselors take steps to ensure that clients understand the implications of diagnosis, the intended use of tests and reports, fees, and billing arrangements. Clients have the right to expect confidentiality and to be provided with an explanation of its limitations, including supervision and/or treatment team professionals; to obtain clear information about their case records; to participate in the ongoing counseling plans; and to refuse any recommended services and be advised of the consequences of such refusal. (See E.5.a. and G.2.)

b. Freedom of Choice. Counselors offer clients the freedom to choose whether to enter into a counseling relationship and to determine which professional(s) will provide counseling. Restrictions that limit choices of clients are fully explained. (See A.1.c.)

c. Inability to Give Consent. When counseling minors or persons unable to give voluntary informed consent, counselors act in these clients' best interests. (See B.3.)

A.4. Clients Served by Others

If a client is receiving services from another mental health professional, counselors, with client consent, inform the professional persons already involved and develop clear agreements to avoid confusion and conflict for the client. (See C.6.c.)

A.5. Personal Needs and Values

a. Personal Needs. In the counseling relationship, counselors are aware of the intimacy and responsibilities inherent in the counseling relationship, maintain respect for clients, and avoid actions that seek to meet their personal needs at the expense of clients.

b. Personal Values. Counselors are aware of their own values, attitudes, beliefs, and behaviors and how these apply in a diverse society, and avoid imposing their values on clients. (See C.5.a.)

A.6. Dual Relationships

a. Avoid When Possible. Counselors are aware of their influential positions with respect to clients, and they avoid exploiting the trust and dependency of clients. Counselors make every effort to avoid dual relationships with clients that could impair professional judgment or increase the risk of harm to clients. (Examples of such relationships include, but are not limited to, familial, social, financial, business, or close personal relationships with clients.) When a dual relationship cannot be avoided, counselors take appropriate professional precautions such as informed consent, consultation, supervision, and documentation to ensure that judgment is not impaired and no exploitation occurs. (See F.1.b.)

b. Superior/Subordinate Relationships. Counselors do not accept as clients superiors or subordinates with whom they have administrative, supervisory, or evaluative relationships.

A.7. Sexual Intimacies with Clients

a. Current Clients. Counselors do not have any type of sexual intimacies with clients and do not counsel persons with whom they have had a sexual relationship.

b. Former Clients. Counselors do not engage in sexual intimacies with former clients within a minimum of two years after terminating the counseling relationship. Counselors who engage in such relationship after two years following termination have the responsibility to thoroughly examine and document that such relations did not have an exploitative nature, based on factors such as duration of counseling, amount of time since counseling, termination circumstances, client's personal history and mental status, adverse impact on the client, and actions by the counselor suggesting a plan to initiate a sexual relationship with the client after termination.

A.8.   Multiple Clients
When counselors agree to provide counseling services to two or more persons who have a relationship (such as husband and wife, or parents and children), counselors clarify at the outset which person or persons are clients and the nature of the relationships they will have with each involved person. If it becomes apparent that counselors may be called upon to perform potentially conflicting roles, they clarify, adjust, or withdraw from roles appropriately. (See B.2. and B.4.d.)

A.9.   Group Work
   a.   Screening. Counselors screen prospective group counseling/therapy participants. To the extent possible, counselors select members whose needs and goals are compatible with goals of the group, who will not impede the group process, and whose well-being will not be jeopardized by the group experience.
   b.   Protecting Clients. In a group setting, counselors take reasonable precautions to protect clients from physical or psychological trauma.

A.10.   Fees and Bartering
(See D.3.a. and D.3.b.)
   a.   Advance Understanding. Counselors clearly explain to clients, prior to entering the counseling relationship, all financial arrangements related to professional services including the use of collection agencies or legal measures for nonpayment. (See A.11.c.)
   b.   Establishing Fees. In establishing fees for professional counseling services, counselors consider the financial status of clients and locality. In the event that the established fee structure is inappropriate for a client, assistance is provided in attempting to find comparable services of acceptable cost. (See A.10.d., D.3.a., and D.3.b.)
   c.   Bartering Discouraged. Counselors ordinarily refrain from accepting goods or services from clients in return for counseling services because such arrangements create inherent potential for conflicts, exploitation, and distortion of the professional relationship. Counselors may participate in bartering only if the relationship is not exploitative, if the client requests it, if a clear written contract is established, and if such arrangements are an accepted practice among professionals in the community. (See A.6.a.)
   d.   Pro Bono Service. Counselors contribute to society by devoting a portion of their professional activity to services for which there is little or no financial return (pro bono).

A.11. Termination and Referral

    a. Abandonment Prohibited. Counselors do not abandon or neglect clients in counseling. Counselors assist in making appropriate arrangements for the continuation of treatment, when necessary, during interruptions such as vacations, and following termination.

    b. Inability to Assist Clients. If counselors determine an inability to be of professional assistance to clients, they avoid entering or immediately terminate a counseling relationship. Counselors are knowledgeable about referral resources and suggest appropriate alternatives. If clients decline the suggested referral, counselors should discontinue the relationship.

    c. Appropriate Termination. Counselors terminate a counseling relationship, securing client agreement when possible, when it is reasonably clear that the client is no longer benefiting, when services are no longer required, when counseling no longer serves the client's needs or interests, when clients do not pay fees charged, or when agency or institution limits do not allow provision of further counseling services. (See A.10.b. and C.2.g.)

A.12. Computer Technology

    a. Use of Computers. When computer applications are used in counseling services, counselors ensure that: (1) the client is intellectually, emotionally, and physically capable of using the computer application; (2) the computer application is appropriate for the needs of the client; (3) the client understands the purpose and operation of the computer applications; and (4) a follow-up of client use of a computer application is provided to correct possible misconceptions, discover inappropriate use, and assess subsequent needs.

    b. Explanation of Limitations. Counselors ensure that clients are provided information as a part of the counseling relationship that adequately explains the limitations of computer technology.

    c. Access to Computer Applications. Counselors provide for equal access to computer applications in counseling services. (See A.2.a.)

Section B: Confidentiality

B.1. Right to Privacy

    a. Respect for Privacy. Counselors respect their clients' right to privacy and avoid illegal and unwarranted disclosures of confidential information. (See A.3.a. and B.6.a.)

    b. Client Waiver. The right to privacy may be waived by the client or their legally recognized representative.

    c. Exceptions. The general requirement that counselors keep information confidential does not apply when disclosure is required to prevent clear and imminent danger to the client or others or when legal requirements demand that confidential information be revealed. Counselors consult with other professionals when in doubt as to the validity of an exception.

d. Contagious, Fatal Diseases. A counselor who receives information confirming that a client has a disease commonly known to be both communicable and fatal is justified in disclosing information to an identifiable third party, who by his or her relationship with the client is at a high risk of contracting the disease. Prior to making a disclosure the counselor should ascertain that the client has not already informed the third party about his or her disease and that the client is not intending to inform the third party in the immediate future. (See B.1.c. and B.1.f.)

e. Court Ordered Disclosure. When court ordered to release confidential information without a client's permission, counselors request to the court that the disclosure not be required due to potential harm to the client or counseling relationship. (See B.1.c.)

f. Minimal Disclosure. When circumstances require the disclosure of confidential information, only essential information is revealed. To the extent possible, clients are informed before confidential information is disclosed.

g. Explanation of Limitations. When counseling is initiated and throughout the counseling process as necessary, counselors inform clients of the limitations of confidentiality and identify foreseeable situations in which confidentiality must be breached. (See G.2.a.)

h. Subordinates. Counselors make every effort to ensure that privacy and confidentiality of clients are maintained by subordinates including employees, supervisees, clerical assistants, and volunteers. (See B.1.a.)

i. Treatment Teams. If client treatment will involve a continued review by a treatment team, the client will be informed of the team's existence and composition.

B.2. Groups and Families

a. Group Work. In group work, counselors clearly define confidentiality and the parameters for the specific group being entered, explain its importance, and discuss the difficulties related to confidentiality involved in group work. The fact that confidentiality cannot be guaranteed is clearly communicated to group members.

b. Family Counseling. In family counseling, information about one family member cannot be disclosed to another member without permission. Counselors protect the privacy rights of each family member. (See A.8., B.3., and B.4.d.)

B.3. Minor or Incompetent Clients

When counseling clients who are minors or individuals who are unable to give voluntary, informed consent, parents or guardians may be included in the counseling process as appropriate. Counselors act in the best interests of clients and take measures to safeguard confidentiality. (See A.3.c.)

B.4. Records

a. Requirement of Records. Counselors maintain records necessary for rendering professional services to their clients and as required by laws, regulations, or agency or institution procedures.

b. Confidentiality of Records. Counselors are responsible for securing the safety and confidentiality of any counseling records they create, maintain, transfer, or destroy whether the records are written, taped, computerized, or stored in any other medium. (See B.1.a.)

c. Permission to Record or Observe. Counselors obtain permission from clients prior to electronically recording or observing sessions. (See A.3.a.)

d. Client Access. Counselors recognize that counseling records are kept for the benefit of clients, and therefore provide access to records and copies of records when requested by competent clients, unless the records contain information that may be misleading and detrimental to the client. In situations involving multiple clients, access to records is limited to those parts of records that do not include confidential information related to another client. (See A.8., B.1.a., and B.2.b.)

e. Disclosure or Transfer. Counselors obtain written permission from clients to disclose or transfer records to legitimate third parties unless exceptions to confidentiality exist as listed in Section B.1. Steps are taken to ensure that receivers of counseling records are sensitive to their confidential nature.

B.5. Research and Training

a. Data Disguise Required. Use of data derived from counseling relationships for purposes of training, research, or publication is confined to content that is disguised to ensure the anonymity of the individuals involved. (See B.1.g. and G.3.d.)

b. Agreement for Identification. Identification of a client in a presentation or publication is permissible only when the client has reviewed the material and has agreed to its presentation or publication. (See G.3.d.)

B.6. Consultation

a. Respect for Privacy. Information obtained in a consulting relationship is discussed for professional purposes only with persons clearly concerned with the case. Written and oral reports present data germane to the purposes of the consultation, and every effort is made to protect client identity and avoid undue invasion of privacy.

b. Cooperating Agencies. Before sharing information, counselors make efforts to ensure that there are defined policies in other agencies serving the counselor's clients that effectively protect the confidentiality of information.

Section C: Professional Responsibility

C.1. Standards Knowledge

Counselors have a responsibility to read, understand, and follow the Code of Ethics and the Standards of Practice.

C.2. Professional Competence

    a. Boundaries of Competence. Counselors practice only within the boundaries of their competence, based on their education, training, supervised experience, state and national professional credentials, and appropriate professional experience. Counselors will demonstrate a commitment to gain knowledge, personal awareness, sensitivity, and skills pertinent to working with a diverse client population.

    b. New Specialty Areas of Practice. Counselors practice in specialty areas new to them only after appropriate education, training, and supervised experience. While developing skills in new specialty areas, counselors take steps to ensure the competence of their work and to protect others from possible harm.

    c. Qualified for Employment. Counselors accept employment only for positions for which they are qualified by education, training, supervised experience, state and national professional credentials, and appropriate professional experience. Counselors hire for professional counseling positions only individuals who are qualified and competent.

    d. Monitor Effectiveness. Counselors continually monitor their effectiveness as professionals and take steps to improve when necessary. Counselors in private practice take reasonable steps to seek out peer supervision to evaluate their efficacy as counselors.

    e. Ethical Issues Consultation. Counselors take reasonable steps to consult with other counselors or related professionals when they have questions regarding their ethical obligations or professional practice. (See H.1.)

    f. Continuing Education. Counselors recognize the need for continuing education to maintain a reasonable level of awareness of current scientific and professional information in their fields of activity. They take steps to maintain competence in the skills they use, are open to new procedures, and keep current with the diverse and/or special populations with whom they work.

    g. Impairment. Counselors refrain from offering or accepting professional services when their physical, mental, or emotional problems are likely to harm a client or others. They are alert to the signs of impairment, seek assistance for problems, and, if necessary, limit, suspend, or terminate their professional responsibilities. (See A.11.c.)

C.3. Advertising and Soliciting Clients

    a. Accurate Advertising. There are no restrictions on advertising by counselors except those that can be specifically justified to protect the public from deceptive practices. Counselors advertise or represent their services to the public by identifying their credentials in an accurate manner that is not false, misleading, deceptive, or fraudulent. Counselors may only advertise the highest degree earned which is in counseling or a closely related field from a college or university that was accredited when the degree was awarded by one of the regional accrediting bodies recognized by the Council on Postsecondary Accreditation.

b. Testimonials. Counselors who use testimonials do not solicit them from clients or other persons who, because of their particular circumstances, may be vulnerable to undue influence.

c. Statements by Others. Counselors make reasonable efforts to ensure that statements made by others about them or the profession of counseling are accurate.

d. Recruiting through Employment. Counselors do not use their places of employment or institutional affiliation to recruit or gain clients, supervisees, or consultees for their private practices. (See C.5.e.)

e. Products and Training Advertisements. Counselors who develop products related to their profession or conduct workshops or training events ensure that the advertisements concerning these products or events are accurate and disclose adequate information for consumers to make informed choices.

f. Promoting to Those Served. Counselors do not use counseling, teaching, training, or supervisory relationships to promote their products or training events in a manner that is deceptive or would exert undue influence on individuals who may be vulnerable. Counselors may adopt textbooks they have authored for instruction purposes.

g. Professional Association Involvement. Counselors actively participate in local, state, and national associations that foster the development and improvement of counseling.

C.4. Credentials

a. Credentials Claimed. Counselors claim or imply only professional credentials possessed and are responsible for correcting any known misrepresentations of their credentials by others. Professional credentials include graduate degrees in counseling or closely related mental health fields, accreditation of graduate programs, national voluntary certifications, government-issued certifications or licenses, ACA professional membership, or any other credential that might indicate to the public specialized knowledge or expertise in counseling.

b. ACA Professional Membership. ACA professional members may announce to the public their membership status. Regular members may not announce their ACA membership in a manner that might imply they are credentialed counselors.

c. Credential Guidelines. Counselors follow the guidelines for use of credentials that have been established by the entities that issue the credentials.

d. Misrepresentation of Credentials. Counselors do not attribute more to their credentials than the credentials represent, and do not imply that other counselors are not qualified because they do not possess certain credentials.

e. Doctoral Degrees from Other Fields. Counselors who hold a master's degree in counseling or a closely related mental health field, but hold a doctoral degree from other than counseling or a closely related field do not use the title "Dr." in their practices and do not announce to the public in relation to their practice or status as a counselor that they hold a doctorate.

C.5. Public Responsibility

a. Nondiscrimination. Counselors do not discriminate against clients, students, or supervisees in a manner that has a negative impact based on their age, color, culture, disability, ethnic group, gender, race, religion, sexual orientation, or socioeconomic status, or for any other reason. (See A.2.a.)

b. Sexual Harassment. Counselors do not engage in sexual harassment. Sexual harassment is defined as sexual solicitation, physical advances, or verbal or nonverbal conduct that is sexual in nature, that occurs in connection with professional activities or roles, and that either: (1) is unwelcome, is offensive, or creates a hostile workplace environment, and counselors know or are told this; or (2) is sufficiently severe or intense to be perceived as harassment to a reasonable person in the context. Sexual harassment can consist of a single intense or severe act or multiple persistent or pervasive acts.

c. Reports to Third Parties. Counselors are accurate, honest, and unbiased in reporting their professional activities and judgments to appropriate third parties including courts, health insurance companies, those who are the recipients of evaluation reports, and others. (See B.1.g.)

d. Media Presentations. When counselors provide advice or comment by means of public lectures, demonstrations, radio or television programs, prerecorded tapes, printed articles, mailed material, or other media, they take reasonable precautions to ensure that (1) the statements are based on appropriate professional counseling literature and practice; (2) the statements are otherwise consistent with the Code of Ethics and the Standards of Practice; and (3) the recipients of the information are not encouraged to infer that a professional counseling relationship has been established. (See C.6.b.)

e. Unjustified Gains. Counselors do not use their professional positions to seek or receive unjustified personal gains, sexual favors, unfair advantage, or unearned goods or services. (See C.3.d.)

C.6. Responsibility to Other Professionals

a. Different Approaches. Counselors are respectful of approaches to professional counseling that differ from their own. Counselors know and take into account the traditions and practices of other professional groups with which they work.

b. Personal Public Statements. When making personal statements in a public context, counselors clarify that they are speaking from their personal perspectives and that they are not speaking on behalf of all counselors or the profession. (See C.5.d.)

c. Clients Served by Others. When counselors learn that their clients are in a professional relationship with another mental health professional, they request release from clients to inform the other professionals and strive to establish positive and collaborative professional relationships. (See A.4.)

Section D:
Relationships with Other Professionals

D.1.   Relationships with Employers and Employees

  a.   Role Definition. Counselors define and describe for their employers and employees the parameters and levels of their professional roles.

  b.   Agreements. Counselors establish working agreements with supervisors, colleagues, and subordinates regarding counseling or clinical relationships, confidentiality, adherence to professional standards, distinction between public and private material, maintenance and dissemination of recorded information, workload, and accountability. Working agreements in each instance are specified and made known to those concerned.

  c.   Negative Conditions. Counselors alert their employers to conditions that may be potentially disruptive or damaging to the counselor's professional responsibilities or that may limit their effectiveness.

  d.   Evaluation. Counselors submit regularly to professional review and evaluation by their supervisor or the appropriate representative of the employer.

  e.   In-Service. Counselors are responsible for in-service development of self and staff.

  f.   Goals. Counselors inform their staff of goals and programs.

  g.   Practices. Counselors provide personnel and agency practices that respect and enhance the rights and welfare of each employee and recipient of agency services. Counselors strive to maintain the highest levels of professional services.

  h.   Personnel Selection and Assignment. Counselors select competent staff and assign responsibilities compatible with their skills and experiences.

  i.   Discrimination. Counselors, as either employers or employees, do not engage in or condone practices that are inhumane, illegal, or unjustifiable (such as considerations based on age, color, culture, disability, ethnic group, gender, race, religion, sexual orientation, or socioeconomic status) in hiring, promotion, or training. (See A.2.a. and C.5.b.)

  j.   Professional Conduct. Counselors have a responsibility both to clients and to the agency or institution within which services are performed to maintain high standards of professional conduct.

  k.   Exploitative Relationships. Counselors do not engage in exploitative relationships with individuals over whom they have supervisory, evaluative, or instructional control or authority.

  l.   Employer Policies. The acceptance of employment in an agency or institution implies that counselors are in agreement with its general policies and principles. Counselors strive to reach agreement with employers as to acceptable standards of conduct that allow for changes in institutional policy conducive to the growth and development of clients.

D.2. Consultation (See B.6.)

    a. Consultation As an Option. Counselors may choose to consult with any other professionally competent persons about their clients. In choosing consultants, counselors avoid placing the consultant in a conflict of interest situation that would preclude the consultant being a proper party to the counselor's efforts to help the client. Should counselors be engaged in a work setting that compromises this consultation standard, they consult with other professionals whenever possible to consider justifiable alternatives.

    b. Consultant Competency. Counselors are reasonably certain that they have or the organization represented has the necessary competencies and resources for giving the kind of consulting services needed and that appropriate referral resources are available.

    c. Understanding with Clients. When providing consultation, counselors attempt to develop with their clients a clear understanding of problem definition, goals for change, and predicted consequences of interventions selected.

    d. Consultant Goals. The consulting relationship is one in which client adaptability and growth toward self-direction are consistently encouraged and cultivated. (See A.1.b.)

D.3. Fees for Referral

    a. Accepting Fees from Agency Clients. Counselors refuse a private fee or other remuneration for rendering services to persons who are entitled to such services through the counselor's employing agency or institution. The policies of a particular agency may make explicit provisions for agency clients to receive counseling services from members of its staff in private practice. In such instances, the clients must be informed of other options open to them should they seek private counseling services. (See A.10.a., A.11.b., and C.3.d.)

    b. Referral Fees. Counselors do not accept a referral fee from other professionals.

D.4. Subcontractor Arrangements

When counselors work as subcontractors for counseling services for a third party, they have a duty to inform clients of the limitations of confidentiality that the organization may place on counselors in providing counseling services to clients. The limits of such confidentiality ordinarily are discussed as part of the intake session. (See B.1.e. and B.1.f.)

Section E:
Evaluation, Assessment, and Interpretation

E.1. General

    a. Appraisal Techniques. The primary purpose of educational and psychological assessment is to provide measures that are objective and interpretable in either comparative or absolute terms. Counselors recognize the need to interpret the statements in this section as applying to the whole range of appraisal techniques, including test and nontest data.

b. Client Welfare. Counselors promote the welfare and best interests of the client in the development, publication, and utilization of educational and psychological assessment techniques. They do not misuse assessment results and interpretations and take reasonable steps to prevent others from misusing the information these techniques provide. They respect the client's right to know the results, the interpretations made, and the bases for their conclusions and recommendations.

E.2. Competence to Use and Interpret Tests

a. Limits of Competence. Counselors recognize the limits of their competence and perform only those testing and assessment services for which they have been trained. They are familiar with reliability, validity, related standardization, error of measurement, and proper application of any technique utilized. Counselors using computer-based test interpretations are trained in the construct being measured and the specific instrument being used prior to using this type of computer application. Counselors take reasonable measures to ensure the proper use of psychological assessment techniques by persons under their supervision.

b. Appropriate Use. Counselors are responsible for the appropriate application, scoring, interpretation, and use of assessment instruments, whether they score and interpret such tests themselves or use computerized or other services.

c. Decisions Based on Results. Counselors responsible for decisions involving individuals or policies that are based on assessment results have a thorough understanding of educational and psychological measurement, including validation criteria, test research, and guidelines for test development and use.

d. Accurate Information. Counselors provide accurate information and avoid false claims or misconceptions when making statements about assessment instruments or techniques. Special efforts are made to avoid unwarranted connotations of such terms as IQ and grade equivalent scores. (See C.5.c.)

E.3. Informed Consent

a. Explanation to Clients. Prior to assessment, counselors explain the nature and purposes of assessment and the specific use of results in language the client (or other legally authorized person on behalf of the client) can understand, unless an explicit exception to this right has been agreed upon in advance. Regardless of whether scoring and interpretation are completed by counselors, by assistants, or by computer or other outside services, counselors take reasonable steps to ensure that appropriate explanations are given to the client.

b. Recipients of Results. The examinee's welfare, explicit understanding, and prior agreement determine the recipients of test results. Counselors include accurate and appropriate interpretations with any release of individual or group test results. (See B.1.a. and C.5.c.)

E.4. Release of Information to Competent Professionals

    a. Misuse of Results. Counselors do not misuse assessment results, including test results, and interpretations, and take reasonable steps to prevent the misuse of such by others. (See C.5.c.)

    b. Release of Raw Data. Counselors ordinarily release data (e.g. protocols, counseling or interview notes, or questionnaires) in which the client is identified only with the consent of the client or the client's legal representative. Such data are usually released only to persons recognized by counselors as competent to interpret the data. (See B.1.a.)

E.5. Proper Diagnosis of Mental Disorders

    a. Proper Diagnosis. Counselors take special care to provide proper diagnosis of mental disorders. Assessment techniques (including personal interview) used to determine client care (e.g. locus of treatment, type of treatment, or recommended follow-up) are carefully selected and appropriately used. (See A.3.a. and C.5.c.)

    b. Cultural Sensitivity. Counselors recognize that culture affects the manner in which clients' problems are defined. Clients' socioeconomic and cultural experience is considered when diagnosing mental disorders.

E.6. Test Selection

    a. Appropriateness of Instruments. Counselors carefully consider the validity, reliability, psychometric limitations, and appropriateness of instruments when selecting tests for use in a given situation or with a particular client.

    b. Culturally Diverse Populations. Counselors are cautious when selecting tests for culturally diverse populations to avoid inappropriateness of testing that may be outside of socialized behavioral or cognitive patterns.

E.7. Conditions of Test Administration

    a. Administration Conditions. Counselors administer tests under the same conditions that were established in their standardization. When tests are not administered under standard conditions or when unusual behavior or irregularities occur during the testing session, those conditions are noted in interpretation, and the results may be designated as invalid or of questionable validity.

    b. Computer Administration. Counselors are responsible for ensuring that administration programs function properly to provide clients with accurate results when a computer or other electronic methods are used for test administration. (See A.12.b.)

    c. Unsupervised Test-Taking. Counselors do not permit unsupervised or inadequately supervised use of tests or assessments unless the tests or assessments are designed, intended, and validated for self-administration and/or scoring.

    d. Disclosure of Favorable Conditions. Prior to test administration, conditions that produce most favorable test results are made known to the examinee.

E.8. Diversity in Testing
Counselors are cautious in using assessment techniques, making evaluations, and interpreting the performance of populations not represented in the norm group on which an instrument was standardized. They recognize the effects of age, color, culture, disability, ethnic group, gender, race, religion, sexual orientation, and socioeconomic status on test administration and interpretation and place test results in proper perspective with other relevant factors. (See A.2.a.)

E.9. Test Scoring and Interpretation
a. Reporting Reservations. In reporting assessment results, counselors indicate any reservations that exist regarding validity or reliability because of the circumstances of the assessment or the inappropriateness of the norms for the person tested.
b. Research Instruments. Counselors exercise caution when interpreting the results of research instruments possessing insufficient technical data to support respondent results. The specific purposes for the use of such instruments are stated explicitly to the examinee.
c. Testing Services. Counselors who provide test scoring and test interpretation services to support the assessment process confirm the validity of such interpretations. They accurately describe the purpose, norms, validity, reliability, and applications of the procedures and any special qualifications applicable to their use. The public offering of an automated test interpretations service is considered a professional-to-professional consultation. The formal responsibility of the consultant is to the consultee, but the ultimate and overriding responsibility is to the client.

E.10. Test Security
Counselors maintain the integrity and security of tests and other assessment techniques consistent with legal and contractual obligations. Counselors do not appropriate, reproduce, or modify published tests or parts thereof without acknowledgment and permission from the publisher.

E.11. Obsolete Tests and Outdated Test Results
Counselors do not use data or test results that are obsolete or outdated for the current purpose. Counselors make every effort to prevent the misuse of obsolete measures and test data by others.

E.12. Test Construction
Counselors use established scientific procedures, relevant standards, and current professional knowledge for test design in the development, publication, and utilization of educational and psychological assessment techniques.

Section F: Teaching, Training, and Supervision

F. 1. Counselor Educators and Trainers
a. Educators As Teachers and Practitioners. Counselors who are responsible for developing, implementing, and supervising educational programs are

skilled as teachers and practitioners. They are knowledgeable regarding the ethical, legal, and regulatory aspects of the profession, are skilled in applying that knowledge, and make students and supervisees aware of their responsibilities. Counselors conduct counselor education and training programs in an ethical manner and serve as role models for professional behavior. Counselor educators should make an effort to infuse material related to human diversity into all courses and/or workshops that are designed to promote the development of professional counselors.

b. Relationship Boundaries with Students and Supervisees. Counselors clearly define and maintain ethical, professional, and social relationship boundaries with their students and supervisees. They are aware of the differential in power that exists and the student's or supervisee's possible incomprehension of that power differential. Counselors explain to students and supervisees the potential for the relationship to become exploitative.

c. Sexual Relationships. Counselors do not engage in sexual relationships with students or supervisees and do not subject them to sexual harassment. (See A.6. and C.5.b.)

d. Contributions to Research. Counselors give credit to students or supervisees for their contributions to research and scholarly projects. Credit is given through coauthorship, acknowledgment, footnote statement, or other appropriate means, in accordance with such contributions. (See G.4.b. and G.4.c.)

e. Close Relatives. Counselors do not accept close relatives as students or supervisees.

f. Supervision Preparation. Counselors who offer clinical supervision services are adequately prepared in supervision methods and techniques. Counselors who are doctoral students serving as practicum or internship supervisors to master's level students are adequately prepared and supervised by the training program.

g. Responsibility for Services to Clients. Counselors who supervise the counseling services of others take reasonable measures to ensure that counseling services provided to clients are professional.

h. Endorsement. Counselors do not endorse students or supervisees for certification, licensure, employment, or completion of an academic or training program if they believe students or supervisees are not qualified for the endorsement. Counselors take reasonable steps to assist students or supervisees who are not qualified for endorsement to become qualified.

F.2. Counselor Education and Training Programs

a. Orientation. Prior to admission, counselors orient prospective students to the counselor education or training program's expectations, including but not limited to the following: (1) the type and level of skill acquisition required for successful completion of the training, (2) subject matter to be covered, (3) basis for evaluation, (4) training components that encourage self-growth or self-disclosure as part of the training process, (5) the type of supervision settings and requirements of the sites for required clinical field experiences, (6) student and supervisee evaluation and dismissal policies and procedures, and (7) up-to-date employment prospects for graduates.

b. Integration of Study and Practice. Counselors establish counselor education and training programs that integrate academic study and supervised practice.

c. Evaluation. Counselors clearly state to students and supervisees, in advance of training, the levels of competency expected, appraisal methods, and timing of evaluations for both didactic and experiential components. Counselors provide students and supervisees with periodic performance appraisal and evaluation feedback throughout the training program.

d. Teaching Ethics. Counselors make students and supervisees aware of the ethical responsibilities and standards of the profession and the students' and supervisees' ethical responsibilities to the profession. (See C.1. and F.3.e.)

e. Peer Relationships. When students or supervisees are assigned to lead counseling groups or provide clinical supervision for their peers, counselors take steps to ensure that students and supervisees placed in these roles do not have personal or adverse relationships with peers and that they understand they have the same ethical obligations as counselor educators, trainers, and supervisors. Counselors make every effort to ensure that the rights of peers are not compromised when students or supervisees are assigned to lead counseling groups or provide clinical supervision.

f. Varied Theoretical Positions. Counselors present varied theoretical positions so that students and supervisees may make comparisons and have opportunities to develop their own positions. Counselors provide information concerning the scientific bases of professional practice. (See C.6.a.)

g. Field Placements. Counselors develop clear policies within their training program regarding field placement and other clinical experiences. Counselors provide clearly stated roles and responsibilities for the student or supervisee, the site supervisor, and the program supervisor. They confirm that site supervisors are qualified to provide supervision and are informed of their professional and ethical responsibilities in this role.

h. Dual Relationships As Supervisors. Counselors avoid dual relationships such as performing the role of site supervisor and training program supervisor in the student's or supervisee's training program. Counselors do not accept any form of professional services, fees, commissions, reimbursement, or remuneration from a site for student or supervisee placement.

i. Diversity in Programs. Counselors are responsive to their institution's and program's recruitment and retention needs for training program administrators, faculty, and students with diverse backgrounds and special needs. (See A.2.a.)

F.3. Students and Supervisees

    a. Limitations. Counselors, through ongoing evaluation and appraisal, are aware of the academic and personal limitations of students and supervisees that might impede performance. Counselors assist students and supervisees in securing remedial assistance when needed, and dismiss from the training program supervisees who are unable to provide competent service due to academic or personal limitations. Counselors seek professional consultation and document their decision to dismiss or refer students or supervisees for assistance. Counselors assure that students and supervisees have recourse to address decisions made, to require them to seek assistance, or to dismiss them.

    b. Self-Growth Experiences. Counselors use professional judgment when designing training experiences conducted by the counselors themselves that require student and supervisee self-growth or self-disclosure. Safeguards are provided so that students and supervisees are aware of the ramifications their self-disclosure may have on counselors whose primary role as teacher, trainer, or supervisor requires acting on ethical obligations to the profession. Evaluative components of experiential training experiences explicitly delineate predetermined academic standards that are separate and not dependent on the student's level of self-disclosure. (See A.6.)

    c. Counseling for Students and Supervisees. If students or supervisees request counseling, supervisors or counselor educators provide them with acceptable referrals. Supervisors or counselor educators do not serve as counselor to students or supervisees over whom they hold administrative, teaching, or evaluative roles unless this is a brief role associated with a training experience. (See A.6.b.)

    d. Clients of Students and Supervisees. Counselors make every effort to ensure that the clients at field placements are aware of the services rendered and the qualifications of the students and supervisees rendering those services. Clients receive professional disclosure information and are informed of the limits of confidentiality. Client permission is obtained in order for the students and supervisees to use any information concerning the counseling relationship in the training process. (See B.1.e.)

    e. Standards for Students and Supervisees. Students and supervisees preparing to become counselors adhere to the Code of Ethics and the Standards of Practice. Students and supervisees have the same obligations to clients as those required of counselors. (See H.1.)

Section G: Research and Publication

G.1. Research Responsibilities

    a. Use of Human Subjects. Counselors plan, design, conduct, and report research in a manner consistent with pertinent ethical principles, federal and state laws, host institutional regulations, and scientific standards governing research with human subjects. Counselors design and conduct research that reflects cultural sensitivity appropriateness.

b. Deviation from Standard Practices. Counselors seek consultation and observe stringent safeguards to protect the rights of research participants when a research problem suggests a deviation from standard acceptable practices. (See B.6.)

c. Precautions to Avoid Injury. Counselors who conduct research with human subjects are responsible for the subjects' welfare throughout the experiment and take reasonable precautions to avoid causing injurious psychological, physical, or social effects to their subjects.

d. Principal Researcher Responsibility. The ultimate responsibility for ethical research practice lies with the principal researcher. All others involved in the research activities share ethical obligations and full responsibility for their own actions.

e. Minimal Interference. Counselors take reasonable precautions to avoid causing disruptions in subjects' lives due to participation in research.

f. Diversity. Counselors are sensitive to diversity and research issues with special populations. They seek consultation when appropriate. (See A.2.a. and B.6.)

G.2. Informed Consent

a. Topics Disclosed. In obtaining informed consent for research, counselors use language that is understandable to research participants and that: (1) accurately explains the purpose and procedures to be followed; (2) identifies any procedures that are experimental or relatively untried; (3) describes the attendant discomforts and risks; (4) describes the benefits or changes in individuals or organizations that might be reasonably expected; (5) discloses appropriate alternative procedures that would be advantageous for subjects; (6) offers to answer any inquiries concerning the procedures; (7) describes any limitations on confidentiality; and (8) instructs that subjects are free to withdraw their consent and to discontinue participation in the project at any time. (See B.1.f.)

b. Deception. Counselors do not conduct research involving deception unless alternative procedures are not feasible and the prospective value of the research justifies the deception. When the methodological requirements of a study necessitate concealment or deception, the investigator is required to explain clearly the reasons for this action as soon as possible.

c. Voluntary Participation. Participation in research is typically voluntary and without any penalty for refusal to participate. Involuntary participation is appropriate only when it can be demonstrated that participation will have no harmful effects on subjects and is essential to the investigation.

d. Confidentiality of Information. Information obtained about research participants during the course of an investigation is confidential. When the possibility exists that others may obtain access to such information, ethical research practice requires that the possibility, together with the plans for protecting confidentiality, be explained to participants as a part of the procedure for obtaining informed consent. (See B.1.e.)

   e. Persons Incapable of Giving Informed Consent. When a person is incapable of giving informed consent, counselors provide an appropriate explanation, obtain agreement for participation and obtain appropriate consent from a legally authorized person.

   f. Commitments to Participants. Counselors take reasonable measures to honor all commitments to research participants.

   g. Explanations after Data Collection. After data are collected, counselors provide participants with full clarification of the nature of the study to remove any misconceptions. Where scientific or human values justify delaying or withholding information, counselors take reasonable measures to avoid causing harm.

   h. Agreements to Cooperate. Counselors who agree to cooperate with another individual in research or publication incur an obligation to cooperate as promised in terms of punctuality of performance and with regard to the completeness and accuracy of the information required.

   i. Informed Consent for Sponsors. In the pursuit of research, counselors give sponsors, institutions, and publication channels the same respect and opportunity for giving informed consent that they accord to individual research participants. Counselors are aware of their obligation to future research workers and ensure that host institutions are given feedback information and proper acknowledgment.

G.3. Reporting Results

   a. Information Affecting Outcome. When reporting research results, counselors explicitly mention all variables and conditions known to the investigator that may have affected the outcome of a study or the interpretation of data.

   b. Accurate Results. Counselors plan, conduct, and report research accurately and in a manner that minimizes the possibility that results will be misleading. They provide thorough discussions of the limitations of their data and alternative hypotheses. Counselors do not engage in fraudulent research, distort data, misrepresent data, or deliberately bias their results.

   c. Obligation to Report Unfavorable Results. Counselors communicate to other counselors the results of any research judged to be of professional value. Results that reflect unfavorably on institutions, programs, services, prevailing opinions, or vested interests are not withheld.

   d. Identity of Subjects. Counselors who supply data, aid in the research of another person, report research results, or make original data available take due care to disguise the identity of respective subjects in the absence of specific authorization from the subjects to do otherwise. (See B.1.g. and B.5.a.)

   e. Replication Studies. Counselors are obligated to make available sufficient original research data to qualified professionals who may wish to replicate the study.

G.4. Publication

    a. Recognition of Others. When conducting and reporting research, counselors are familiar with and give recognition to previous work on the topic, observe copyright laws, and give full credit to those to whom credit is due. (See F.1.d. and G.4.c.)

    b. Contributors. Counselors give credit through joint authorship, acknowledgment, footnote statements, or other appropriate means to those who have contributed significantly to research or concept development in accordance with such contributions. The principal contributor is listed first and minor technical or professional contributions are acknowledged in notes or introductory statements.

    c. Student Research. For an article that is substantially based on a student's dissertation or thesis, the student is listed as the principal author. (See F.1.d. and G.4.a.)

    d. Duplicate Submission. Counselors submit manuscripts for consideration to only one journal at a time. Manuscripts that are published in whole or in substantial part in another journal or published work are not submitted for publication without acknowledgment and permission from the previous publication.

    e. Professional Review. Counselors who review material submitted for publication, research, or other scholarly purposes respect the confidentiality and proprietary rights of those who submitted it.

Section H: Resolving Ethical Issues

H.1. Knowledge Of Standards
Counselors are familiar with the Code of Ethics and the Standards of Practice and other applicable ethics codes from other professional organizations of which they are members, or from certification and licensure bodies. Lack of knowledge or misunderstanding of an ethical responsibility is not a defense against a charge of unethical conduct. (See F.3.e.)

H.2. Suspected Violations

    a. Ethical Behavior Expected. Counselors expect professional associates to adhere to the Code of Ethics. When counselors possess reasonable cause that raises doubts as to whether a counselor is acting in an ethical manner, they take appropriate action. (See H.2.d. and H.2.e.)

    b. Consultation. When uncertain as to whether a particular situation or course of action may be in violation of the Code of Ethics, counselors consult with other counselors who are knowledgeable about ethics, with colleagues, or with appropriate authorities.

    c. Organization Conflicts. If the demands of an organization with which counselors are affiliated pose a conflict with the Code of Ethics, counselors specify the nature of such conflicts and express to their supervisors or other responsible officials their commitment to the Code of Ethics. When possible, counselors work toward change within the organization to allow full adherence to the Code of Ethics.

    d.   Informal Resolution. When counselors have reasonable cause to believe that another counselor is violating an ethical standard, they attempt to first resolve the issue informally with the other counselor if feasible, providing that such action does not violate confidentiality rights that may be involved.

    e.   Reporting Suspected Violations. When an informal resolution is not appropriate or feasible, counselors, upon reasonable cause, take action such as reporting the suspected ethical violation to state or national ethics committees, unless this action conflicts with confidentiality rights that cannot be resolved.

    f.   Unwarranted Complaints. Counselors do not initiate, participate in, or encourage the filing of ethics complaints that are unwarranted or intend to harm a counselor rather than to protect clients or the public.

H.3.   Cooperation with Ethics Committees

Counselors assist in the process of enforcing the Code of Ethics. Counselors cooperate with investigations, proceedings, and requirements of the ACA Ethics Committee or ethics committees of other duly constituted associations or boards having jurisdiction over those charged with a violation. Counselors are familiar with the ACA Policies and Procedures and use it as a reference in assisting the enforcement of the Code of Ethics.

APPENDIX B
Sample Counselor-Client Agreement and Initial Interview

Our Agreement to Work Together

My job as your counselor is to provide you with quality service. I am a member of the American Psychological Association, and the responsibilities I have to you are outlined in their ethical code. This agreement covers the basics of that code. Even if you believe that the situations described do not apply to you, please read the agreement carefully. Please ask me questions about what I have written and discuss with me any changes you may want to make in the agreement before signing it.

Confidentiality

One of the primary reasons you come to see me is to have a private place to talk about a problem. I understand that you may talk to me about experiences that you do not share with anyone else and may express feelings and thoughts you do not share with others. I want to give you a safe place to think and feel and make decisions and will not discuss what you tell me with others, except in the situations outlined below.

Limitations to Confidentiality

In certain situations I will not be able to keep what you tell me confidential and may not be able to obtain your permission before talking to someone else about what you tell me. First, according to my ethical code and state law, I have the responsibility to take action when anyone's life is threatened. If you threaten harm to yourself or to someone else, I will inform your family and call the police if the threat is eminent. I am also required by state law to call Child Protective Services to report any incident of child abuse reported to me by a child and must discuss any life-threatening situations with the child's parent or guardian. Whenever possible, I will ask you to make the call to prevent violence and advise you to discuss the situation with a lawyer, but if you are unwilling to prevent the violence, I will take action myself. I will notify any potential victim of violence as well as family members if the individual is a minor.

The second limitation to confidentiality is based on my need to consult with other therapists in order to provide you with quality care. I receive assistance on a regular basis from _____ and from time to time will consult with other therapists about my work. I do not reveal the names of my clients during these consultations. If there is a reason you do not want me to talk to the specific individuals I have named, I am willing to arrange consultation with other professionals. If I do need to use your name in coordinating services with another professional, I will ask you to sign a release of information before I talk with the other therapist.

The third limitation is that I take notes of our sessions together, including information about homework assignments and progress you are making, what assistance I offered to you, situations when I was required to break confidentiality, and any conflicts between us that may arise as we work together. If a lawyer asks for these records in connection with a court case, I will first talk to you about the request and ask the lawyer to accept a summary of our work together rather than my notes. I will do what I can to minimize the information I give, but I am bound by the same restrictions in legal areas that apply to any other citizen. Also, if you submit a claim to an insurance company to cover my fee, the company will likely ask me for a psychological diagnosis, which will mean information about you will be stored in the company computer. If your carrier is part of a managed care company, I will also be required to release information about our treatment plan and your progress as we work together in order to receive authorization to continue to work with you and be paid by the insurance company.

The fourth limitation occurs when your counseling takes place with other family members or in a group setting. I will emphasize the importance of confidentiality to everyone involved and ask for a commitment to keep information disclosed confidential, but I will not be able to prevent others from disclosing information outside the counseling session. Please report any such violation to me, and we will discuss what your options are at that time.

Types of Services I Provide

I am trained to attend to your thoughts, feelings, and behavior related to the issue you bring to counseling. To help me provide quality service to you, I have completed a Ph.D. in Counseling and Guidance at the University of Arizona and I am currently a licensed psychologist in the State of Arizona. I have training in cognitive, behavioral, and expressive methods and have more than twenty years of experience working with individuals, couples, families, groups, and counselors-in-training. I have helped people with issues including work performance, career changes, addictions, childhood traumas and violent experiences as adults, restricted and impulsive expression of feelings, developmental disabilities, and conflict resolution and communication processes in heterosexual and homosexual relationships. I have experience responding to life crises such as the death of a loved one, the loss of a job, or the end of an intimate relationship. If I do not have the skills and experiences to provide you with help, I will assist you in finding another therapist who is qualified.

Structure of Our Relationship

Our professional relationship is different from a relationship you may have with a family member or a friend. I am willing to listen and to help you with important parts of your life, but we will not have a social relationship either during the time we are working together or after we stop working together. We make a trade: I give you a safe place to talk, and you decide at some point that you no longer need my help.

If we are likely to meet at social gatherings in the community, we can discuss that ahead of time. If we meet accidentally in a public place, I will say "hello" but not encourage conversation with you, unless you initiate such conversation. Remember that I am not judging you or thinking about what you have told me in my office in these situations. During sessions, we can talk about these social contacts if either of us needs to.

I will not agree to meet with you outside my office unless we agree that working in a setting other than my office is necessary to meet a specific counseling goal. I might, for example, go with you to a shopping mall to help you overcome a fear of being in a public place. Under no circumstances is it appropriate for us to have sexual contact. Under no circumstances is it appropriate for us to barter or develop a relationship other than the one I have described here.

My Availability in Addition to Our Counseling Appointments

When I am not working with you, I am working with another client, completing business tasks, or taking time to rest and rejuvenate. The boundaries I set with you about telephone contact between sessions may vary, depending on your needs and mine.

You may call and leave messages on my answering machine at any time. You may need to call for these reasons:

1. Make appointments or change appointment times.
2. Report the results of an agreement we made during session about something you would do after session. For example, we practice a conversation you are to have with a friend and later you call me to report how the conversation actually turned out.

3. Report emotional reactions or experiences that may happen between sessions that you want to tell me about but that do not require any action on my part except to listen.
4. Report progress you make or frustrations you may feel with the plan we made in session.

I return calls between 9:00 A.M. and 8:00 P.M., Monday through Thursday, during my regular working hours. Friday, Saturday, and Sunday I check my machine and return calls at least once a day. I may ask you to discuss with me a specific agreement about our contact between sessions. For example, we may need to meet more frequently, or you may need to call me regularly the day after each session. I will encourage you to develop a support system with other people in your life and to establish ways to support yourself. If I am not able to provide sufficient care to meet your needs, I will help you find another counselor or an inpatient facility that will be helpful to you.

There will be times when I will be on vacation or unavailable because of a family emergency. When I am, another counselor will take over for me and will be identified on my answering machine message. I will prepare this counselor if possible, and, when I return to work, I will review with this counselor any contact with you during my absence.

Payment for Services

My fee is $70.00 per session, and I ask that you pay each time we meet. I do not work on a sliding scale. I do not charge for canceled appointments, but I will discuss your canceling appointments if that occurs repeatedly. If you make an appointment and do not call to cancel the appointment, I will charge you for the session. If a portion of my fee is paid by an insurance carrier or another third party, I will not be able to bill the carrier for an appointment you did not keep, and you will be responsible for paying my entire fee for that session. I do not charge for time we spend talking on the telephone, but I ask that you make your calls as brief as possible.

If you have insurance coverage for mental health services, I will give you a bill when you pay me each time, and you can submit that bill with your insurance form to be reimbursed. You need to check with your insurance company to learn whether your coverage includes the services of a licensed psychologist in private practice. If the insurance company will not reimburse you and requires me to submit bills and reports to them, I charge an additional $10.00 processing fee per session if I am required to do the paperwork. (Please ask me for an additional information sheet if you plan to use your insurance coverage to pay for my services.)

Evaluation of Counseling Services

Even though you and I work together in good faith, there is no guarantee that you will make all the changes we identify that you want or need to make. My job is to help you identify goals and develop plans to reach them. Your job is to decide what plans will be useful to you and to carry out these plans as you see fit. You have the right to stop working with me or to ask to renegotiate our agreement at any time.

If at any time you have questions about what I am suggesting to you, please talk to me. If you do not feel safe talking to me, talk to another therapist or a friend and decide what action to take in regard to our work together. If there is a conflict between us that we cannot resolve, I will ask if you are willing to meet with me and another therapist you feel safe with. We will ask that person to help us work out any differences and make a decision about continuing to work together.

About two months after we complete our work, I will send you an evaluation form to complete. This feedback will help me to do a better job with you and others I work with. Please return the completed form.

Ending Our Work Together

When we agree to end our work together, we will discuss what has been helpful and what has not, what further support you will need to continue to work on your goals, and how you might decide to resume working with me or another therapist.

We may also stop working together because we have agreed that a referral to another therapist will help you to reach your goals more quickly or because you choose to stop using therapy as a way to reach your goals. No matter what the circumstances of our ending our work together, I want to know about your experience of working with me and ask that you give me feedback directly.

Signatures

Please decide whether you are prepared to sign this agreement now. We can discuss the details before you sign it.

I understand and agree to the statements in this document and have decided to work with _____.
                                              Counselor's name

Signed _____
                                              Client

I understand and agree to the statements in this document and have decided to work with _____.
                                              Client's name

Signed _____
                                              Counselor

FORM B.1 Sample Initial Interview Form

INITIAL INTERVIEW INFORMATION

Information you give me on this form is confidential unless you tell me your life or someone else's life is in immediate danger. If a question is too difficult to write about, you can talk to me about it instead.

The following questions are designed to help us begin. You may feel that many of these questions are personal and unrelated to why you are here. However, these questions are important for me to ask so that I may give you the best possible service.

Please ask me any questions that you may have related to my training and skills. You may want to know about the different kinds of work I have done, my fees, and my expectations about our work together.

Date _____

Name _____

Address _____ ZIP _____

Phone (home) _____ (work) _____

Age _____

REASONS FOR MAKING THIS APPOINTMENT

1. What brings you to counseling at this time?

    _____

    _____

    _____

2. If this problem has been ongoing, please describe the history briefly.

   _____

   _____

   _____

   _____

   _____

PREVIOUS COUNSELING EXPERIENCES

1. Who suggested that you come to see me?

   Name _____

   Address _____

   Telephone _____

2. Have you ever been in counseling before?   Yes   No

   If yes, please answer questions 3–6.

3. Please list names and information about each counselor, if you have seen more than one.

Name	# Sessions	How Successful?*
_____	_____	_____
_____	_____	_____
_____	_____	_____
_____	_____	_____

   *Rate the experience on a scale of 1–10.

(continued)

FORM B.1 *(continued)*

Not successful   Very successful

  1   2   3   4   5   6   7   8   9   10

4.   What was helpful about seeing the counselors? _____

_____

5.   What was not helpful? _____

_____

PERSONAL INFORMATION

1.   Please describe any changes in your actions and emotions that are presently making you uncomfortable as well as any recent changes in you that other people in your life have noticed. For example, you realize you are much more irritable than usual or a friend might tell you how tired you look.

_____

_____

_____

2.   When was your last medical exam? _____

What was the reason for the exam? _____

3.   Please describe any medical problems you have.

_____

_____

_____

_____

4. If you use caffeine (coffee, colas, chocolate), sugar, or tobacco, describe how much you use on a daily basis.

   _____

   _____

5. Describe your general eating habits.

   _____

   _____

6. Describe any special dietary needs you may have.

   _____

7. Describe any recent change in your weight.

   _____

   _____

8. Describe any problems you have sleeping or any recent change in your sleeping patterns.

   _____

   _____

9. Describe any regular exercise you do.

   _____

   _____

10. Please list and explain the purpose of any medications you are taking, including over-the-counter drugs. Include the names of prescribing physicians for prescription drugs. (Use the back of the page if necessary.)

(continued)

the back of the page if necessary.)

_____

_____

_____

_____

11. Do you drink alcohol or use recreational drugs?   Yes   No
    If so, please describe frequency and nature of use.

    _____

    _____

    _____

12. If there is a history of substance abuse in your family, please
    describe.

    _____

    _____

13. If there is a history of psychiatric disorders in your family,
    please describe. _____

    _____

14. Have you been hospitalized for a psychiatric disorder or
    received treatment in an inpatient facility for alcohol and
    drug abuse?   Yes   No   If so, please describe.

    _____

    _____

    _____

15. Have you or has anyone in your family attempted suicide?

    Yes   No   If so, please describe.

    _____

    _____

16. Have you or has anyone close to you been a victim of sexual abuse or assault?   Yes   No   If so, please describe.

    _____

    _____

17. Have you or has anyone close to you been a victim of physical violence? Yes No If so, please describe.

    _____

    _____

18. Have you witnessed any physical or sexual violence?

    Yes No If so, please describe.

    _____

    _____

19. Have you caused physical harm or been sexually abusive to anyone else?   Yes   No   If so, please describe.

    _____

    _____

    _____

    _____

(continued)

20. Please give the name and phone number of someone to contact in case of an emergency.

21. Please identify the people who are your primary emotional supports. Your list might include family, friends, social or religious organizations, and any other formal or informal counseling you may be involved with.

COUNSELING GOALS

Please complete as much of this as you can. We may add to this page during our first meeting.

During our first meeting, we will begin to discuss our purpose in working together. The questions that follow are designed to help us agree on what our job is together. We will write out an agreement about your counseling goals and will need to continue to talk about goals and progress for as long as we work together.

1.   What would you like to change?

2.   What is stopping you from changing?

3.   How will we know if our work together is helping you to make the changes you want to make?

(continued)

MUTUAL GOALS AND PLAN TO REACH GOALS

Goals:

Plan:

Benefits:

Risks:

Alternative plans considered:

Estimated number of sessions:

APPENDIX C
Sample Counselor-Client Agreement and Precounseling Information Form

Christian Counseling Agreement

Confidentiality and Its Limitations

In our working together as counselor and client, anything that you share with me will be considered confidential. Before sharing any of the content of our sessions with someone else, I will seek your permission to do so. The counseling session is meant to be a safe place to talk about unsafe things. There are certain limitations to confidentiality.

1. It is my primary intention and duty to preserve God's gift of life. If I believe that you are a danger to your own life, or to that of another, it is my duty to inform the appropriate authorities. I am also required to notify Child Protective Services about any incident of child abuse. It is also my duty to warn any potential victim of pending danger. I will ask you to make the call, or to notify a lawyer to that effect. If you will not do so, I will take action myself.
2. During sessions, I make brief notes, which are for my professional use only. If you are involved in a court case, release of these notes may be court ordered, and I am required to comply.
3. Insurance companies require a psychological diagnosis for the insurance claim. I will discuss the diagnosis with you, as it becomes a part of your permanent medical record.
4. As part of my desire to serve you in the best possible way as a professional, I receive supervision from other professionals. What is discussed is considered to be confidential.

5.   It is possible, even probable, that you will meet someone in the waiting room that you know. This is unavoidable and has not proved to be a problem in the past.
6.   Should you desire my giving/receiving information to/from someone else, I will request from you a signed form of consent for the release of that information.
7.   In keeping with the concept that this counseling ministry is an extension of your congregation's ministry, while still respecting your right of confidentiality, may I release information about your counseling progress to your pastor, if your pastor so requests it? Please initial.

Yes, you may speak with my pastor. _____   No, you may not. _____

Informed Consent

You have a right to receive any necessary information from me that will allow you to make a reasonable decision about your participation in the counseling process. If anything that we are doing is not clear to you, please feel free to ask for further explanation.

The Counselor-Client Relationship

Ours is a professional relationship between counselor and client. It is different from that of family or friends. This relationship does not extend outside the counseling sessions on a social basis. I will not meet with you anywhere other than in my office, unless it is therapeutically necessary to meet a specific counseling goal. When necessary, you may call me at my office between sessions (1) to change an appointment; (2) in time of crisis; or (3) as mutually agreed upon in a previous session. If these calls become inappropriately frequent or lengthy, I reserve the right to charge you for my time (see Professional Fees).

My Professional Training and Approach to Counseling

I have been a Wisconsin Synod Lutheran pastor since 1974. I am a national and state board certified professional counselor (M.A. in Counseling, University of Arizona, 1991). I am a Bible-based, Christ-centered Lutheran counselor. I hold the Bible to be the inspired Word of God and our guide for this life and for eternal life. My Christian values and beliefs have a strong influence on my counseling approach and purpose.

As we seek to clarify our personal relationship with God spiritually, we are able to clarify our ways of feeling and thinking about ourselves and others and our ways of behaving and interacting with others. I will seek to help you on a spiritual, cognitive, emotional, and behavioral level. If necessary, we may invite others involved in your relationships to participate in our counseling sessions.

If I am unable to serve your counseling needs, I will provide you with the names of other counselors who may better help you.

Professional Fees

The undersigned client agrees to be responsible for payment of the full amount of the agreed-upon fees (and any attorney and/or collection fees resulting from unpaid fees). The following is the current LCSSA fee schedule.

1. $75.00 per session hour (50 minutes). A mutually agreed-upon longer session will be charged for accordingly.
2. There is a $15.00 discount per session hour when payment is made at the session.
3. Members of LCSSA receive an additional discount when payment is made at the session.
4. Should you not keep an appointment without prior notification at least by the day before (other than for illness or emergency), you will be responsible for payment of the fee for the session time that had been reserved for you.

The undersigned has read and understands the above statements and agrees to work with _____ in a counselor-client relationship under the above-stated conditions.

Client _____ Date _____

FORM C.1   Sample Precounseling Information Form

LUTHERAN COUNSELING SERVICES SOUTHWEST ASSOCIATION
380 East Fort Lowell Road, Suite 122
Tucson, Arizona 85705
(520) 882-3773

PRECOUNSELING INFORMATION

Please complete this form. Some questions are of a personal nature. This is necessary for a helping relationship. All information is confidential within the limits of the law (see page headed "Christian Counseling Agreement"). If you do not wish to answer a question in writing at this time, we can talk it over together in our first session.

Date _____ Church affiliation _____

Name _____ Age _____ Birth date _____

Address _____

City _____ State _____ ZIP _____

Phone: Home (___)_____ Work _____ Pager _____

Occupation _____ Employer _____

Education: No. of yrs completed _____ Degree/cert. earned _____

Marital status: S ___ M ___ Widowed ___ (19 ___) Dvrcd/Sprtd _____

Any prior marriage/relationship? Y N What years? _____

(Ex-)Spouse's name _____ Years married _____

Children/names (ages) _____

Parent/Guardian (if minor) _____

Primary physician _____ Phone _____

Person responsible for payment of fees _____

Insurance company _____

Group # _____ Certificate # _____

In case of emergency, contact _____ Phone _____

Referred by _____

REASONS FOR SEEKING COUNSELING

What is happening in your life at this time, that you are seeking counseling? How long has this been going on?

_____

_____

_____

PREVIOUS COUNSELING EXPERIENCE

1. Have you ever been in counseling before?   Yes   No

2. Dates and duration of counseling: _____

3. What was helpful to you? _____

PERSONAL INFORMATION

1. Please check any recurrent feelings, thoughts, or experiences.

___ sadness/depressed mood

___ irritability

___ loss of interests or pleasure

___ hopelessness/helplessness

___ unplanned weight gain/loss

___ appetite increase/decrease

___ insomnia (lack of sleep)

___ hypersomnia (too much
   sleep)

___ numbness/tingling feeling

___ hot flashes/chills

___ sensation of shortness of
   breath

___ sweating

___ chest pain or discomfort

___ accelerated heart rate

___ trembling or shaking

___ dizziness or faintness

(continued)

___ sleep interruption

___ decreased need for sleep

___ more talkative than usual

___ fatigue/loss of energy

___ sense of worthlessness

___ low self-esteem

___ feeling guilt/shame

___ loss of concentration

___ inability to think

___ racing thoughts

___ distractibility

___ thinking about death

___ impaired functioning (at home/work/school)

___ lack of emotional responsiveness

___ sense of numbing or detachment

___ reduction in awareness of surroundings

___ marked symptoms of increased arousal

___ nausea or abdominal distress

___ intense fear or discomfort

___ derealization (feelings of unreality)

___ depersonalization (feeling detached from self)

___ fear of going crazy or losing control

___ fear of dying

___ feeling "on edge"

___ restless, unsatisfying sleep

___ mind going blank

___ muscle tension or soreness

___ excessive anxiety or worry

___ difficulty controlling the worry

___ experienced traumatic event

___ intense psychological distress when reminded of the traumatic event in any way

___ marked avoidance of things related to the traumatic event

___ sense of foreshortened future

___ inability to recall important details of the traumatic event

___ persistent reexperiencing of the trauma (e.g., flashbacks, intrusive thoughts)

___ recurrent distressing dreams of the traumatic event

___ feeling of detachment from others

___ restricted range of emotions and feelings

___ exaggerated startle response

___ outbursts of anger

___ hypervigilance

___ restlessness/fidgeting

2. When was your last medical examination? _____

3. Please mark what you use currently with a "C" and those used in the past with a "P." Estimate your quantity and frequency of use (q/f). Example: coffee . . . (q/f = 3 cups/day)

___ caffeine

___ coffee (q/f = _____)

___ colas (q/f = _____)

___ chocolate (q/f = _____)

___ sugar (q/f = _____)

___ tobacco (q/f = _____)

___ alcohol

___ beer (q/f = _____)

___ wine (q/f = _____)

___ liquor (q/f = _____)

___ marijuana (q/f = _____)

___ cocaine (q/f = _____)

   (in what form? _____)

other chemical use:

___ _____ (q/f = _____)

___ _____ (q/f = _____)

___ _____ (q/f = _____)

___ _____ (q/f = _____)

(continued)

4. Is there a history of alcohol or drug problems in your family? Y N

5. Is there a history of psychiatric disorders in your family? Y N

6. Have you ever been hospitalized for a psychiatric disorder, or have you been in a substance abuse treatment center? Y N

7. Please list any prescribed and over-the-counter medications you are taking, the daily dosage, and the purpose for their use.

   _____

   _____

   _____

8. Are you on a special diet? Y N If yes, for what purpose?

   _____

   _____

9. Have you contemplated or attempted suicide? Y N

10. Have you been a victim of sexual abuse or assault? Y N

11. Have you been a victim of physical violence? Y N

12. Have you witnessed any physical abuse or violence? Y N

13. Have you witnessed any sexual abuse or assault? Y N

14. Have you ever caused physical harm? Y N

15. Have you ever sexually abused or sexually assaulted someone? Y N

16. Please identify several people who give you emotional
    support:

    _____

    _____

COUNSELING GOALS

What changes would you like to make in your life at this time?

_____

_____

_____

_____

_____

_____

(continued)

Index

TO THE OWNER OF THIS BOOK:

We hope that you have found *The Practical Counselor: Elements of Effective Helping* useful. So that this book can be improved in a future edition, would you take the time to complete this sheet and return it? Thank you.

School and address: ───────────────────────────────

Department: ──────────────────────────────────

Instructor's name: ─────────────────────────────────

1. What I like most about this book is: ─────────────────────

───────────────────────────────────────

───────────────────────────────────────

2. What I like least about this book is: ────────────────────

───────────────────────────────────────

───────────────────────────────────────

3. My general reaction to this book is: ─────────────────────

───────────────────────────────────────

4. The name of the course in which I used this book is: ──────────

───────────────────────────────────────

5. Were all of the chapters of the book assigned for you to read? ──────────

    If not, which ones weren't? ──────────────────────

6. In the space below, or on a separate sheet of paper, please write specific suggestions for improving this book and anything else you'd care to share about your experience in using the book.

───────────────────────────────────────

───────────────────────────────────────

───────────────────────────────────────

───────────────────────────────────────

───────────────────────────────────────

Optional:

Your name: _____ Date: _____

May Brooks/Cole quote you, either in promotion for *The Practical Counselor: Elements of Effective Helping* or in future publishing ventures?

Yes: _____ No: _____

Sincerely,

Philip Lauver
David R. Harvey

FOLD HERE

- -

Brooks/Cole Publishing is dedicated to publishing quality books for the helping professions. If you would like to learn more about our publications, please use this mailer to request our catalogue.

Name: _____

Street Address: _____

City, State, and Zip: _____

FOLD HERE

BUSINESS REPLY MAIL

FIRST CLASS   PERMIT NO. 358   PACIFIC GROVE, CA

POSTAGE WILL BE PAID BY ADDRESSEE

ATT: _Human Services Catalogue_

Brooks/Cole Publishing Company
511 Forest Lodge Road
Pacific Grove, California 93950-9968

FOLD HERE

f.